POLAND,
What Have I To Do With Thee...

POLAND,
What Have I To Do With Thee...

Essays without Prejudice

RAFAEL F. SCHARF

VALLENTINE MITCHELL
LONDON • PORTLAND, OR

Originally published in 1996 in a joint Polish–English edition by
Fundacja Judaica, Kraków as
Co Mnie I Tobie Polsko...Eseje bez uprzedzeń
(Poland, What Have I To Do With Thee...Essays without Prejudice).

Published in English in 1998 in Great Britain by
VALLENTINE MITCHELL
Crown House, 47 Chase Side,
London N14 5BP

Website: http://www.vmbooks.com

Copyright © 1998 Rafael F. Scharf
Reprinted 2002

British Library Cataloguing in Publication Data

Scharf, Rafael F.
Poland, what have I to do with thee: essays without prejudice. – 2nd ed.
1. Scharf, Rafael F. 2. Jews – Poland – Biography
I. Title
943.8'004924

ISBN 0 85303 350 1 (paper)

Library of Congress Cataloging-in-Publication Data

Scharf, Rafael F.
 [Co mnie i Tobie Polsko. English]
 Poland, what have I to do with thee – : essays without prejudice / Rafael F. Scharf.
   p. cm.
 ISBN 0-85303-350-1 (pbk. : alk. paper)
 1. Jews – Poland – Kraków – History – 20th century.
2. Holocaust, Jewish (1939–1945) – Poland.
3. Scharf, Rafael F. 4. Poland – Ethnic relations.
I. Title
DS135.P62K737613   1998
940.53'18'094386–dc21   98-30088
                                                                                                     CIP

All rights reserved. No part of this publication may be reproduced, stored in or introduced into a retrieval system, or transmitted, in any form or by any means, electronic, mechanical, photocopying, recording or otherwise without the prior written permission of the publisher of this book.

Printed in Great Britain by Bookcraft (Bath) Ltd,
Midsomer Norton, Somerset

For my family and friends — with gratitude
Felek

Contents

Foreword
Rafael Scharf: Chronicler of Kraków Jewry ANTONY POLONSKY   ix

1	Poland, what have I to do with Thee ...	1
2	What shall we tell Miriam?	52
3	Kraków – blessed its memory	63
4	*Cum ira et studio*	71
5	Let us talk ...	80
6	As in a dream	89
7	From the abyss	94
8	The lesson of Auschwitz	104
9	On the 50th anniversary of the Warsaw Ghetto Uprising	109
10	Rumkowski of the Łódź ghetto	115
11	Janusz Korczak and his time	121
12	Warsaw ghetto	134
13	Witnesses	142
14	Saints or madmen? A meditation on Ephraim Oshry's *Responsa from the Holocaust*	148

15	All our yesterdays ... On the album by Roman Vishniac	156
16	Reflections on the unspeakable	162
17	A peculiar people	167
18	A Beloved Teacher	173
19	Booksearch! From Przemysl to the British Library	178

Rafael Scharf: Chronicler of Kraków Jewry

No more will you find in Poland Jewish shtetlach
Hrubieszów, Karczew, Brody, Falenica
In vain will you seek in the windows lighted candles
And search for the sound of chants from the wooden synagogue
The last scourings, the Jewish rags have vanished,
They sprinkled sand over the blood, swept away the footprints
And whitewashed the walls with bluish lime
As after a plague or a great day of fasting.
One moon shines here, cool, pale, alien,
Outside the town, when the night lights up,
My Jewish kinsmen with their poetic fancies
Will find no more Chagall's two gold moons.
They have flown away, frightened by the grim silence.
No more will you find those towns, where the cobbler was a poet,
The watchmaker a philosopher, the barber a troubadour.
No more will you find those towns where biblical psalms
Were linked by the wind with Polish laments and Slavic ardour,
Where old Jews in the orchard, under the shade of cherry trees,
Wept for the sacred walls of Jerusalem.
No more will you find those towns where poetic mist,
The moon, winds, lakes and the stars above
Wrote in blood a tragic story
The history of the world's two saddest nations

THIS POEM, *Elegy for the Shtetl*, written in 1946 by the Polish–Jewish poet, Antoni Słonimski, encapsulates the two main themes of this important and moving book: regret for the loss of the multi-faceted world of Polish Jewry and reflections on why the history of the 'world's two saddest nations' diverged so drastically and led to so much misunderstanding, bitterness and hatred. There can be few people better qualified to reflect on these complex and perplexing themes than Rafael Scharf. Born into a relatively comfortable but still observant Jewish family in Kraków in 1914, he attended the Hebrew High School in Kraków (which he describes in a number of these essays) where he obtained both a thorough general education and an abiding love of Polish literature as well as a deep grounding in Jewish history, the Hebrew language and modern Hebrew literature. From there he went to the Jagiellonian University where he graduated in law. Already committed to revisionist Zionism and uneasy about the future of Poland, he left for England in 1938 and went to the London School of Economics ostensibly to study colonial administration, hoping to make his future in the emerging Jewish state. Seduced by the calm and order of England, he settled permanently in London where he married and raised a family working as a printer and as a dealer in watercolours.

Yet his real vocation was always as a writer. Already in Poland, as a journalist for the Polish-language Jewish daily newspaper *Nowy Dziennik*, he had demonstrated his literary skills. He took a long time to find his voice. Partly this was because of the need to establish himself in his adopted country and to support his growing family. But there were deeper reasons. He felt a strong desire to become English. As he writes in the introductory essay in this volume:

> There was a time when I would have given my right arm (or some other part of the anatomy) to speak English without a foreign accent and not to be recognised as a 'foreigner' the moment I opened my mouth. (p.5)

He found, as so many have before, that while England is hospitable to exiles, it is much harder to become English and he came to see the futility of his desire to achieve this goal: 'I now think that that wish was misplaced, not to say pitiful. I have cured myself of that feeling of inferiority and see that the object of my admiration was not essentially better but only different from me' (p.5).

He also found that he could not abandon his Jewish and Polish roots and slowly his interest in them resurfaced. In the case of his Polish background, this seems to have occasioned some irritation, as is suggested by the title of this volume, 'Poland, what have I to do with Thee…', which he glosses in the introductory essay as 'Your concern, Poland, is not mine'. In another passage, he refers to Poland as a 'stepmother' (p.3). As he explains, he speaks for those Jews who have some connection not only with the Jewish, but also with the Polish world, no matter how deep or tenuous. As he writes: 'I feel I have special qualifications in this area. I was an eye-witness to a singular period of Polish and Jewish history, one of the last still surviving' (p.2). Yet, in spite of his bitterness at the strength of anti-Jewish prejudice in his native country, he came to feel that he had no desire, as he puts it, to 'convert' from his Polishness. Were he to be stripped of all that is Polish in him, he would lose too much: the Polish language, Polish poetry, the Polish landscape, the good and not so good memories of the common past, those parts of one's personality which reflect the Polish character. Were this to occur, 'one would feel bereft, impoverished, incomplete' (p.4).

His Jewish feelings were more complex. As a young man, he became a radical Zionist because he believed that the condition of the Diaspora Jew required drastic, indeed revolutionary, modification. He felt little sympathy for normative Jewish religious belief or practice. In a moving passage, he describes an encounter with his father, when he questioned why he spent his Saturday afternoons attempting to make his way, not very successfully, through the dense pages of the Talmud:

> He wished to persuade me to share his outlook but we did not know how to talk to each other, and he realized that an argument with a precocious know-all only led to an aggravation of spirit. Only once, I remember, he exploded when I asked him: 'What is all this for?' 'What is all this *for*, fool? The whole of life is for *this*!' (p.56)

He also felt little empathy for the mass of Jews in Poland. As he explains:

> To many of us who grew up within or next to that human landscape and who remember it lovingly, these people – shameful to confess – did not at that time look attractive. These misty eyes, beards, sidelocks, crooked noses – one looked away, embarrassed by what a non-Jewish onlooker might feel or say. It now seems clear that these faces, etched with worry and wisdom, lit with inner light, otherworldy, Rembrandtesque, were inexpressibly beautiful. (p.140)

Their language also did not arouse his sympathy:

> There was a time when Yiddish was denied even the dignity of being called a 'language' – in the eyes, or rather ears, of the Poles, and also many of the so-called 'assimilated' Jews, it was a jargon, gibberish, used by those black-bearded, 'sidelocked' Jews, who were no doubt plotting something sinister or casting spells. Those harsh, throaty sounds, accompanied by this wild gesticulation, bode no good. (p.6)

Yet as he came to see himself as one of the last representatives of this now almost entirely destroyed world, he came to see its deep inner spirituality:

> The community was fragmented and torn by internal strife, but there was one unifying factor – a sense of sharing a common fate which transcended social and political differences. There was a marked spirituality, even among the non-religious, an instinctive allegiance and response to what was felt to be the Jewish ethos: a deeply ingrained, universal conviction that, beyond the mundane, man had to aspire to higher things, however defined. (p.60)

Poland, what have I to do with Thee ...

Discussing Rabbi Oshry's responsa during the Holocaust, he comments:

> To the lay, secular, rational mind the questions and the responsa might appear absurd, grotesque, eerie, not to say insane. But one would have to be quite devoid of feeling not to perceive that we witness here a dimension of spirituality which is transcendental. One may not be able to comprehend it or even remotely empathize with it but it is impossible to shrug it off. Whether one is inclined to shake one's head in disbelief or weep with compassion, one cannot but stand in awe in the face of this degree of devotion and trust in God. (p.155)

The earliest piece in this volume dates from 1977, nearly forty years after Scharf came to England. It is an account of 'Janusz Korczak and his Time', which he wrote for the *Jewish Quarterly*, that indispensable journal whose survival and flourishing owes so much to him. As one of the founders of the International Janusz Korczak Society, he feels deep sympathy for Korczak: for his humanism, his attempt to combine Jewishness and Polishness, and for his tragic death. But the essay also adumbrates in an early form the two main themes which dominate this volume. Scharf discusses the question of Korczak's Polishness in a way which suggests how strongly he identified with it and with its fate:

> Korczak grew up feeling Polish to the core. In his attachment to the Polish soil, history, literature and language nobody could be more so. In this he was typical of a segment of Jewish society in love with the *idea of Poland*. It was only by a gradual and painful process, in the cooling moral climate, that he was forced to recognise that his case was one of love unrequited, and no matter how pure and worthy his devotion he would stay condemned by the sheer fact of his origin. The unhealed wound of this rejection never ceased to plague him. (p.125)

Scharf then uses the peg of Korczak to explain why the integration of the Jews into Polish society did not succeed, describing the separateness of the two groups on the Polish lands and the difficult situation of the minority of Jews who wished to transform themselves into 'Poles of the mosaic faith'. He links the fate of the Jews in Poland during the Second World War, as Błoński was later to do, to this separateness from the majority:

> The time has come to face the obstinate fact that the stage for the extermination of the Jews proved to be conveniently chosen. It is clear that the genocide could not have been carried out with the same implacable thoroughness and efficiency, down to the last child, if it had not been correctly assumed that the victims would be considered strangers in their own land, with whose fate their co-citizens would not

identify. The searching out, the assembly, the transport, the poisoning and the burning would not have been possible if the local population had felt that this was being done to their own flesh and blood. (p.128)

This sense of grievance at Polish behaviour during the Shoah pervades Scharf's earlier writings. It receives its finest articulation in the speech he gave at the Oxford Conference on Polish–Jewish history held in September 1984, and is found in this volume with the telling title *'Cum ira et studio'*. In it, he expresses his pain at the fact that the 'fabric of Polish–Jewish cohabitation on Polish soil has been irreversibly destroyed', and refers to the 'trauma of unreciprocated love' of the Jews of 'this last generation, nearing its close', who 'cannot erase from their hearts this country where "they were born and grew up", where ... they loved the landscape, the language, the poetry; where they were ready to shed their blood for Poland to be her true sons. That this was evidently not enough leaves them broken-hearted.' He concluded:

> The paths of 'two of the saddest nations on this earth' have parted for ever. I wonder how far the Poles are aware of the fact that with the Jews an authentic part of *their* Poland was obliterated. The question begs to be asked: Will that Poland one day be better, richer in spiritual and material goods, without the Jews? (p.79)

This article evoked a highly significant response in the form of Jan Błoński's piece 'The Poor Poles look at the ghetto' in which he called on the Poles to accept some degree of responsibility for the fate of their Jewish fellow citizens under Nazi occupation, to stop 'haggling, trying to defend and justify ourselves. To stop arguing about the things that were beyond our power to do, during the occupation and beforehand. Nor to place blame on political, social and economic conditions. But to say first of all, "Yes, we are guilty".' Błoński explicitly referred to Scharf's speech in Oxford as the spur which led him to take up his pen:

> I recall one moving speech at the Oxford Conference, in which the speaker started by comparing the Jewish attitude to Poland to unrequited love. Despite the suffering and all the problems which beset our mutual relations, he continued, the Jewish community had a genuine attachment to their adopted country. Here they found a home, a sense of security. There was, conscious or unconscious, an expectation that their fate would improve, the burden of humiliation would lighten, that the future would gradually become brighter. What actually happened was exactly the opposite. 'Nothing can ever change now', he concluded. 'Jews do not have and cannot have any future in Poland. Do

tell us, though', he finally demanded, 'that what has happened to us was not our fault. We do not ask for anything else. But we do hope for such an acknowledgement.'[1]

Scharf was deeply affected by Błoński's article, which certainly changed significantly the way in which the 'Jewish issue' was discussed in Polish circles. He commented on it in his contribution to the discussion on 'Ethical Problems of the Holocaust' at the International Conference on the History and Culture of Polish Jewry held in Jerusalem in February 1988:

> I read Błoński's article, for the first time, with growing excitement and quickened pulse. At one point he makes reference to one of the speakers at the conference in Oxford in 1984, whose words, he said, inspired him to ponder these matters. From the words quoted by him it was clear that he was referring to me. I was startled and also moved to see how one word, a sentence, a thought can strike another man's mind, can germinate there and bear fruit beyond expectation. I was talking then, at least that is how Błoński understood it, to the effect that we Jews no longer expected anything from the Poles but the admission that they have been, in some way, at fault. For many years, we listened, waited for a sign – but we heard no voices. In the end, I had thought that we would be straining our ears in vain. But now, at last – we hear the voice of Błoński. (...)
>
> More than a year has passed since Błoński's voice sounded. I would like to assure all those who feared that it would have a harmful effect on Poland, that quite the opposite has occurred. His article is seen, in itself, as a certain rehabilitation of sorts. When, paradoxically and undeservedly, I am put in the role of an *advocatus Poloniae*, I myself, in many instances, recall this article and those which followed. I maintain that one can no longer speak loosely about the Poles' opinion on the subject without taking into consideration these new voices, which save the reputation of Poland. (p.86)

This issue is not resolved and Scharf's concluding reflections on it in his introductory essay, while stressing the importance of the new democratic framework for a more open discussion of the character and extent of Polish anti-semitism, do not hesitate to attack the persistence of primitive forms of hostility to the Jews in Poland and to expose the apologetic tone in relation to this issue all too often encountered even among otherwise well-intentioned individuals.

The second theme of Scharf's writing, his evocation of the lost world of Cracovian and Polish Jewry, has played a larger role in his writing in recent years and is very well represented in this volume. Already in his Korczak essay, he stressed the scale of what has been destroyed:

Rafael Scharf: Chronicler of Kraków Jewry

> But for the Jews, let there be no mistake, the loss of Poland is incalculable. For despite the chequered fortunes, despite the vicissitudes, or perhaps because of them, the Jews in Poland through generations formed the most energetic, resilient and productive, the most 'Jewish' part of the Diaspora. Deep roots were struck and they nourished abundant growth. (p.131)

His recall is almost Proustian. It is a unique privilege to have accompanied him as he strides (for an octogenarian he is remarkably spry) round the streets of Kazimierz and recalls their former inhabitants and the various exploits of his youth, now divided from us by half a century and the abyss of the Shoah. In the words of the Polish literary critic, Jan Błoński:

> Who on earth, today, walking along Dietla Street in Kraków, can still recall any of its former inhabitants? They have virtually all perished for Dietla Street, with its avenue of trees, was the very heart of the Jewish quarter. The only person, perhaps, who recalls not just one, but all these people is Rafael Scharf ... and so he [has taken] upon himself the role of guardian of Cracovian and Jewish memory, the role, as it were, of the last witness, who strives to record this Jewish–Cracovian particularity. Like Gebirtig in his songs, Scharf bears live, authentic testimony to the character of that city and its community, which filled these walls to the roof, in a state of more or less peaceful cohabitation with their Polish fellow-citizens.[2]

This is an elegiac and sad book. Scharf provides a moving and detailed description of all the inhabitants of the apartment block at the corner of St Sebastian and Berek Joselöwicz Street, which was a microcosm of the many-sided Jewish life of Kraków and which culminates with a description of the non-Jewish janitor, Rehman, whose son, a chimney-sweep, kept Scharf's mother's possessions during the war, selling some to provide her with an income in hiding and returning the rest after the war, 'which perhaps would not deserve mention if not for the fact that the opposite was the rule'. He concludes:

> Such was just one, ordinary tenement house, one strand in a patchwork, a tiny stone in a crazy paving. Nothing, nothing remains of it all. (p.17)

This is not a book about the Holocaust, but it is preoccupied with the consequences of the mass murder of the Jews of Poland and of Europe. As Scharf comments, 'The period of German occupation in Poland dominates my internal landscape and casts a shadow over everything that happened to me before and after ... Some people may say that all this was a long time ago, but there has not been a day in my life that I have not reverted in my thoughts to those events.' Like many of those who survived, he feels guilt at his survival and burdened by the need to bear witness to the ordeal of those who did not survive, in his own family, the only exception apart from himself being his mother. He writes:

> How does one cope with that sort of knowledge, that almost everybody one knew – family, friends, teachers, neighbours, shopkeepers, beggars – all died some horrible death and it is only due to some accidental twist of fate that one has not gone the same way. When I want to recall a face I knew, I see it contorted, gasping for breath, in a mass of swirling bodies. (...)
>
> The generation of Jews of the post-holocaust era, the 'survivors' in the broadest sense, are a people apart. Burdened by their memory, walking wounded in eternal mourning. I do not think that an outsider can understand this condition. (p.37)

The book's sadness derives too from Scharf's sense of the enormous mass of talent destroyed by the Nazi genocide:

> One third of the Jewish people perished, were gassed, extirpated, turned into ashes. In those ashes how many potential Einsteins and Freuds, Heines and Mendelssohns, Gottliebs and Chagalls, Tuwims and Korczaks – people burdened with that genetic endowment which gives rise to genius. (p.114)

Is it fanciful also to think of Felek himself as one of the victims of this catastrophe? The move to England has made him a bilingual writer, capable of expressing his many and complex thoughts in both English and Polish. But the destruction and the move have robbed him of what every writer needs, an audience. As he admits:

> I haven't got a clear image of my reader. The majority of those who might have formed the natural readership have perished; a great many of those who survived the cataclysm are also no longer with us. (p.1)

It is clear too that he fears that he has been unable fully to communicate, even to his own children, what he feels is important to him – a failure he attributes at its deepest level to the problem of 'how to present the boundless horror of those events which have no analogy in history and at the same time not to undermine the belief in the sense of creation, in human values, in justice'.

It may be, too, the move to bilingualism has robbed him of fluency. How moving and important are these essays, 'a small plot on Mount Parnassus'! But with his enormous talents, is it not possible to imagine him in other circumstances as another Stryjkowski, Rudnicki or Grynberg?

Rafael Scharf: Chronicler of Kraków Jewry

When reflecting on Polish behaviour during the Shoah, he always recalls the exceptions to those who were indifferent or even rejoiced at the murder of the Jews, the chimney-sweep Rehman, who assisted his mother, the anti-semite Jurczyga who, during the war, assisted his former Jewish adversary Staszek K. He also reminds us of Jewish swinishness, of Jewish collaboration as of that of his friend Arthur Loeffler, who disgraced himself in the 'Jewish Police' in the Kraków ghetto.

He sees the Holocaust as a perilous portent for mankind:

> What lesson humanity will draw from that cataclysm; how it will cope with the awareness of the depth to which man showed himself capable of sinking; how man will renew belief in basic moral values, in a world possessing means of destruction, by comparison with which even the gas chambers pale into insignificance: on answers to these questions depends the future of humankind. (p.120)

His prevailing tone, however, faced with the incomprehensible character of the Shoah and of the evil which man is capable of, is to mourn, to regret the loss of 'the world of European Jewry, a thousand-year-old civilization' wiped out in four years. In this way his work is closest to another Polish–Jewish writer, with whom he certainly felt a special kinship, Stanisław Wygodzki. I know that Felek believes that poetry can perhaps articulate feelings inexpressible in other form. So let me conclude with some of Wygodzki's verses:

I am a father to you
Rachel, Sulamit, Rebecca
I am a tomb and quietness
Miriam, Esther, Ruth
A father for Malka and Chana

Not like a pilgrim do I stand here
A pilgrim has a time of rest
... Even deeper I go into sadness
Into an ever larger cemetery

The song of the wounded heart does not seek revenge
... Wrong is overcome by the force of grief

I do not come as an avenger, or a judge
I do not come as a preacher to sow poison and wormwood in the heart
How can one place flowers on a grave in the air?

Antony Polonsky

Poland, what have I to do with Thee ...

NOTES

1. Jan Błoński, 'The Poor Poles look at the ghetto', in Anthony Polonsky (ed.), *My Brother's Keeper? Recent Polish Debates on the Holocaust* (London: 1990) pp.44–5.
2. Jan Błoński, 'Przedmowa', in Rafael F. Scharf, *Co mnie i tobie Polsko ... Eseje bez uprzedzen* (Kraków: 1996) p.7.

1 • Poland, what have I to do with Thee ...

A FEW words of explanation concerning the somewhat unusual form of this book: it was written in Polish and in English, in turns. Thus it reflects accurately the individuality of the author, the dual track of his life, the entanglements of roots. In the course of writing I felt that Polish served me better in describing some periods and themes, English seemed to serve better for others. Subsequently, what I wrote in Polish I translated into English and vice versa. These translations were not always literal: on occasion, when I felt it would be better thus, I departed from 'the original', most often when some quotations of Polish poetry would have had little meaning for the English reader, or where I felt that a different style of utterance would be closer to the spirit of the language.

This collection is not conceived as a book with a specific beginning, middle or end, to be read in a prescribed sequence. Its fragments were written at different times, on different occasions, as casual comments, reflections, *pensées*, material for discussion.

I haven't got a clear image of my reader. The majority of those who might have formed the natural readership have perished; a great many of those who survived the cataclysm are also no longer with us. Years have flown past, as is their wont, quickly and imperceptibly; former girlfriends, if lucky, have become grandmothers, the snows of yesteryear have melted.

In Jewish folklore there is a myth that when the Angel of Death comes to do his worst and finds the intended victim preoccupied with something important, like writing a book, he relents, for the time being, and fills in the quota with someone else who appears idle – hence the rabbis always pretend to be so busy (perhaps, subconsciously, I act from a similar motive).

When I was very young, I was in the habit, in the company of adults, of speaking out of turn (some of this appears to have survived till old age). My Mother used to cool down my excess of zest: 'Do not open your mouth till you think what to say.' To which I used to reply with iron, childlike logic: 'How am I to know what I think until I've said it?' Such a Cartesian thesis: 'I speak therefore I think – loquor ergo cogito.'

Poland, what have I to do with Thee ...

I have given these pages a title: 'Poland, what have I to do with Thee ...', an echo of St. John (2. 4) where Jesus rebukes his Mother for urging him to perform a miracle. (This passage has always struck me as not ringing true – a Jewish boy would not have addressed his Mother so arrogantly. In fact, looking at the original Greek τι ἐμοι και σοι γύναι, the passus does lend itself to a much milder translation than the commonly used, brash, 'What have I to do with thee, Woman?' or 'Your concern, Mother, is not mine.')

I have a need to clarify once and for all (no, not once and for all – only to the next, deeper clarification) what sort of a Pole I am, what my connection with Poland is, how I view Polish matters, the old ones and the current ones, from the perspective of a Jewish émigré. What still moves me, to what have I grown indifferent? I am using the personal pronoun 'I' here, but the matter is not about me alone – were it so, I would not have cared to put pen to paper.

I attempt to speak of people of a specific formation. There are many of us, spread across the world, whose identity is not easily defined. The spectrum of Polish Jews, or Jews of Polish origin, is wide and not clear cut, from the strictly orthodox to those completely assimilated. There are those who have consciously severed their ties with their country of origin, who want to have nothing to do with it. Others, to whom the labels and the definitions mean little, who have merged with their surroundings, have no need of introspection or stating of position. There are also those who have genuine affection for Poland. All of these groups, with their nuances and shadings, have their conscious and subconscious reasons for relating to these matters thus and not otherwise. The fact that I have the need to delve into some of these issues would point to my position in the spectrum. What additional light I shall be able to throw on these complex matters remains to be seen – I can hardly contain my own curiosity.

I hope this will not sound immodest – I feel I have special qualifications in this area. I was an eyewitness to a singular period of Polish and Jewish history, one of the last still surviving. Soon the field will be open to a different, indirect kind of account and analysis. Our children and grandchildren may want to know how it appeared to us, a future historian might reproach us that we did not leave enough evidence, the passage of time will bring a different perspective. I feel free to speak openly and without constraint and whilst I do so I may rethink some of my own views.

The personal pronoun is the most suspect part of speech. How we

Poland, what have I to do with Thee ...

relate to the 'I' defines our personality. For the sake of objectivity its use should be reduced to the minimum. In the English mode of expression self-depreciation is commonly acceptable. It is not quite so in America. Before one of my lectures at a conference in New York, my friend who knows the local custom warned me against it. It appears that if you declare in front of your audience that you are not the greatest expert in your subject and your utterance is not the definitive word in the matter, they will take you at your word and wonder why you have invited them to listen to you.

This reminds me of a Jewish anecdote – how on the Day of Atonement, as is the habit, the Rabbi steps in front of the Ark, beats his breast and says: 'God, forgive me my sins, I am a mere nothing.' After him, the head of the community does the same – beats his breast and says: 'God forgive me – I am a mere nothing.' Then the beadle steps out, beats his breast and says: 'God forgive me my sins, I am a mere nothing.' Whereupon the head of the community nudges the Rabbi and whispers: 'Look at him. What cheek, he also fancies himself a nothing!'

In that heartrending lament which the great Polish poet Julian Tuwim wrote in exile, when he first heard the news of what was happening to Jews in Poland, a lament to which he gave the title 'We, Polish Jews,' there is the following statement: 'I am a Pole because I like it that way.' Some variation on that theme, for example: 'I am a Pole even though I don't like it' or 'I am a Pole even though they don't like it' or 'I am a Pole because I don't know how to cease to be one' might well serve as a motto for these reflections.

These variants show how complicated is the definition of identity of a Jew of Polish origin. In my case, not as dramatic, of course, as that of Tuwim, the problem has an additional twist. Poles have always taken me for a Jew, Jews for an Englishman, the English for a Pole. I myself, in turn, could say that I look upon England as a wife, on Israel as a lover, on Poland as a stepmother.

This is written half in jest to illustrate the depth of these dilemmas but, in fact, personally, I have no difficulties with it. I feel no internal split of any sort. I know perfectly well who I am, irrespective of what others might take me for. I am a Jew, *tout court*, completely, openly and naturally. In contradistinction to this, my 'Polishness' does require proofs, and if called upon, I could produce them aplenty. The great Polish journalist and essayist, Stefan Kisielewski, has written that 'Poland is Catholic not only by faith and tradition. A Pole is a Catholic by temperament, by choice and most importantly – by his perception of the world.' That concept of course, says nothing to me and of me, an unbridgeable gap separates me from it.

Is it possible to 'convert' from being Polish? Consciously, by an act of will, by a declaration of intent, to shed it for ever? I think it is possible, particularly if one lives abroad, if one has been wounded by the way many Poles have treated Jews, if one remembers what happened to Jews who lived in Poland – it is possible to turn one's back on it, sever all emotional connection, no longer feel any common bond with that country. Many people within my circle of friends have done just that. I see nothing wrong or unworthy in such an attitude; all I want is for them to show similar tolerance to my attitude. I have lived for over half-a-century outside Poland; nobody in my family speaks Polish, not my wife, not my children, not my grandchildren. I have not taken part in the life of the Polish community in exile, have no input into the Polish heirdom – but do not want to 'convert' from my 'Polishness.' Certain thoughts about Poland drive me to distraction, and many things which I see and remember fill me with aversion – but to 'convert'? No.

I am thinking what would be left of me if by some ungodly edict I were to be stripped of all that is Polish in me. First, of the language, which – although somewhat rusty and neglected – remains part of the furniture without which the inner space would be empty; of the poems and verses with which I lull myself to sleep; of the recollection of the landscape, its singular sights and smells. (Janusz Korczak remarked, during his stay in Palestine, that the eucalyptus speaks to him differently from the pine.)

Were one to lose the link with that language and landscape, with the good and not-so-good memories of the common past, and with that part of one's personality which reflects the Polish character (for – contrary to appearances – the long, multifaceted relationship of the Poles and their Jewish co-citizens resulted in some remarkable resemblances) – one would feel bereft, impoverished, incomplete. This Polish facet, or its residue – it is not easy to quantify it – gives life an added dimension. Who of us is so richly endowed as to afford the loss of this heritage?

I must be grateful to fate, not altogether blind, which made me live the greater part of my life in England. England has proved, on the whole, a hospitable land to a stranger (particularly if he is white-skinned) with that civilised lack of curiosity about the neighbour, not prying into his private matters (or parts). There used to be a widespread feeling of superiority with regard to foreigners. Slowly, through frequent contacts with people of different nationalities, the influx of tourists, mass tourism abroad, and also due to a manifest lack of commercial success in a global sense, that feeling of superiority has been knocked out of the English, the pendulum has swung the other way. They have become very self-critical, and thereby also more human and 'sympathique'.

It has been a life-enhancing experience to find oneself in the orbit of Anglo-Saxon culture and gain direct access to the treasures of the English language and literature, which are amongst the greatest achievements of the human spirit.

There was a time when I would have given my right arm (or some other part of the anatomy) to speak English without a foreign accent and not to be recognised as a 'foreigner' the moment I opened my mouth. I now think that that wish was misplaced, not to say pitiful. I have cured myself of that feeling of inferiority and see that the object of my admiration was not essentially better but only different from me. I have recognised that greater value lies in colourful differentiation than in grey uniformity. Today, perhaps to spite myself, when I have very nearly lost the traces of the foreign accent, I purposely cling to its remnants to sound a bit different from the rest.

It seemed to me, at first, that these recollections were somehow too fragmentary and amounted to little, that all of this took place in a very distant past, before the flood, the other side of the nightmare. But nothing is ever lost in memory, not even that which we push into the subconscious and try to forget. It only requires a trigger – like, for me, a walk through these little streets of Kraków – to bring it all whirling and bubbling to the surface, forming a continuous flow.

However, I shall restrict myself to talking only about such aspects as throw some light on this period of history, on Jewish society, its features and habits, and shall postpone the merely personal to some later date, *sine die*.

We had, in my time, in Kraków a rabbi by the name of Szmelkes. He gave 'religious instruction' to Jewish students from state schools – that was a part of the compulsory curriculum. A story went round that when he was being engaged to deliver an occasional speech at a wedding or some other festive occasion, he would say: 'I can offer you a speech for which I charge 150 zloty, I can offer you a speech for which I charge 100 zloty. I can also offer you a speech for which I only charge 50 zloty. But I wouldn't advise you to take the one for 50 zloty.'

Poland, what have I to do with Thee ...

I have the ambition to serve up something for, say, no less than 100 zloty.

* * *

There was a time when Yiddish was denied even the dignity of being called a 'language' – in the eyes, or rather ears, of the Poles, and also many of the so-called 'assimilated' Jews, it was a jargon, gibberish, used by those black-bearded, 'sidelocked' Jews, who were no doubt plotting something sinister or casting spells. Those harsh, throaty sounds, accompanied by this wild gesticulation, bode no good.

In fact it is a language whose early forms were created and developed by the 'ashkenasi' Jews ('ashkenaz' in Hebrew means Germany) inhabiting territories in Upper Rhineland, including towns like Mainz, Worms and Regensburg, who, in the course of their wanderings, had settled in Central and Eastern Europe. Here they further developed the language, enriching it with the vocabulary of the local population.

The dictionary *Der groyser Verterbuch fun der yidisher Sprach* contains 180,000 words. The greater part derives from various German dialects, but Yiddish changes their style, structure, pronunciation and grammar. The second part is drawn from Hebrew sources, namely from the Old Testament, liturgy and medieval literature. Finally, the third part is taken from the languages of the countries where Jews lived, mainly from Polish, Russian, Ukrainian and Byelorussian. It became the lingua franca of the Jews of Europe, from Holland to Poland, Rumania, Hungary and the Balkan Countries and was carried across the Ocean in the immigrants' luggage to North and South America. It is estimated that on the eve of the outbreak of the Second World War 11 million people spoke Yiddish. The figure diminished dramatically as the result of the extermination of the Jews and also through cultural changes.

There was a time, at the dawn of Zionism and the pioneering effort in Palestine, when Yiddish was considered, and for good reason, to be a threat to the revival of the Hebrew language. The rebirth of Hebrew was, as a matter of principle, to go hand-in-hand with the rebirth of the Nation in its own Land, with the conquest of the desert, with breaking away from the way and tradition of the Diaspora.

In that conflict the opposing forces were uneven. Almost everybody spoke or at least understood Yiddish – this was so easy. Very few spoke Hebrew – this was so difficult. For two thousand years

Poland, what have I to do with Thee ...

Hebrew was a dead language – at the time of Jesus it was already not Hebrew but Aramaic which was in daily use in Palestine. The fact that from that battle, against overwhelming odds, Hebrew emerged victorious is one of the miracles of modern times and living proof of the hard-necked obstinacy of the Jewish people. In that early period in Palestine whoever ventured to speak Yiddish in public invited contempt. There were no publications of any sort in Yiddish. When in 1927 there was an attempt to introduce Yiddish as a subject at the University, there was an almighty outcry that 'pagan gods are being brought into the Temple' and the project had to be withdrawn. It was only in 1951, when there was already a third generation that considered Hebrew to be their mother-tongue, that Yiddish was accepted as a legitimate subject at the University. The circle was squared – nostalgia for the past, idealised and irretrievably lost, a recognition of the beauty and value of the treasures of the Yiddish literature, embodied in the works of Jehuda Leib Perec, Shalom Aleichem, Mendele Mojcher Sforim, Szalom Asz, the Singer Brothers and others, the awareness that this was an integral part of the national heritage, that this was the language on the lips of the people who perished – all this combined to surround Yiddish with an aura of prestige.

Isaac Bashevis Singer declared in his acceptance speech of the Nobel Prize for Literature that the honour bestowed upon him was really a recognition of the Yiddish language – 'a language without land, without frontiers, a language not supported by any government, a language not supported by the rulers and the mighty of this world, a language which is the expression of thousands of years' experience of the Jewish people.' So said Bashevis Singer, and nobody knew more about these things than he.

The language is pithy, colourful, expressive, earthy – and at the same time poetic, full of singular turns of phrase, metaphors, proverbs, wit. It reflects the spirit of the societies which used it – their character, disposition, way of thinking, sense of humour. It is warm, full of diminutives. Martin Buber remarked that when a Jew addresses himself to God with the word 'Gotteniu' this marks as intimate a relationship to God as man is capable of achieving.

A curiosity: the highest compliment, distinction, homage to another person which can be expressed in Yiddish is the phrase 'Er iz a mensch' – he is a man, such as a person should be, such as can be relied upon in all circumstances.

Poland, what have I to do with Thee ...

In one sense Yiddish is unique among languages. It is a language – please consider this – in which it is virtually impossible to make a grammatical error. However you say it, provided it is clear what you mean to say, even if only with the help of the accompanying gesture, it will pass as acceptable, without a censorious comment. If you want an object to be of a feminine gender, even though it is normally considered to be of a masculine gender – 'zoll zajn', let it be so. If you want to alter the sequence of words in a sentence, introduce a neologism, known only to you or invented by you – it's fine, it's not the end of the world (and the end of the world, in Yiddish, is also not the end of the world!), nobody will take you on account of this for an ignoramus or simpleton. It will not be 'classical' Yiddish, not everybody has aspirations to be a Perec or a Singer. If you consider how much suffering has been caused to humanity by efforts to master articles, cases, declensions, how people who commit grammatical errors or have the wrong accent are looked down upon by their fellow creatures, you will realise what a marvellous invention this is, this independence, freedom and tolerance, which may be the envy of other languages but which can never be imitated.

* * *

We lived in a three room flat, with balcony, on the third floor, in a tenement house, on the corner of St. Sebastian Street and Berek Joselewicz Street. As in most houses in that district, with the exception of the caretaker who lived with his family in the basement, and one other of whom more later, all the tenants were Jewish – the wealthier ones in the front, the poorer in the back – a microcosm of the Jewish community. On each floor some little world of its own, some human comedy, loving, feuding, intriguing, gossiping – a seething cauldron.

When one talks of those better-off and those poorer, one has to bear in mind the Yiddish proverb 'm'kennish shetzen a yiddishe kishke', which means – if those peculiarities can be translated – that it is hard to guess the contents of a Jewish purse. Indeed, whilst everyone knew what was cooking in one's neighbour's pot (even if nothing was cooking), it was customary to keep one's financial status secret, mainly from the tax inspector, but also from a jealous neighbour; showing off one's wealth was deemed to be vulgar and stupid. Many Jews used to invest their savings in bricks and mortar, even property abroad, in Berlin or Vienna. Hence the disproportionate number of properties in Jewish hands.

To illustrate the point – a small digression. One of the janitors at the

Poland, what have I to do with Thee ...

Hebrew School in Brzozowa Street was a man called Hamer. He kept a tuck-shop in a niche on the ground floor, open during the breaks and afternoon activities; this was to compensate him for his beggarly wage. His son, not a high-flyer, in fact a bit of a dunce, was accepted after his matriculation for medical studies at the Jagiellonian University. It was obvious that this could only have been achieved by way of a substantial bribe to an official in that department's administration. In fact such a scam came to light in a subsequent investigation – no one was in the least surprised. The surprise was – where did Hamer get the money from?

Bribery, using influence, exploiting connections, was an integral part of daily life, it was accepted as normal (*plus ça change?*), it alleviated, in a way, the full rigour of the law. It was known that most problems could be settled for money, one only had to know the right channel and the current tariff. Mrs Lustig knew who mattered at the town hall, Mr Buchholz at the police, Mr Bader at the courts-of-law. I remember how one such go-between was relating to my Father a conversation he had had with an Inland Revenue official: 'We stood on the corner of Dietla and Starowislna Street, at the Koerner family's apartment house. I told him – take a good look at this building, it could be yours if you settle this matter we are discussing favourably. Imagine – here his voice trembled with indignation – he refused. Refused! Dirty dog! Now I shall have to find someone else, it will cost more.'

Money mattered, as always, as everywhere (it mattered also later, up to a point, in the ghettos). But there is an old Jewish tradition, expressed in a saying from the Talmud, that a learned person takes precedence over the chief priest. This ethos, in a vestigial form, was maintained. True respect was accorded to Osias Thon, to Rabbi Kornitzer, to Chaim Hilfstein – not to Mr Wasserberger, the milling magnate, or Mr Lachs of the Suchard Chocolate Factory.

On the ground floor, in the courtyard, there was a 'cheder', a Jewish elementary school for boys, where reading the Bible was taught. Boys from the neighbouring houses were brought there by a 'belfer', often by force, against their will. All day long, through the half-closed windows, the courtyard was filled with a rhythmic sing-song, children repeating after the teacher, the 'melamed', verses from the Scriptures. Now and again there was a shriek, some kid being beaten by the 'melamed' with a belt or a whip – the traditional teaching method.

I went to 'cheder' once only; my Father considered this to be my

Poland, what have I to do with Thee ...

(or rather his) duty, although my Mother protested. I did not like it – and refused to go again. The few prayers for daily use my Father taught me gently – they sufficed for a long time (though not for life). Worse than that – I ended, after one attempt, my piano lessons. I did not like the teacher, he threatened, the imbecile, to box my ears if I didn't practise – again, a teaching method, but in my case the least effective. On such details depends, sometimes, the course of one's life – what would I not have given later for the facility, like my brother, to sit down to the piano and strum Chopin's Etudes. I hold it against my parents that they indulged me too much, for a bit more strictness would have produced, perhaps, a better end-product. Apparently they saw no cause to be strict: at school I was always top of the class, things appeared to come easily, too easily. My Mother used to show off to neighbours my end-of-term reports : 'My Felus', she used to say, 'has 'tenacious' for application, 'commendable' for behaviour and 'very good' from top to bottom.'

The ground floor flat was occupied by the Einhorn family, a couple with two sons – Oscar, a contemporary of my older brother, and Bruno, slightly my junior. Mr Einhorn came to Kraków from abroad, probably from Czechoslovakia. He spoke Polish with a funny accent, although that alone would not mark him out; many Jews, if they spoke Polish at all, spoke with a funny accent. The names of the boys – Oscar, Bruno – sounded more 'progressive' than those in common usage, derived from the Bible. One could deduce a great deal from the sound of first names. My brother, four years my senior, had in his birth certificate as first names 'Jechiel Kalman'; inheriting them, as was the custom, from one of his grandfathers. I had in my birth certificate 'Rafael' after no one in particular; my Mother fancied that it sounded 'modern' and yet was within the Jewish tradition – after all an archangel he (true, only one of four, and the one who guarded 'the rear' – as my brother was fond of reminding me). The fact that 'Rafael' soon and irreversibly changed into 'Felek' is due to the tendency of the Polish language to diminutivise – a suffix makes an object smaller and smaller, a caressing gradation. (The English language lacks this, one has to labour: table, little table, sweet little table.) One cannot call a child 'Rafael', it gets softened into 'Rafael-ek'; from there it is only a step to 'Felek.' Between my brother's 'Jechiel Kalman' and my 'Rafael' there are four years during which my Mother, a 'modern' woman, enlightened and widely read, waged a battle, step by step, against the tradition of my Father's home. Father would voice, now and again, a

Poland, what have I to do with Thee ...

token protest, but deep down he agreed with her and submitted to the progressive change.

Something must have been known about Mr Einhorn's past, for my Mother was less than delighted when I visited their flat to play with the boys. They had a huge box of building bricks from which we used to erect fortresses and ramparts for our armies of lead soldiers – I brought with me my own contingent. Rumour had it that Mr Einhorn had gambled away a fortune at cards and had had to flee Prague, for such 'debts of honour' could have serious consequences, outside the law.

Kraków had its own quota of such gamesters of whom it was known that they neglected their families and lost fortunes playing cards (we never heard of those who won, which was puzzling). One of the scenes where these card-games were played was Hotel City at the Wawel end of the Plantations. When, occasionally, I would accompany my Mother on a walk through that neighbourhood, she would command me to look away from that place of iniquity, which, of course, had just the opposite effect.

The idea that cards were the invention of the devil meant that there was not a pack at home, not even for playing children's games, and to this day I don't distinguish clubs from spades. Later, when the game of bridge reached Kraków and took it by storm, my early aversion prevented me from learning that splendid game and deprived me of a social asset. I was left with an undying passion for chess. If not for that early, puritanical idea that moving little pieces over a chessboard, no matter how clever, is ultimately a waste of time, I felt I could happily have devoted most of my time to the game of chess. Today this passes for a respectable activity, one can earn a living thereby, or even make a fortune. In those days there was absolutely no money in it, great masters played in tournaments for a pittance.

(A little glimpse from the past: A few days after our arrival in this country, in May 1938, my friend Joe and I spotted a notice in the paper: Alexandre Alekhine will be playing a simultaneous game, against all comers, in the National Liberal Club in Northumberland Avenue in London. Wow! There's London for you, we thought excitedly, you can see the legendary Alekhine in person. We rushed there, of course, at the appointed time and not only did we see him but we bought ourselves a place at a chessboard, one of twenty, to play against him. We paid for it (I swear my memory does not deceive me, unlikely as it sounds) one shilling between us, sixpence each. The play lasted 2½ hours. Joe and I on board 20 were the last to finish the game, we drew (I knew we should not have taken that 'poisoned' pawn, but Joe thought otherwise). This means that Alekhine, one of the greatest masters of all time, played, in the year 1938, for 2½ hours, to earn himself one pound sterling. I know about inflation and all that, but...)

That puritanical streak which coloured our lives extended to alcohol. There was always a bottle of vodka on the sideboard from which Father would pour out a glass to the rare, non-Jewish visitor whom he happened to entertain, whilst for himself he would fill a glass of water from an identical bottle. Maybe this was not typical, for in the Jewish tradition alcohol is not condemned – the hassids, egging themselves on to a state of ecstasy, found a measure of slivovitz helpful. In the Bible, references to the consumption of wine vary. Total abstinence is regarded as retrograde, and the Book of Proverbs contains warnings but also encouragement. The Talmud says, light-heartedly, that at the Feast of Purim, one should drink until the distinction between the blessing of Mordechai and the cursing of Haman becomes blurred. Drunkenness among Jews was unknown. It was unthinkable to find a Jew in one of the drinking dens, even those in Jewish quarters. He might be an inn-keeper but would rarely touch vodka himself. Perhaps this was a reaction against the widespread and vulgar drunkenness around. A Jewish song ran something like this: *Shiker is a goy – Shiker is er – trinken miz er – weil er is a goy* (A goy is a drunkard – but drink he must – because he is a goy).

I revert to the house. On the first floor, on the right, lived the Zuckermans. The father had a timber-yard in Podgorze, and also a saw-mill somewhere in the Carpathian mountains. There was a large radio-receiver in the flat, allegedly for listening to foreign stock exchange quotations. There were four children in the family, all of whom went to the Hebrew school round the corner. The oldest, Baruch, was in the same form as my brother and was a member of the Communist Party. One day, there pulled up in the front of the house a Black Maria; two civilian police agents came out, knocked at Zuckerman's door and conducted a search, by turning the flat upside down looking for illegal publications, arrested Baruch and took him to the local prison, the so-called St. Michael's, whose iron-grilled windows gave on to the Plantations. We used to go to 'visit' him, gathered in a small group outside. We saw him at the window and waved to him. He would respond, clenching his fist.

The fact that his parents were dying a thousand deaths was less

Poland, what have I to do with Thee ...

important to him than the advancement of the world revolution. Soon after there was a court case (because in that fascist pre-war Poland one could not be kept in custody without trial, and during the trial one could defend oneself and make communist propaganda). The case went under the name of 'Henner and associates', against a few students from the University, a few from high-schools. The public prosecutor was the notorious Mr Szypula, who deplored the corruption of the young men, stressing their Jewish origin. They were defended by the able advocate Mr Bross, eloquently but to no good purpose. They all got sentenced to a few years in prison, the normal tariff. The war opened the gates of prisons. I met Zuckerman after the war, under a different name; he was some high dignitary – rightly so, who else? A pre-war sentence for 'subversion' served as unquestionable qualification for office.

On the same floor lived many members of the family Apfelbaum, very orthodox, three generations, bearded men in kaftans, women in wigs, youngsters in black caps, with shoulder-length sidelocks. I don't know how they made a living. It was noticeable how clean they were, one could say elegant, in a sort of way. I never exchanged a single word with any of them, although I prowled through that staircase ceaselessly and brushed against them, but with some sense of embarrassment, uncertain how to relate to them. They, wrapped up in their own world, walked past, hardly noticing our existence. I remember how one day I passed their door and from behind it I heard loud laughter. A shiver ran down my spine – they are capable of laughter? What were they laughing at?

A floor above lived Mr Danziger with wife and son. Mr Danziger was portly, wore pince-nez, had a waxed, turned-up moustache. During the First World War he had been a 'Feldwebel', a sergeant-major in the Austrian Army. On the sideboard in their dining-room, in a glass showcase, there was his photograph in uniform and with an Iron Cross. He was a teacher by profession, at the red-brick school in Miodowa Street. His son, Zygmunt, a good-looking youngster, was a student in the 'St. Jacek' high school in Sienna Street. Our housemaid, Emilia, said of him, with a sneer, that he was 'spoilt'; presumably he made passes at her, but fruitlessly. She was like a nun and, despite my Mother's warnings, ended up in a nunnery.

Zygmunt had more luck with his own housemaid, the comely Wanda. Mrs Danziger made no secret of it – like a latter-day Mrs Dulska she explained that she had hired her so that Zygmunt should not have to loiter the streets for pick-ups. When the housemaid became pregnant Mrs Danziger grew indignant that Wanda had cheated her, because when questioned about her sex life she had assured her that she was clean, healthy and had three abortions behind her. With these credentials she received a better wage than the usual, and despite that – look what happened... She was, of course, dismissed on the spot. What would follow in a case like that – and it was by no means exceptional – is a matter for speculation. She might return to her village to give birth or to abort or – if she was afraid to show herself on her home ground – she would find the woman in the back street who advertised her services with the notice 'Cups, leeches applied' and would, for a small sum, do what was necessary.

There was a sequel to this story. I remember how, one day, Wanda appeared in front of the Danzigers' flat, wrapped in a shawl, with a child at her breast, banged at the door with her fists and screamed: 'Take this bastard from me.' The doors remained shut, Wanda got hoarse, she sat on the doorstep of the house barring the entrance, no one dared go past her. She was not there next morning; one assumed the Danzigers had bought her off with a hefty ransom. Zygmunt told me later that he had threatened his parents that he would marry Wanda.

On the same floor, at the other end of the corridor, lived the Bertrams. The lady of the house was Salcia Bertram, a corset-maker. That was, in those days, an important and difficult craft. We are not talking of these airy-fairy girdles and bras of today, bought ready-made, but of those artful suits-of-armour, made to measure, with stays and whale-bones, frills, buckles, ribbons and strings to tighten the waist. That part of a lady's wardrobe was no trivial matter, for it required expert craftsmanship to make sure that it fitted here and there, and advise on how to put it on and, more importantly, how to take it off. Mrs Bertram had a small shop-atelier in Szewska Street, under the sign of 'Gracja'; she had a select clientelle and not every woman could afford a corset from Mrs Bertram. The trouble was that in the same limited space her husband plied his trade as a watchmaker. When a lady came in for a fitting, Mr Bertram hid behind a screen and held his breath.

The younger daughter in the Bertram's household was Olga, the most beautiful maiden of her generation in the whole neighbourhood – nobody would dispute that. (Whether she was the most beautiful in the whole of Kraków would have been disputed by some, since the

Poland, what have I to do with Thee ...

competition for that title was fierce.) Olga learned her trade at her mother's knee and learned it well, which – as it turned out later – was providential. Olga was the childhood sweetheart of my friend Johnny Erteszek from Brzozowa Street Number 13. A year before the outbreak of war Johnny went to the United States, obtained the so-called 'first documents' which entitled him to re-entry and in August 1939 arrived in Kraków in order to marry Olga and carry her away to the Golden Land. The outbreak of war thwarted that plan but after some wandering through Russia, through Japan, with some strange adventures and coincidences, the young couple landed in California. Now the story developed a twist worthy of a Hollywood scriptwriter. Olga made up a sample of a new model bra, Johnny offered it to one of the biggest department stores – Macy's or Bloomingdales – and got a substantial order. One has to know how to exploit such opportunities; they built a small factory, then a bigger one, naturally under the trademark 'Olga.' The firm prospered and grew into a public company with shares on the stock exchange. Every garment produced in the line of 'intimate apparel' – corsets, girdles, brassieres – carried a label with Olga's photograph and the slogan 'Behind every Olga garment, there is a real Olga.' Her face became known in America like that of a film-star.

Johnny came from a fairly orthodox family – they had a shop, a ladies' outfitters in Grodzka Street, closed, of course, on Saturdays. Father would go to the synagogue on important holidays, the kitchen was kosher, Johnny was a pupil at the Hebrew School. When I received the first letter from Johnny and Olga after their arrival in America I was overjoyed to hear that they were alive. Some time later, Johnny mentioned that he and Olga had become members of a church (Episcopalian? Congregational? I did not know the difference). I was a bit startled but assumed that they had had good utilitarian reasons for such a step. I only knew converts of that kind, and although I had a distaste for such a procedure I was not censorious. However, it transpired from further correspondence, and later in personal encounters, that we were facing a different phenomenon. Johnny asserted that he had converted out of conviction, that he had had a revelation of a new, great, blinding Truth.

I do not know why it was, and is, so difficult for me to accept such a statement at face value. Millions of people change their faith and convert from one set of beliefs to another. It would be arrogant to doubt the sincerity of their motives.

But with Johnny, no, I simply could not believe in the authenticity of his revelation. I am naturally sceptical of such phenomena and deeply suspicious of 'inner voices'. All the more so when this goes, as it did in this case, with an aggressive condemnation of Judaism. Since that time our discussions, verbally and in writing, turned solely around this topic, Johnny tried to persuade me of the truth of his new faith. This had just the opposite effect: in search of arguments I delved deeper into the principles and practice of Judaism and blunted somewhat my uncompromising agnosticism. When I begged of Johnny to cease to practice on me his missionary zeal, he used to say: 'Do not ask this of me, I do it out of friendship and respect for you, I have seen the light, you remain in darkness, I have the inner compulsion to open your eyes.'

There is no denying that this different outlook on basic questions cooled our relationship a little, which saddened me for I have great affection for friends with whom I went to school, to university, and with whom I shared a happy past in Kraków. Only a few of them survived, many have since died the unnatural Jewish death in their own beds – I cherish every one of them.

To revert to the story of the house. On the second floor, overlooking the courtyard, there was a room occupied by a small, portly, middle-aged man who lived alone. His name was Itzie Mann and he was a cantor in one of the synagogues. He had a beautiful, powerful voice. From that room often rose the sounds of Italian operatic arias: 'Vesta la giuba' or 'La donna e mobile'. One day Mr Mann disappeared and gossip had it that he was performing in the Metropolitan Opera in New York. A little ditty was composed, making fun of him, reminding him of the days when he was a poor, Jewish cantor.

On the third floor – Scharfs, Fischers, Rehmans. About Fischer the shoemaker, who occupied a tiny flat, one room and kitchen, with his wife, six sons and a daughter ('There is no shortage of space in mother's home' – he used to quote from the Talmud) I write in another place.

Rehman, except for the janitor the only non-Jew in that house, was a chimney-sweep. His mother, by appearance and disposition a witch-like figure, had the concession to sweep chimneys in a prescribed district – that was a source of a small but secure income. Young Rehman had to learn the trade, formal qualifications had to be acquired, exams had to be passed. He went to some school in Austria.

Poland, what have I to do with Thee ...

Whilst there he learned to speak German and, through close contacts with his Jewish neighbours, Yiddish.

He was a broad-shouldered youth, bright, intelligent, good-humoured. In his free time he would sit on the balcony reading or solving crossword puzzles which at that time began to feature in newspapers. He was on the best of terms with my family and the other tenants and best of all – the house was no place for keeping secrets – with Mrs Glass in the neighbouring house. When she gave birth to a boy, people discerned resemblance.

I remember him in his full regalia, all in black, soft cap on his head, scoop on one arm, a coil of wire ending with a brush and a heavy metal ball on the other – like a figure in old photographs. (Meeting a chimney-sweep was considered to be a good omen.) I saw him climbing on roofs, letting the ball fall through the chimney to displace the soot, then pushing the brush. He used to come home smeared from head to foot, face covered with soot, only the whites of his eyes gleaming.

When Jews were being ordered to move to the ghetto and my Mother decided to move to Warsaw where she thought it would be easier for her to hide, she left everything of value, mainly paintings of which there were many, in Rehman's safe-keeping, as he was one of the few gentiles she knew. He had her address in Warsaw; from time to time he would sell a painting and send her the money.

He himself did not have an easy time. With a German-sounding name and his knowledge of the language he could have improved his lot by passing himself off as a 'Volksdeutsch', and indeed there was pressure put on him to, but he resisted and damned the consequences. After the war he handed back all that was left – which, perhaps, would not deserve mention if not for the fact that the opposite was the rule. Those poor wretches who came up to claim their possessions were often shown the door or worse. Men such as Rehman were a rarity.

Such was just one, ordinary tenement house, one strand in a patchwork, a tiny stone in a crazy paving. Nothing, nothing remains of it all.

* * *

Young women of marriageable age were divided between those of whom it was known that they had a dowry and those who had none.

It was understood that the dowry should be in an inverse ratio to the beauty of the bride. That was a theme of interminable chit-chat and gossip in the homes and coffee-houses, which seemed to exist for precisely this purpose. Guessing the size, the whereabouts, the form, was fun. Mr F., for instance, gave his daughter as dowry a tenement house in which, allegedly, many years ago there was a brothel – that was a long time ago, but such things Cracovians do not forget. This caused much titter and amusement (perhaps prompted by jealousy, for the bride was very beautiful and would have found many a suitor) – it was said that Frederica received as her dowry a brothel. It was known who among the eligible men was a particularly avid 'dowry chaser', what the tariff was for professional degrees – doctors, lawyers, engineers. What also counted a little was 'yichus', that is 'noble birth' of sorts, a good name derived from rabbinical descent or old-established, not a newly acquired wealth.

When my parents got married, the match was, of course, 'brokered'. The story was that my Father sought assurance that the bride-to-be was not a red-head – and he went to get a glimpse of her from afar. It was known that the females in the Loewy family were ginger, but they were only half-sisters to my Mother.

Marriage-broking in that society was an indispensable institution. How otherwise would a female 'from a good home' find a suitable husband? Opportunities to meet, to talk to, to make friends – not to mention other things – with the opposite sex, were very limited outside the family circle. Young maidens in those days (I speak of the turn of the twentieth century – after that progress, or regress if you will, was rapid) grew up not merely as virgins, but often in ignorance of the facts of life. One of the older aunts would instruct the bride about what to expect on the wedding night, sometimes only when it was no longer prudent to delay. Whether the male would also grow up in such a state of innocence one can only surmise – I suspect that the more gregarious life-style, in the 'cheder' and the yeshiva, gave many opportunities to talk these things over; it would not be surprising if, besides the disputations over the holy texts, sex were the main topic under discussion. What, in those conditions, went on in bed on wedding nights is today hard to imagine – it is unlikely that there was a great deal of mutual pleasure. (In some communities the groom's parents were entitled to and did inspect the sheet.)

A marriage broker would bring together couples who, according to his knowledge of matters human and financial, were likely to get on.

He would take into account social standing, education and money, and would negotiate the delicate subject of the dowry.

It was obvious that at the base of this transaction was not 'love' – the very notion as we understand it belonged to a different planet – but the acceptance of a working convention. To remain unmarried was considered the worst thing that could happen to a woman. The threat 'you will grow a grey-haired tress' had to be taken seriously. The community felt responsible for marrying off those who had no one to take care of them – to whom they were given in such cases is another matter, but even this was better than nothing.

The husband was the one who, above all, was to earn a living and provide for the family: the wife was to look after the home, prepare meals, bear children and bring them up. That was the basic division of labour – life, of course, played variations on the theme. It happened, not all that infrequently, that the burden of earning a living would fall on the wife.

Among the Orthodox there was still another practice. The girl's father, if he could afford it, would travel round yeshivas and inspect students of a suitable age to choose his future son-in-law. It was understood that such a young man would be kept, for life, by the father-in-law. He would have no other duties but to study the holy books and produce children in the intervals.

Divorces were rare. The expectation of 'happiness' in marriage was low; husbands, as a rule, were not drunkards or wife-beaters; opportunities for infidelity were hard to come by; censoriousness by family and neighbours was strict, concern for the welfare of children deep. Above all – what would a divorcee do with herself, what would her lot be?

All this contributed to the stability of marriages. According to Jewish law it is only the husband who has the power to divorce his wife if he wishes (we know how our forefather Abraham sent away his wife Hagar with the little boy Ishmael – the Arab–Jewish hatred has ancient roots), he may grant or refuse a divorce as he wishes. In Orthodox Jewish circles these laws have caused a lot of misery to women and have been subject to fierce controversy as to how they are to be applied and interpreted.

In that system a woman often married beneath her station: her choices were limited and pressure to marry irresistible. Thus also my Mother, who had only a stepmother, could not afford to be unduly fussy and accepted her lot with good grace. She covered up the differences in the level of culture between the spouses. She came from a fairly prosperous home; her father had been a wine merchant. She had a good upbringing, went to a German school, was well-read in German literature (which proved, in the event, a life-saver) and also, though somewhat less so, in Polish. She exercised a civilising influence on the home and on my Father. She had, one has to say, more time than he had. Running a small household was not very time-consuming, there was always a housemaid, time was left for reading books from the lending library and working for charities – she was active in the Orphan's Home, and the Parent–Teacher Committee of the Hebrew High School. She cooked and delivered meals to some old people in the neighbourhood. In the afternoons she often spent an hour or two in a coffee-house, meeting friends, chatting about children, about housemaids, gossiping.

There were many subjects to dwell on. You've heard about it, haven't you? Yesterday Mrs N. burst into the coffee-house across the road where Mr N. was playing cards and made such a scene that the poor man dare not show himself in the street, she's ruined his life... This could not have happened to Mr K. who was also there; he would have broken her bones... You know to whom the Nattels want to marry off their daughter, the one with the squint? To Dr S. from Przemysl; people say he will soon get a chair at the Kraków University. Our maid who is friendly with the one in service with the Nattels told us that he was at a party there last night celebrating the engagement, and on departure he slipped her a large tip and pinched her bottom hard... Mr B. who lost his wife recently is courting the young actress who lodged with them; he should allow for a decent interval at least, but he cannot wait to get his paws on her, shame... Have you read, it was on the first page of the Illustrated Courier, Mr G., the lawyer, brought home some whore and she bit his tongue. He will no longer be the silver-tongued orator he fancied himself to be... You know the Latin teacher at the Hebrew High School, Bronstein? Pupils adore him. He was dismissed by Dr Hilfstein who thought he might be a communist. With a name like that, probably a relative of Trotsky... And young Bader, who shot his rival dead, got away with it scot free, he pleaded it was a duel, no way, it must have cost a small fortune in bribes... Mrs Lustig's son, a known dumbhead, got accepted to study medicine, that woman knows every back door. And so it went on. Nobody was safe from the wagging tongues.

My Father was severe, there was no arguing with him. He thought it was his birthright to have the first and last word on every issue. It was totally inconceivable that he should change nappies when the baby cried or push the pram or carry a shopping basket with provisions. He never looked into the kitchen, he would put his shoes there for cleaning before going to bed and pick them up highly polished next morning. He would come home for lunch from his office which was not far away (in Kraków nothing was far away) and have his afternoon nap; we would then walk on tiptoe and speak in whispers.

He concentrated entirely on the business of making a living and improving his and our material lot, and in this he had a measure of success. He first served as a salesman in a leather store and soon after, as often was the case with Jewish employees, opened a little store of his own in competition with his former boss. His boss, a Mr Nebenzahl, had a reputation for shrewdness. It was said that he developed his own method of personnel selection. He watched his employees like a hawk. Whenever a clerk went to the toilet, Mr N. would look at the watch and count the time of his absence – if the man ran to his desk quickly, buttoning up his fly (that was before the zip-fastener era), it earned him good marks, ahead of his less nimble colleagues. My Father clearly was one of those who would take too long over his business and so was quickly dismissed. A few years on and he advanced to be a manufacturer – 'The Viennese Factory of Leather Belting' proclaimed the sign over the door. It had nothing to do with Vienna, other than that capital being a symbol of excellence.

Money for housekeeping was dispensed in small doses; Father never lost the feeling of insecurity, the anxiety that there would be a shortfall, that the rainy day could not be far away. In the thirties, the word which was continually on people's lips was 'the crisis'. The object of awe was the so-called *Wechsel*, a promissory note; there was a pile of them on Father's desk, the shaky foundation of the family's fortune. If a 'promise to pay' embodied in such a document was not honoured, the note – lengthened by a slip of paper with a seal – was added and the note was presented to the first 'guarantor' on the list. If he refused to pay, a further slip of paper with a seal was added and the note was presented to the second guarantor and so on. Sometimes such a 'Wechsel' with its 'protests' stretched for yards. I remember these rolls of paper as the symbol of 'the crisis'. Bankruptcies of individuals and firms, genuine and fraudulent, abounded, causing a chain reaction. 'A Scharf does not go bankrupt' – my Father would pronounce with pride, as if the mere fact that one paid one's debts was, in contrast with others, especially praiseworthy.

Poland, what have I to do with Thee ...

Even in a small place like Kraków, where Kazimierz, the Jewish quarter, existed cheek by jowl with the non-Jewish, the lives of those neighbouring communities were, in many important senses, separate. It was possible for a Jew to grow up in a family circle, study, or prepare for a trade yet not cross the border dividing the Polish and Jewish communities. A great many Jews, in the district of Nalewki in Warsaw, in the hundreds of 'shtetlach', besides a sporadic contact with a supplier or a client lived thus – not together, but next to each other, on parallel lines, in a natural, contented isolation. During my whole life in Kraków, till my departure before the war, I was never inside a truly Polish home, whose smell, caught in passing, was somehow different, strange. I did not miss it, considered this division natural. I also do not remember whether in our home, always full of people, guests, visitors, passers-by, friends of my parents, my brother's and mine, there ever was a non-Jew, except for one neighbour and the caretaker who would come to collect his tips, and, of course, the maid who inhabited the kitchen.

The kitchen was large, more interesting than the drawing-room. I spent a lot of my time there, learned a great many things from one or another of the maids, of whom some were in our service for a number of years, sometimes till they got married. They were mainly peasant girls for whom there was no room in their village home – service with a middle-class Jewish family in a town was for them a social advancement and offered shelter from the dangers of city-life into which they otherwise might have drifted. They would acquire 'manners', would learn to speak 'properly'. They worked hard – cleaning, scrubbing floors, beating carpets on the stand in the courtyard, carrying coal from the cellar, making fires in the huge, tiled stoves, and cleaning out the ashes afterwards. When the washer-woman would come and do the monthly laundry in a giant tub, they would hang up the washing in the attic at the top of the house, then carry it in a wicker basket to a nearby mangle, after which they would do the ironing. They got up early and went to bed after all the members of the family, leaving their shoes for cleaning behind the kitchen door, had retired.

They had their 'free' day on Sundays – they would go to church, often bringing back with them devotional broadsheets full of ugly cartoons of Jews and poisonous articles – the church's calculated antidote to their contacts with Jews, whom they had a chance to observe at close quarters and see that they were not as black as painted. Afterwards, Mary, Catherine or Wanda would meet her swain, usually a soldier (Kraków was a garrison city), and go with him, arm in arm, for long walks through the Plantations or along the bank of the River Vistula. Towards the evening she would bring him home – they would sit, till late, on the back stairs, where she would feed him with delicacies from the larder, the like of which were not on the menu in the barracks – a reward and a bait for the future.

When I was a small boy my Mother would sometimes take me shopping for poultry in the 'New Square', in the heart of the Jewish quarter, with its market-stalls and the butchers and fishmongers in the round brick building in its centre. I recall the procedure – first the purchase, after a bit of haggling, of a live bird, a chicken or goose, from the country-woman by the kerbside (a fraction cheaper than from the butcher's). The bird would be handed over to a ritual slaughterer nearby who would slit its throat with one, deft move of the knife – the blood would squirt into the gutter. The desperate screeching and cackling of birds provided musical background to the whole scene. From there, on to the stall of the pluckers – a few women with kerchiefs, on low stools, would pluck the bird, feathers would fly around, and the operation would be over in a few minutes. Payment was in kind – the down and feathers were valuable merchandise in the hands of big exporters. The naked, repulsive corpse, wrapped in newspaper, would be thrown into the capacious shopping bag to re-appear on the kitchen table, awaiting further developments skilfully performed by my Mother.

Many memories connect with the sports ground of the Makkabi club, at the end of Dietla and Koletek streets, the scene of football matches in summer and an ice-rink in winter. To play football for that club was the dream of every aspiring Jewish youngster, the players were famous, I could name the team today. There was also a second Jewish club, Jutrzenka (Morning Star), playing in black-and-white shirts (Makkabi played, of course, in blue-and-white), but that was a workers' club and did not enjoy our fanatical support.

In the wooden fence surrounding the ground there were many cracks and holes and by pressing one eye to them one could see part of the field ('move away you so-and-so, that was my hole'); during matches the ground was thickly surrounded by such viewers. There were a few houses in an enviable position, from whose windows part of the field was visible. I had access to one such window in a flat in **Koletek Street belonging to the family Simanowicz. The father of that** family was partially paralysed. Shortly before the outbreak of war the family obtained a 'certificate' for entry to Palestine, but it would have been unthinkable to leave father behind. One day he got himself, somehow, to the window and fell to his death to free the family from the burden.

'The School' – The Hebrew Primary and Secondary School (Gymnasium) to give it its full title – was an educational establishment with the full curriculum in the Polish language, as prescribed by the Ministry of Education. This, after matriculation, gave automatic access to most departments of the universities. Parallel with the instruction in secular subjects there was a program of studies in Hebrew – the Bible, Jewish history and literature, according to the plan of Hebrew schooling developed and practised in Poland. From its inception till the outbreak of war, this school gave tuition to more than 2000 pupils of both sexes and left its mark on them. The memory of the teachers who virtually all perished in the Shoah is cherished by former pupils to the present day. The school was a sort of oasis where pupils could maintain an illusion that the world was and would remain a benevolent place.

I remember those distant days of my youth and childhood with utter clarity – it is known that with age the long term memory sharpens (whilst it is increasingly difficult to remember what one had for dinner yesterday). And the patchwork of those recollections does not consist of any great historical events but, more often than not, of trivial details, passing shadows, seemingly insignificant happenings, which for no apparent reason left a lasting trace in the grey matter.

The triangular area between Brzozowa, Berka Joselewicza and Sebastiana streets was where young urchins romped all day long, playing cops and robbers or a kind of rounders or kicking around a rag-ball – a real football with an inner tube and a leather cover was quite out of their reach. A rag-ball made from an old sock, packed tight with scraps of textiles into a round shape with string – to make such an object fit to be kicked around in the dust and mud – that was a special art. The best artist in this field and the best player in those games was the son of the concierge of our house – barefoot, in tatters, rachitic, but nimble as a monkey. He used to parade in front of the house walking on his hands – I admired him greatly and envied him, but it was unthinkable that I should be permitted to play with him. The basement, at the rear of the courtyard, where the sun never reached, thronged with families of the poor, often riven by disease due to malnutrition.

Poland, what have I to do with Thee ...

Only once did I penetrate that territory – during the taking of the national census students like myself were engaged in collecting data. After this experience, whoever did not turn into a revolutionary, at least in his mind, and did not want to abolish the system which tolerated such a state of affairs, lost the respect of his peer group. (It was said that the official publication *The Statistical Yearbook*, which used to appear in red covers, was the best recruiting material for the Communist Party.)

I would like to portray myself as a true child of the district of Kazimierz – this would not have been considered, in its day, as something to be proud of, rather the contrary, but with the passing of time we value things for their rarity.

In fact my Kraków (and I use that pronoun without hesitation) was not just Kazimierz. I would go there occasionally, to visit a friend, to attend a performance in the Yiddish theatre in Bochenska Street, or take part in a protest meeting in the large courtyards in Krakowska Street.

But my daily path from school, situated on the corner of Brzozowa Street and Podbrzezie, led from the family home in Dietla Street (third from the corner of Starowislna Street) in the direction of the town centre, towards the main Post Office, to the Rynek – the main town square – under the arcades of the Clothiers' Hall through the Plantations, at the side of the University, to the open spaces of the so-called 'Blonia', the grasslands, or directly through Karmelicka Street to the swimming pool in the Cracovian Park.

It might appear from this long register of streets that they stretch over some vast area – in fact, the space we are talking of was quite small, everything was within walking distance, there was nowhere to hide. On occasions when I used to come home in the late evening, after some assignation on the town's periphery, my Father already knew whom I had been walking with arm-in-arm and there was some evasive explaining to do.

One could have disappeared in the darkness of a cinema – a tactful projectionist in the Promien picture-house would sound a bell to warn that the show was about to end. Early American films were widely shown. We saw Charlie Chaplin and Jackie Coogan, Harold Lloyd, Buster Keaton, Johnny Weissmuller as Tarzan, the cowboy Tom Mix, Greta Garbo. German films with Martha Eggert-Kiepura, Emil Jannings, Marlene Dietrich, Lilian Harvey, Franciska Gaal; French films with Maurice Chevalier, Charles Boyer, Simone Simon, Danielle

Darieux. Also, if one was so inclined – Polish films with Brodzisz, Bodo, Junosza-Stepowski, Smosarska. (Antoni Slonimski asked by *Wiadomosci Literackie* which foreign film and which Polish film he considered best, replied: 'The best foreign film is Renée Claire's *Vive la Liberté*. I do not go to see Polish films.')

Films, generally, were a popular form of entertainment. The Slowacki Theatre was another. No performance was missed although I do not recall ever buying an entrance ticket. We had an arrangement with one of the ushers who, for a small tip, would let us in to the 'gods'. The theatre director in those days was Teofil Trzcinski; after him came Zygmunt Nowakowski (whom I had occasion to meet during the war, in London, as the editor of Grydzewski's *Wiadomosci*); after him, Osterwa. The repertoire was varied, mainly light. I remember seeing there the popular vaudeville *Krakowiacy i Gorale*, an American play *The Artists* with Stefan Jaracz and the adorable Zofia Jaroszewska, and the Hungarian plays of Molnar and Bus-Fekete. Occasionally, there were plays by Shakespeare, Bernard Shaw – interestingly enough some of Shaw's plays had their first showings in Poland, before they appeared in England. (To this day, in productions of *The Applecart*, King Magnus often wears a square hat with a feather, modelled on King Stefan Batory, as painted by Jan Matejko.) And, naturally, there was the whole range of the classic Polish repertoire – Slowacki, Mickiewicz, Wyspianski, Zapolska, Fredro – whose statue stands in front of the theatre, and Balucki, whose statue stands at the back. We greatly admired the leading actors – Solski, Adwentowicz, Zelwerowicz, Nowakowski, Osterwa – their art was equal to the finest on the stages of the West.

From the theatres to the cafés. There was Feniks in the Market Place, Bisanz in Basztowa, Secesja in St. Anne Street, Esplenade on the corner of Straszewski Street, Cyganeria in Szpitalna Street. (That was the one where, in 1942, a few Jewish teenagers threw a bomb, knowing that this was the meeting place of German officers.) In that café, on the few square feet of polished floor, there was dancing every day at five in the afternoon.

The period of University studies was a happy one. This had little to do with the merits of the University – though it had many – but with the fact that if a youngster between his 19th and 23rd year, who has a good home, many friends of both sexes, good health, curiosity and zest is not happy, then there is something very wrong with him. I chose Law for my studies – that was my natural inclination, with a view to practising a 'free profession'. It is worth noting that in pre-war Poland, that backward and undemocratic country, every student who passed his matriculation, irrespective of grades, had automatic access to University – I don't know where else this is or was the case. It is true that there was the so-called *numerus clausus* in the Faculty of Medicine, meaning that only a restricted number of Jewish students were accepted – and we made a great deal of fuss about it. If there had been no restrictions of that kind and if admission had been governed strictly by the excellence of grades, Jewish medics might have greatly outnumbered their non-Jewish colleagues – a situation which, not surprisingly, was not tenable in the prevailing conditions. Considering that sons and daughters of practising Doctors of Medicine could, if they wished, enter the Faculty outside the quota, that *numerus clausus* rule, in retrospect, does not appear so monstrous.

The Faculty of Law had, at that time, many distinguished professors. Wroblewski and Taubenschlag in Roman Law, Krzyzanowski in Economics, Kutrzeba, Vetulani, Gwiazdomorski, Zoll – all worthy teachers to learn from. A few of the professors were Jewish; some were baptised, which made it easier for them.

I completed my four-year studies with the Master's Degree (*Magister Iuris*). I thought that I would write my doctor's thesis, even when my plan to go to England was taking shape. I discussed the choice of subject with Professor Langrod, who suggested that in view of my stay in England I should write 'An Outline of Colonial Administration', no less. This, he thought would be useful and of current interest. In certain political circles in Poland at that time the idea was being propagated that on the international forum Poland should claim for itself colonies in Africa. There was an organisation with branches in various cities called 'The Maritime and Colonial League' – preparing the ground and ready to step in when such plans took shape. Perhaps Professor Langrod saw in me a future governor of Cameroon or Zanzibar. As we know, these plans did not materialise. In any event I did not write that thesis and did not gain such qualifications; other events claimed my attention. When I lecture these days in Poland, in Germany or in the States, I am always addressed as 'Professor' or, at least, as 'Doctor' – it is wearisome to try to set the record straight each time. I am content with my modest title of *Magister Iuris* and only once did I have a pang of regret. Some years ago I was present in the *Aula* of the Jagellonian University at the ceremony of the 'renewal of the Doctorate' of Dr Altschuler from

Jerusalem. It was precisely 50 years after my diploma. Had I been, all those years ago, more diligent and written my thesis, I would also have qualified for the 'renewal of Doctorate' and the ceremonial robes and hat would have fitted me well and made me look uncommonly distinguished.

I have always been a passionate reader of newspapers. There was no shortage of them in Kraków. There was the staid, conservative *Czas* (The Time), the socialist *Naprzod* (Forward), the nationalistic, right-wing *Glos Narodu* (The Nation's Voice) and the popular, pro-government, omnipresent *Ilustrowany Kurier Codzienny* (The Illustrated Daily Courier). The owner of that paper was Marian Dabrowski, a member of the Polish Parliament, a press magnate, who also owned a whole range of other papers and magazines. Considering to what depth the gutter press can sink, fifty years on, in England, *The Ikac*, as it was known for short, does not in retrospect appear so bad. It had to defend itself once in court against the accusation that it was publishing obscene ads. The sample quoted was: 'A hundred-percent virgin looks for a macho-lover' – small beer by today's standards.

At the other end of town, towards the River Vistula, in Orzeszkowa Street, was situated the *Nowy Dziennik* (New Daily), a Jewish daily newspaper in the Polish language (one of three such newspapers in Poland – the other being *Nasz Przeglad* (Our Review) in Warsaw and *Chwila* (A Moment) in Lwow). That newspaper served the Jews of Kraków as the main source of information, reporting events in the wide world, in Poland, in Palestine. The leading articles were often written by Dr Osias Thon, the pride of Kraków Jewry, a member of the Polish Parliament, the chairman of the Jewish Parliamentary Club, the Rabbi of the Progressive Synagogue, the 'Tempel', and an ardent Zionist. The *Nowy Dziennik* was an institution without which the life of Kraków Jewry was unthinkable. I started my journalistic career there and became its foreign correspondent in London.

A small digression: on my last visit to Kraków some months ago, I paid a visit to the reading room of the Jagellonian Library, locus of many happy memories and – on an impulse – requested to be shown the bound folios of *Nowy Dziennik* from the year 1938. I wanted to cast a glance over those pages, re-read the articles which I then wrote to the joy of my Father and, perhaps, some other readers. The folio was put on my desk. With trembling hands I started to turn the flimsy pages. I was overcome with memories. Every headline, every name, every advert ('Buy lottery tickets from Safir Brothers – every other ticket wins'), every small ad ('You will speak English like a native Englishman – Karmel, Koletek Street 3') brought forth a flood of images, faces, scenes, events. Immersing myself entirely in that old world, slowed down by the turning of the pages, I did not get to my own articles before closing time. I had paused too long over a notice, one day in January 1938, which read: 'On Wednesday, at the premises of the Massada youth-group (of which I was then the leader), at 8 pm, Felek Scharf will give a talk titled: 'How to get rid of the British in Palestine'.'

One day, on another visit, I shall get to see the correspondence 'From Our Own Reporter in London'. I happen to remember one article, in particular, the last one I wrote in August 1939, wherein there was a passage saying that 'I stake my journalistic reputation (sic) on the prediction that there will be no war.' At the time when this article would have reached the Editor's desk – the Germans were already in Kraków.

In retrospect this looks as if I had been blind and naive to a degree – which might well have been true, but the prediction by itself is no proof of this. I was in good company. Many prophets, among them the widely circulated *Daily Express* of Lord Beaverbrook, throughout 1938 and until the last day carried a banner headline: 'There will be no war.' It is assumed now that everybody knew, that it was obvious to everyone that war was inevitable. This is not how matters looked then, particularly to an observer newly arrived in England, dazzled by the wealth and apparent power of the Empire, with possessions around the globe, where the sun never set. I saw it – would not Hitler see it? He would not dare...

It follows that it is difficult to predict – particularly the future.

One year and a bit before the outbreak of World War II I left Kraków 'voluntarily' (a good deal could be written about those inverted commas). I was conscious that the decision was irreversible and would decide the future course of my life. It matured slowly, during many a sleepless and talked-through night. It meant parting with a safe and cosy home to which I was greatly attached, particularly to my Mother. Leaving it made me feel guilty. I saw it as a kind of escape from the battlefield, a shedding of responsibility for a common fate. I had a circle of friends of both sexes, such as I have never had since – it was not easy to part company with them.

On the other hand, life in Poland appeared less and less attractive

Poland, what have I to do with Thee ...

to me. Antisemitism permeated the space around. The professional prospects for a newly qualified student of law were gloomy; first five years of 'articles,' then practice in an overcrowded profession. One day I returned from the Courts of Law where I had represented a client whose semitic features were against him, but whose claim was undoubtedly just, even in such inexperienced hands as mine. I lost the case and it was obvious that the judge was biased. One was used to a measure of discrimination by the authorities, but the dispensation of justice was a different matter – it symbolised a qualitative change.

I returned to the office taking a long, roundabout way. I handed the files to my patron and told him I would not come to the office again. He huffed a bit: 'Don't take it so hard, we shall go to appeal and have this decision rescinded. Such things are unpleasant but one must adjust to realities.' 'Let him' – I thought – 'go on adjusting if he wants to, I will not.' That was the end of my career as a lawyer.

The incident, on the face of it, was trivial, but the fact that I have not forgotten it shows how deeply it cut. Whilst I try, as far as possible, to recreate my train of thought and the open and the hidden motives for my departure, the heart of the matter was that I felt constrained and wanted out, into the wide world.

The idea which at that time exercised more than any other the minds and hearts of people in my circles was Zionism. At school and at university I was an active Zionist – I wrote articles, spoke at meetings, agitated for emigration to Palestine, to pioneer, to conquer the desert, to create a Jewish State. (There circulated at that time a definition of a Zionist which had a grain of truth in it: it was a Jew who, using the money of another Jew, sends a third Jew to Palestine.) I was determined to go to Palestine, but like St. Augustine who implored God to make him chaste but not 'just yet', I was not quite ready 'just yet' to sacrifice myself for the great cause, before I had tasted life a bit more, learned a bit more. My contribution, so I argued, would be the more valuable for it. And so the matter got postponed and never realised. There came the war, love, marriage, responsibilties.

Why, when leaving Poland, did I chose England as my port of call? We were persuaded that Great Britain, at that time, was the centre of 'civilisation', and it was necessary for all sorts of reasons to get acquainted with it. I had invested time and money in learning the language. I thought that I had learned a good bit, although it transpired soon after arrival that my teacher in Kraków had been only a few pages ahead of me in the Berlitz primer.

Poland, what have I to do with Thee ...

I read, passionately, a selection of English novels (in Polish translations) – Galsworthy, Somerset Maugham, all of Kipling – Stalky and Co. was one of my favourites; boys at a 'public school', that was the life. Thomas Hardy, P. G. Wodehouse, above all, Aldous Huxley – that sophisticated, intellectual ambience, that modern society, those discussions of profound ideas – these writers formed my view of the land I was heading for.

The year was 1938. To be let into England was by no means simple. I could show a double cause, to be sure. I had been accepted to do a course of post-graduate studies at the London School of Economics, and I was a foreign correspondent for *Nowy Dziennik*. Indeed, soon after arrival, I started sending short articles, snapshots of everyday life, tittle-tattle about English eccentricities, literary gossip. I do not know what my readers made of it; more importantly for me, my Father liked it, was proud to see my name in print, received congratulations for my efforts in the synagogue or the coffee-houses (more often there) and therefore found it easier to send me my monthly allowance. Sterling stood high; the few pounds necessary for a modest upkeep, when translated into Polish zloty, represented in his view a lot of money and he did not suspect that my Mother was sending me some more, saved from her household allowance.

After a long journey by train and boat, I arrived by way of Hook of Holland and Harwich at Liverpool Street Station, then one of the less attractive rail terminals in London. I was laden like a pack-mule with a heavy trunk filled with a carefully planned wardrobe: tailor-made suits (it was habitual for middle class people to have suits and dresses made to measure) from 'Made in England' cloth, according to the latest Cracovian fashion (far ahead, as it appeared, of that prevailing in England). The inevitable 'smoking', or dinner jacket, for those receptions in high society which would come my way thick and fast; 'plus-fours' like those of the Prince of Wales in a photograph which I had passed on to my tailor. I proudly carried a portable typewriter – let it be seen that I am a journalist – an Underwood with Polish letters. It weighed 10.5 kilograms (I had the feeling that the decimal point dropped out en-route.) A small rucksack filled with cakes my Mother gave me for the journey – I ate them all, sitting on the iron steps on a side-platform, enveloped in smoke – the last taste of home. Nothing ever again tasted so heavenly. I was a bit frightened, and excited at the same time – England, here I come: Prepare to be conquered!

I travelled by Underground to the East End; it was then a Jewish district with its famous Whitechapel High Street. I spent the night in a Salvation Army hostel; next morning I went in search of lodgings. There was dense, yellow fog, which I knew from my Sherlock Holmes, settling in the nose and throat; shirt and undershirt were soon blackened with soot. The sun fought feebly to penetrate the cover. I walked around the streets a bit and was startled to see shopsigns with Hebrew letters. But the human landscape was strangely familiar – Jews from Poland, from Russia, trading among themselves and jabbering in their Anglo-Yiddish jargon.

I found a room with a family, dark and poky, unlike the one which I had at home, light years away from Forsytes, Kipling and Huxley (but close to Zangwill). As it turned out it had its compensations. The landlady whose family hailed from Chrzanow took trouble to keep one of my appetites satisfied; her pretty daughter, the other.

Round the corner from where I lodged, in Ridley Road, Dalston, I sometimes observed, in the afternoons, a public meeting, a speaker on a soap-box addressing a score or so of bystanders, who clapped and shouted approval. Ah, I thought, an example of British democracy in action. One day I came closer to pick up the sense of the tirade. I must mention that I was wearing a black shirt, practical and fashionable. Suddenly, from a nearby housing estate there rushed a group of Jewish youngsters, who with a few kicks, blows and shoves set the speaker and the gathering to flight. I remember this, for as I stood near the speaker, somewhat disoriented, I took a knock on the head. It turned out that the speaker was Oswald Mosley, the founder and leader of the British Fascists, Blackshirts as they were called from the colour of their uniforms, and the meeting was a regular provocation of his gang in the heart of the Jewish neighbourhood. Ridley Road became notorious for this. It was somewhat ironical that wanting to observe British democracy at work, I took a blow meant for a fascist.

Life took such a course that England, which was to be a staging-post, became my home, where I have spent my adult life, have children and grandchildren – all of them good, healthy, normal, a veritable God's garden. In the course of that long journey (long according to the calendar though it feels as if it has passed in a flash) I have not become, in any sense, English. I have been spared all ambiguity in this respect by this unflinching and constant awareness that I am, totally, a Polish Jew, and cannot and would not be anything else. I nurture for this, my adopted country, feelings of deep, though not uncritical, affection and am concerned for its well-being; I am grateful to fate for having thrown me here and not elsewhere, but despite my family bonds, ties of true friendship, love of the language and the landscape, I remain a stranger in the land and I find that position on the margin comfortable.

This 'alienation' bears, in some way, on the relationships in my own home, with my own family, with those whom I love and who are closest to me of all. I do not share with them to the full my internal landscape. Matters which preoccupy me the most – Jewish matters, Israeli matters, are not, cannot be central to their being. I have not transmitted to them a great deal of my past, and therefore a great deal of myself. I did not know perhaps how to do it, maybe I thought this to be some sort of burden which should remain private and not be shifted to other people's shoulders.

I do think, sometimes, that had I found myself in the 1930s and 1940s in Palestine, I would have been more useful, whatever part I played; there – there was a time when a mere Jewish presence was useful.

That was also the time – it did not last long and could not have lasted long – when that small settlement of Jews in Palestine, consisting of idealists, inspired by the vision of a physical and spiritual regeneration of the Jewish people in their own country, represented a model of a society which had no equal and deserved one's unqualified admiration.

But it seems to me that had I been at the time in Palestine, taking into account my former ties with the 'Revisionist' movement in Poland, with some of my closest friends in 'Etzel', the fighting group around Begin, I would have *par-force* become a part of that group, with all the consequences that entailed. Even if their methods were against my conviction that the end cannot justify any means, my loyalty to old comrades and solidarity with friends would have probably proved stronger than other principles. I could easily, all too easily, have become a 'terrorist' (but a bad one, *malgré-moi*).

The period of German occupation in Poland dominates my internal landscape and casts a shadow over everything that happened to me before or after. From the moment when the trickle of news about the extermination camps began to reach London, I stood close to the sources of information. I was working at that time with Ignacy Schwarzbart who, until the arrival of Szmul Zygielbojm, was the only Jewish representative in the Polish National Council of the Emigré Government in London and I was with him when he received the first fateful telegram from the Polish Underground and he wrote, with a trembling hand, in his diary: 'This is not possible.' I was with him when later, reports reached him which no longer left room for any doubt, and he wrote in his diary: 'It is true nonetheless.' Some people may say that all this was a long time ago, but there has not been a day in my life that I have not reverted in my thoughts to those events.

My Mother survived the war with the help of false documents, the so-called 'Aryan papers', by a series of miracles – without miracles no Jew survived. She had, in the then current phrase, 'good looks', which in that context meant only the lack of semitic features. She spoke impeccable Polish, and also German, which was her first language. When interrogated by the Gestapo officer into whose hands she was delivered by a blackmailer whom she had ceased paying, knowing that since he knew her address there would have been no end to it, the officer took the view that she did not look or speak like a Jewess; a view influenced perhaps by the fact that during the interrogation my Mother played with her golden wedding ring, which she casually let drop on the carpet.

In 1943, when the ghetto was burning, my Mother lived in a rented room with a Polish family who of course had no notion of her identity, within sniffing distance of the ghetto walls – the acrid smoke floated through the windows. Her hosts, in whose appartment there were frequent conspiratorial meetings, looked on with chilling indifference. How my Mother managed not to give herself away by a twitch of the face or an overflowing tear; how she sharpened her senses to observe and imitate the religious habits during festive meals, visits to church, the kneeling, the crossing oneself, the muttering of prayers, the hundred and one little gestures which belong to a culture not her own, will remain a mystery.

Money for board and lodging came from a gradual disposal of pieces of jewelery – a few rings, brooches, earrings, a pearl necklace – birthday presents or anniversary gifts which she used to receive, as was customary among moderately affluent middle class families. Each sale made it painfully clear that soon there would be nothing more to sell. From time to time she received a small remittance from Kraków – it came from her former neighbour, Rehman, bless him, who occasionally disposed of the paintings which Mother had left in his safe-keeping. The paintings were mainly by contemporary Polish artists, Kossaks – Wojciech and Jerzy, Falat, Wyczolkowski, Malczewski, Wodzinowski, Vlastimil Hofman, Rychter-Janowska. It was the fashion in those days to cover the drawing-room wall with paintings, and I think that the main buyers of paintings were Jews.

To disguise from her hosts the fact that she had some sort of an 'income', Mother acquired a large ball of wool from which she was seen through most of her waking hours to be crocheting a garment. When this was ready she used to go out into the street with the avowed purpose of selling it. She would come back with the bundle in her bag and at night, my Penelope, would unstitch it, in order next morning to be seen at her labour as usual.

Those who survived and described 'life on Aryan papers' conveyed a picture of a haunted, nightmarish existence. The fact that they found themselves in a hostile environment, where a wrong word or gesture was a matter of life or death, meant that many of them who, at enormous cost and risk, had managed to settle on the 'Aryan' side, could not endure the continuous fear and strain and returned to the ghetto, to suffer, starve and eventually perish – but amongst their own people.

When I think what my own chances would have been had I been there, I am convinced that I would not have survived. The options were limited. One was flight eastwards from the advancing German Army. Many people who took that route did survive, even through 'gulags' and 'settlements'; there was in the end the saving grace of General Anders' exodus. My only brother, with his young wife, was not so lucky – they were caught in the German advance and killed. My Father, who in his flight had reached Lwow, was soon after deported by the Russians to the tundra in Karelia, in the Far North, to fell trees – an occupation which he was not used to and could not do, one of the millions of victims of the noble socialist maxim 'who works not eats not' (kto nie rabotajet' nie kushayet'). My Mother, we all thought, was not fit to embark on an arduous trek eastwards and I would not have left without her.

To cross to the 'Aryan side' would not have been a feasible option for me – I had no friends over there and my looks, even though not so strikingly Jewish as to betray me to the Germans, whose discernment in this matter was not great, would undoubtedly have caught the attention of one of the all too many eagle-eyed Poles.

Our housemaid, a peasant woman who would have been glad to go through fire for us and who in fact did give shelter to my Mother for a while, could not have done the same for me – men were more difficult to hide.

Poland, what have I to do with Thee ...

There would have been nothing for me but to go, like the rest of the community, to the ghetto or labour camp and share their fate to the end. It is true that even among those there was a handful of survivors, but that called for enormous endurance and luck (if you could call it that) and above all an iron will to survive which, I am convinced, would not have been at my command, seeing what was happening around me. But one must add this proviso: that no-one really knows beforehand what he can endure and what he is capable of in circumstances which defy all imagining.

When I asked my Mother what gave her the strength and the will to survive, she maintained that it was the thought that I was somewhere far away, safe, and that one day I would return and take her away with me. The moment the war ended she returned to Kraków, to lodgings in one of the houses which, formally, she owned – and waited. Indeed, not too long, for as in a fairy-story, I was soon knocking at her door. Those emotions and the gratitude for my good fortune, one case in a million, I cannot, nor will I try to describe.

I brought my Mother to England, she lived with me and my family for another 10 years, learned the language, managed the household, saw the birth of grandchildren. It would seem, on the surface, that she had wholly recovered and the nightmare of the past was being forgotten. Till the last, however, when there was a ring at the door and I was getting up from my chair to answer it, she would go pale and grab my sleeve: 'Don't go' – she would whisper and then nod her head and smile wanly. For years I sat in the evenings by her bedside, listening, interminably, to her improbable true stories. For her it was a kind of therapy, for me an experience of heartbreaking immediacy. Since then I have read a great deal and even written a little about this subject; nothing has embedded itself so deeply in my consciousness as my Mother's recounting of those consummately hideous times.

The greatest pain to which a human being can be exposed is that of a mother or a father looking on the suffering of their child and not being able to help or relieve it. Think of how much of this kind of pain there was at that time, parents helplessly witnessing their child slowly dying of hunger, parents separated from their offspring during a 'selection', parents, with their child, being pushed into the gas-chamber.

When I think of what my Mother went through in those days – thoughts which I have learned to ward off but which haunt me during

Poland, what have I to do with Thee ...

sleepless nights, I am overcome by a desire to set the world on fire. And that 'only' a mother, not a child.

There were many different ways in which a Jew could have perished in Poland in war-time: from disease, from hunger, during an *Aktion*, from a bullet – because a German had a fancy to shoot him; he could have committed suicide when life became too hard to endure; he could have been worked to extinction in a labour camp or tortured to death in a concentration camp. He could also, lost among the Poles, have died as a Pole.

Tracing the fate of members of my family I discovered a Scharf in every one of those categories. How does one cope with that sort of knowledge, that almost everybody one knew – family, friends, teachers, neighbours, shopkeepers, beggars – all died some horrible death and it is only due to some accidental twist of fate that one has not gone the same way. When I want to recall a face I knew, I see it contorted, gasping for breath, in a mass of swirling bodies. (The Germans also had at their disposal Zyklon C – a poison gas swifter in action but somewhat more expensive to produce. Well, let the Jews suffer a bit longer.)

How does one adjust to what, in ordinary life, passes for 'normality'? How does this awareness shape one's 'Weltanschauung', one's perception of history, of religion, of morality, of man?

The generation of Jews of the post-holocaust era, the 'survivors' in the broadest sense, are a people apart. Burdened by their memory, walking-wounded in eternal mourning. I do not think that an outsider can understand this condition.

* * *

I would like to recall the following story. At one of the summer camps of the Kraków branch of an organisation of university students known by its acronym Z. A. K. M. I. K. (The Jewish Academic Circle of Lovers of Nature!), in Kuznica on the Baltic Coast, a year before the outbreak of war, I struck up a friendship with Staszek K. from Warsaw. He was, like myself, a dedicated 'mountaineer'. We went together for summer and winter holidays to Zakopane, at the feet of the Tatra mountains, for the conquest of the lesser peaks – and women (in both respects there was more talk than real achievement). Staszek was a sturdily built, muscular youngster, blond and blue-eyed. After matriculation he took up a university course in Physical Education. He used to tell me that among his fellow students there was a group of right-wing nationalists who made a habit of taunting him, calling him abusive names, urging him to go to Palestine. This had its own irony, for Staszek came from a very assimilated background: his father was a lawyer, his mother a collector and expert on Sèvres china – his Jewish ties were atrophied and only these racist attacks prevented him from forgetting that he was a Jew and, in the end, turned him into an ardent Zionist.

One student in particular, a Silesian by the name of Jurczyga, was always truculent and enjoyed provoking a quarrel, attacking Staszek physically. Since Staszek was not one to give way easily, it often ended in fisticuffs, a black eye or a tooth knocked out – fairly normal side-effects of university life in those days.

When the ghetto was created in Warsaw, Staszek had not for a moment considered the possibility of being locked in. He foresaw, correctly, that he would have felt totally alienated from his fellows there – it is true to say that at the very bottom of that cauldron of degradation which was the ghetto, were the converts and the assimilationists, who felt no bond of kinship with the surrounding multitude, but only dislike and revulsion for them, a feeling which was heartily reciprocated.

Staszek said good-bye (as it turned out – for ever) to his parents, bought a certificate of baptism (as luck would have it of a person with the same initials – he did not have to remove the embroidered monograms from his shirts) and made his way to Zakopane – where else? He took up lodgings with a peasant whom he knew from our pre-war escapades, on the way to the Koscieliska valley. He acquired two fierce alsatian dogs, partly for company, partly for further disguise – nobody could possibly take for a Jew this athletic, blond young man, with alsatian dogs on a lead, speaking, on occasion, the local argot. In that respect he felt completely safe and preferred not to think what would happen when the money ran out, when the time came to part with the golden cigarette-case, the signet ring, the Waterman fountain-pen, the Omega watch, and how long the money would last.

One day he went out as usual for a walk in the town's centre. Suddenly, as in a bad dream, he came face to face with his persecutor, the Silesian from the Physical Education course. Fright, panic, too late to avoid the clash – this is the end, thought Staszek.

Jurczyga took another step forward, fell on Staszek's neck, gave him a warm hug. 'My friend' – he cried – 'for God's sake, are you afraid of me? What do you take me for? I'll lay down my life for you. Here's money, take it, take it all, here's my address. Whenever you're in need, day or night, just knock at the door, count on me.'

It so happened that soon after, when Staszek, having been denounced, was running away from the Gestapo, Jurczyga saved his life at the risk of his own.

In every discussion of these themes of the German occupation one has to bear in mind that those were apocalyptic times, that the circumstances in which people lived and acted were unprecedented. The decisions which they were often asked to take were so horrifying that one must beware of jumping to conclusions or passing judgement. A mother faced with the choice which of her two children to save if there were a chance of saving only one of them – the very thought of having to make such a choice curdles the blood and renders one helpless. Such situations were frequent – who can put oneself in such a place and enter into a rational discussion of rights and wrongs?

In the years after the war, among my Krakówian contemporaries, there was frequent mention of one Arthur Loeffler. He was a colleague of mine from school and university; we were very close. At school he was known for playing the first trumpet in the school orchestra: at the school's summer-camps the day would begin with Arthur rousing the boys and girls from their sleep with the Krakówian 'trumpeter's call'. After matriculation he turned his musical talent to good use, playing in jazz bands, in cafés, *thé-dansants*, society balls. He was not a high-flyer, not known for special gifts, but an ordinary, popular, good chap.

During the war Arthur was recruited to serve in the OD, the 'Jewish police'. How much recruitment to the OD was voluntary and how much compulsory is a moot point. It was clear that the role of the 'Jewish police' was solely to serve the Germans and do their dirty work for them – nobody expected to go through that service with their hands clean. Nonetheless there were many cases where the presence and the action of Jewish policemen tempered somewhat the frightfulness of the situation.

We know from the accounts of eye witnesses that Arthur in the course of his duties behaved badly; that, above all, he traced and delivered to the Gestapo people whom he recognised as Jews, among them some of his former school friends. In the interminable discussions and recollections of those times, the question would crop up again and again: 'How could he, how could he?'

Poland, what have I to do with Thee ...

That question 'How could he?' concerns, of course, not only Arthur Loeffler, but thousands of others whose actions and decisions seem to us now incomprehensible and contemptible. There is no need to justify such deeds – there are moral limits which must not be exceeded in any circumstances. But we must bear in mind what physical and mental pressure the German monster could and did exercise to get his way. And when one puts the question of how could he take some of his former friends to the Gestapo, a Waechter or a Schenker, one must remember that before he was sent out on his deadly hunt to fill the quota of victims, he was told in no uncertain terms that should he return empty-handed, his father or mother, his sister or his brother would be killed instead. Let those who can pass a moral judgement.

* * *

The 'Shema', the key text of the Jewish liturgy, contains a commandment to teach the next generation, ceaselessly, the essence of Judaism. In the 'Haga-da', the story commemorating the exodus from Egypt, recited during the feast of Passover, there is a demonstration of how to instruct all of them – those who are keen to learn, and those who want no part in it, those who are indifferent, and those who do not even know what questions to ask.

The extermination of Jews in Europe during the last war is the most tragic event in the whole, long martyrology of the Jewish people. The recollection of it dominates my internal landscape – everything I think and do, my view of everything around me is filtered through this awareness. And yet, despite these commands and instructions, I do not know how much of this awareness I have passed on to my children.

The motives for this reticence were diverse, not always clear even to myself. They know, of course, that I am a Jew, I have always stressed it. They know of my origin, my connection with Israel, with Poland – such always was and is the climate of my family home. But the extermination of the Jews, of my family, of what this means to me – these matters were seldom raised. I thought, perhaps, that they were growing up free from that trauma, cheerful, carefree, normal – why influence their disposition, cast the shadow which has darkened my life?

Another probable reason was that I found talking about these matters exceedingly difficult and had no language which I thought adequate or appropriate. I feel a bit guilty on this account. I did not appreciate, perhaps, that the past is not only a burden but also a

Poland, what have I to do with Thee ...

heritage and that in shielding them from the pain, I also deprived them of something of value. A generation which does not know its roots, which is not in dialogue with its past, is, in some way, not whole. And if the awareness of that past is painful, it is, perhaps, a price worth paying.

How to do the 'passing on'? There are many professionals in this field, but the majority of us are amateurs who have to find their own way (but I console myself with the thought that the Titanic was built by professionals and the Ark by an amateur). The greatest difficulty, as I see it, is how to present the boundless horror of those events which have no analogy in history and at the same time not to undermine the belief in the sense of creation, in human values, in justice.

Individual testimonies, which are legion, strike deeper than mere statistics, however stark. There are many sources of great value – one must learn how to use them, the timing, the dosage.

I have a friend, a woman writer, who lost her whole family in the Shoah. She told me that many years ago she was on vacation in Spain with her 10-year-old son. In that holiday resort, at that time, there was a veritable plague of insects, which made their stay well-nigh intolerable. One day she shut tight all the doors and windows of their apartment, sprayed every nook and cranny with insecticide and took her son for a long walk. When they returned after some hours and opened the door to the apartment to verify the efficacy of the operation the floor and the walls were covered with insects, dead or twitching in their last throes. At this sight the boy asked her: 'Mummy, is this how Jews were poisoned? Is this how they died in the gas chambers?'

What had she told her son once, what picture had entered his little head, that he should come out with a remark like that? What scar did this image leave on him for life? Did she have the right to mark him so? Did she have the right not to?

I read somewhere an aphorism which amused me: 'Love is a physiological function which made a career.' It could be said that antisemitism is a primitive idea which made a career. (Another definition is 'A Christian disease of which Jews die.')

The target is well chosen – Jews have this mysterious gift of provoking jealousy and contempt at the same time. They are weak (despite the myth of their power) and dispersed: it is easy to get at them. Antisemitism is a light sleeper and it is a very durable product – it survived the destruction of millions of Jews, it appears that it can thrive even in their absence. The Poles did not invent antisemitism – it is an ancient phenomenon, religious, social, economic, political – but this last variant, that is antisemitism without Jews, can be called a Polish invention.

In various essays in this small collection, in my discussion with Andrzej Szczypiorski in the Paris *Kultura*, in my utterances at conferences in Oxford and Jerusalem, I have given expression to my thoughts on this subject. In a sense, everything I write revolves around this theme.

I am prompted here to add to this some further thoughts because during my recent visits to Poland I have been struck by the fact that, despite the passage of time, when a new generation has grown up, changes for the better have not been blindingly apparent. There is still a thicket of prejudice, ignorance and ill-will. There persists the demonisation of the Jew, the thought that there must be some truth in the accusation that Jews commit ritual murder; that Jews as a race, nation, community, have in them an ineradicable element of evil. There lives a mere handful of Jews in Poland today, a sorry remnant of a 3½ million strong presence, and yet many Poles cultivate their grudges against them and are ready to activate their hostility. That phrase which one heard after the war – 'For one thing Hitler should be thanked: he did leave Poland free of Jews' is the most odious expression to which human thought and language can sink. If this in any way reflects the prevailing mentality, then the moral devastation of which it is an example does indeed bode ill for the future of the country.

What have the Jews done, what unpardonable sins have they committed, that such should be their picture in the mind and the subconsciousness of many Poles? Is this merely an expression of the common, ordinary hatred of 'the other', 'the alien', the target of the traditional Christian doctrine of deicide, or is it something more, something specifically Polish, the roots of which must be sought not in Jewish characteristics but in the Polish psyche?

Whatever the case, the effect is a psychopathic phenomenon, a neurosis of a sick organism, which obscures a true picture of the world. Were I a 'true' Pole (in the definition of President Walesa) I would deplore this national obsession, not on account of the Jews to whom this no longer matters very much, but because I care for the health of the nation. I would grieve not only because of the misdirected energy and the sheer stupidity of it all, but because of the

Poland, what have I to do with Thee ...

nagging question: whose side are you on in this matter? On the side of Hitler?

Yet another approach is possible. If Poles (many of them) are so hostile to Jews and hate them so, and the hatred is so deeply rooted and long lasting – perhaps there are good reasons for such feelings and if so, what are they and can they be removed?

It seems to me that posing the question thus is based on a false premise. It assumes that Jews are hated because they exhibit such and such failings – remove those failings and Jews will be hated no longer: I do not believe that such a proposition reflects reality. Where Jews are hated, they are hated because they are, because they exist – and the only remedy would be to cease to exist (at times, it has seemed, even that would not suffice). Their great, incurable failing (and they have many) is their Jewishness. Who among them would not wish that they were better? Room for improvement is vast (although it is not quite clear what precisely would constitute improvement and how one would go about achieving it). It is an illusion to think that if they were better they would have avoided their worst fate. To wish that they were different is to wish they ceased to be themselves.

An inviolate dogma of Polish perception is the view that POLAND is without blemish. Nobody in Poland will deny that Poles are capable of committing deeds foul, shameful or treacherous – Poles are prone to self-criticism. But, paradoxically, POLAND, independently of Poles, as it were, remains unsullied, is always the innocent victim, the Christ of Nations, and woe unto those who attempt to tarnish that dogma.

Many Poles will confess openly (some with pride) that Poland was and is the home of many antisemites. But the accusation that POLAND was an antisemitic country surprises them, they resent it, seem not to understand why their country should have this reputation. They believe it is the Jews who spread this opinion, repaying with ingratitude the good they received, villains that they are. And why, indeed, should Jews be doing this (except that it is in their nature to pervert the truth)? Because they feel guilty about the role some of them played in Poland – Rozanski, Swiatlo, Brystygierowa and their ilk. Moreover, Jews in America and in the West are ashamed that they did nothing to save their fellow Jews during the war. (What, precisely, they could have done and what sin of omission they are supposed to be ashamed of is not clear. One of the then leaders of American Jewry, Rabbi Stephen Wise, confessed after the war that he regretted not having blockaded the entrance to

Poland, what have I to do with Thee ...

The White House with his own body. That would have been a gesture but it would have had no effect. Roosevelt had the same answer to all Jewish appeals – Allied victory will bring release to all, including Jews.)

That mental muddle, the non-sequiturs and ignorance of facts are typical of Polish apologetics in Jewish matters. The awareness that there are real charges to be answered, and the unwillingness to enter into a serious, informed discussion, cause them to side-track the issues, to pursue false trails, to settle for arguments *ad personam*.

For many years there was in Poland no possibility of free, honest, open discussion of many issues. There was a rigid frame of official doctrine, misrepresentation and bending of facts, outright, brazen lies. Mental habits engendered by such practice die hard. It is necessary to learn anew, to face the truth, even if Poland does not always emerge from this process unsullied.

I will not, once again, go over the whole range of issues arising from the history of the Jews in Poland, but would like to make it clear to my Polish friends who often do not know the facts that in the short inter-war period, when the Poles were at last responsible for their own fate and the fate of their ethnic minorities, the Jews were left in no doubt that they were not fully-fledged citizens, equal in all respects – that was the basic fact of their existence in the diaspora. Their formal equality was guaranteed by the constitution, there was also the greatly resented Minority Treaty for their protection, but a Jew, even one who to all outer appearance was indistinguishable from his Polish neighbour, knew in his heart of hearts that he was considered to be here as a guest and not as of right. Should he want to forget it for a while, reminders of it would meet him at every step – at school, on the street, in the press, in every professional and political walk of life.

Were one to compound an anthology of articles and statements from the newspapers and publications of all sorts, often illustrated by cartoons that could have been copied from Streicher's *Der Stuermer*, it would serve as an antidote to any sentiment which tended to look at the past through rose-tinted glasses.

In the image of Poland engraved in the Jewish consciousness there are also events from post-war history – the pogroms in Kraków and in Kielce, the loathsome campaign of the late 1960s which forced the final Jewish exodus from Poland. What would have happened after the war if Jews, many of them, had returned to the places of their birth and habitation and had claimed their property? The reception they

Poland, what have I to do with Thee ...

got in those rare cases when they did so fills one with a melancholy view of human nature.

It is true that many Jews, after their experiences in this century, conceive the whole world as being set against them and they see no reason for excluding Poles from that picture.

This view is unselective, one-sided and unjust. It is incumbent upon us to remember that Polish antisemitism, even in its ugliest and most brutal manifestations, was a phenomenon of a different order and category from the Nazi doctrine and practice. What the Germans did was outside the mental horizon and imagination of even the most rabid Polish antisemite.

* * *

It behoves me to say something about being an émigré, since that notion has formed a significant part of my state and existence.

What marks an immigrant is the fact that he is not greatly concerned or preoccupied with the events in the country around him while at the same time he has grown a bit cool about what is going on in his country of origin. This means a general drop in emotional temperature. Life is probably, in the material sense, better and safer here, but also emptier. Even though the thought of 'return' has long been abandoned; the whole existence here has been, as it were, 'temporary', 'provisional' – and never had the French saying: *Rien ne dure que le provisoire* a truer confirmation.

The core of one's personality is memory. What we remember of our past and how we relate to it make us what we are. The interruption of the flow of one's existence is the definition of the fate of an émigré. The mother-tongue becomes gradually less vivid, fluent and proficient, an impoverishment of one's personality follows – that is part of the price, a huge one, paid for the new status. To what extent one manages to compensate for that loss with new knowledge, new language, new interests is the measure of the quality of this second life.

It is one of the stark facts of social behaviour that an immigrant is viewed with dislike by the native population – that is how the herd instinct manifests itself. That dislike, paradoxically, is often strongest in an environment which contains a large section of recent immigrants and also not-so-recent immigrants who feel threatened by the new influx. Jews who came to England a long time ago and acquired good protective colouring often viewed with unease and resentment Jews arriving from Russia, or later, from Germany. They were a little ashamed of them, afraid of the responsibility for them.

In the early days of our stay in Great Britain our relationship with the native population was marked by a degree of insincerity on our part – it would have been impolite and also imprudent to voice openly what our thoughts of them were. And they were, naturally enough, disparate: we envied them their normal, stable existence, admired some of the traits of character and behaviour, wanted to get included in the stream of their lives, to earn a good opinion in their eyes. We would flatter them if that was going to help. On the other hand we were critical of them; they appeared to be cold and remote, with a feeling of natural superiority; we often felt we were being patronised. The elementary fact escaped us that – as in every nation and society – there were among them all sorts of people – warm and cold, stiff and accessible, wise and stupid, good and bad.

At the time of our arrival Great Britain's rule extended over a large part of the globe. Now it is a small country, struggling with economic and social problems, uncertain of its role in Europe and the world. It would appear that the British, as a nation, as people, have in the light of these changes altered for the better. One could say that the pendulum has swung the other way. Instead of the stereotypical self-confident, somewhat arrogant, superior being, one meets all too often those who are self-disparaging, severely and unjustly critical of their country and their fellow men.

I realised, relatively early, that there was no need for me to feel inferior, to imitate the native, to strive to be like him and in the deepest sense of the word his equal, although he and his parents were born here and this is 'his' country and I have only been thrown here by fate.

In the course of years, on various occasions, a question has come to the fore: how would the British have behaved if the war had been lost and the country occupied by Hitler? After all, it was not such a fanciful thing to imagine. How would the British have behaved towards the German occupier and – what is to me of greater interest still – towards the Jews? Would they have behaved like the Poles, or like the French, or the Italians or differently from all those? It is a painful speculation, fortunately only theoretical. Were I pressed to express an opinion on this, based on my understanding of the ways of the British and of human nature, I would incline to the view that they, like others, would not have emerged from such a devillish trial with credit (a small object-lesson from the Channel Islands destroys all illusions).

Poland, what have I to do with Thee ...

There is no doubt that a Quisling or a Petain would quickly have emerged from the ranks of the Mosleys or Halifaxes or Ravensdales to 'save' Britain through collaboration with the Nazis and at their bidding would have delivered to them first the 'foreign' Jews, those who had come from Germany recently, and then 'their own', i.e. those who had come somewhat earlier.

I think, however – and this is the measure of my respect for my adopted country – that when it came to private succour, saving individuals, hiding them, helping small groups to escape – the proportion of such people would have been larger, maybe significantly so, than in other countries. (Such a statement is, of course, without proof and throws light not on the British but only on my view of them.)

A Jew, no matter of what origin, makes a different immigrant from a Pole. An émigré Pole looks at such a turn of events as a passing phase, does not on the whole think that this may extend to the second or third generation, to eternity. He does not think about striking root, about assimilation, about 'going native' – what purpose would that serve? A Jewish émigré sees it differently. There is no thought in his head of 'returning', he accepts immediately that emigration means a new beginning and believes that the new country may be for him, and certainly his children, better than the one he left behind. He also often has in his new abode some community, near or more distant relatives from previous waves of emigration. But even without relatives in the strict sense of the word there would be, everywhere, a 'native' Jewish community, towards which he would gravitate and where he would expect support. ('Jews hold together' – the Poles would say, reproachfully. In fact this is a fine quality, not to be sneered at.) Even though emigration is not a phenomenon unknown to Polish history, Jews are, one could argue, historically better equipped to cope with it – until recently the Diaspora, a state of dispersion, was the natural condition of their existence. It follows also that Jews quickly create an input into the host culture, whilst Poles rarely do so, their creativity finding expression in their own language and own culture.

If, after spending some years in a Wellsian time-machine, I had landed now, in the nineties, in Poland, unaware of recent events, I would have looked round and to my indescribable joy have realised that I was in a free and independent country, not threatened by neighbours from the East or from the West. Moreover, that the geopolitical conditions had changed to such an extent that such a threat could be eliminated from any political prognosis. (I nearly said 'for ever', but 'for ever' means a very, very long time and we have observed how unimaginable changes can and sometimes do take place unexpectedly and rapidly.)

I would see that Poland is ethnically and religiously united, without the problems with minorities which were her blight before the war and with which she could not cope. She finds herself within physical and political borders more favourable than any in previous history (if we are not to return to the bombastic concept of 'from the Baltic to the Black Sea').

Never before have such favourable conditions prevailed for Poland to be master of its own fate and decide its own future.

Seeing all this, assuring myself that I was not dreaming, I would fall to my knees and be in ecstasy. Why do I not see around me Poles jumping for joy?

Is it possible that in their subconscious there lingers a thought that this ethnic and religious homogeneity does not represent a gain, but an awesome, irreparable loss which will lead to a cultural and spiritual impoverishment?

* * *

To stimulate conversation in good company and to give food for thought, I sometimes throw in the following question: Have you ever met, face to face, somebody who is out of the ordinary, exceptional, qualitatively different from the rest of us, unquestionably above the common herd – in one word: great? People seldom come up with a ready example, which only goes to show the fairly obvious point that such persons are rare and that opportunities to brush against them do not often come our way.

I myself have no hesitation in giving a positive answer. A number of times I found myself in the presence of Vladimir Jabotinsky and I was acutely aware, every time, that I was in the presence of a phenomenon, in the magnetic field of an overpowering personality, whom I admired, respected and owed allegiance to; more – a feeling that I would have been ready to go through fire at his behest.

That was partly due to a kind of brainwashing to which I was submitted in my youth. Jabotinsky was the founder and leader of the Zionist-Revisionist party (whose 'fighting arm' was the organisation Brit Trumpeldor or Betar). From early days I was a member of the Masada student organisation within that party. The vigorous, aggressive programme and the fiery rhetoric of Jabotinsky, positing 'a Jewish State on both sides of the River Jordan' appealed to my youthful patriotic fervour more than the diplomatic play and the 'leftish', too peacable – as it seemed to me – policy of Chaim Weizmann, Nahum Sokolow or, later, David Ben-Gurion, Shertok or Arlossorof. We sang, enthusiastically, the 'Hymn of Betar' composed by Jabotinsky, of the great, courageous generation, which would raise the flame of rebellion, conquer the mountain or die – that was the way and the spirit. In the thirties Jabotinsky sent weekly articles to the Jewish newspapers in Poland (first to *Der Hajnt*, then to *Der Moment*). These articles were very influential in forming Jewish public opinion. This was journalism at its best, persuasive and prophetic.

In the late 1930s there appeared in Kraków a journal called *Trybuna Narodowa*, the organ of the Revisionist Party. I was on the editorial board of that paper and one of my functions was to translate from Yiddish into Polish Jabotinsky's articles sent to us from his office in Rue de la Boétie in Paris.

One of our 'achievements' was the publication of a 'special supplement' to the conservative Polish daily *Czas*; they agreed to print material supplied by us. The main article, on the front page, was written by Jabotinsky (translated by me), entitled 'A Favourable Storm'. For it he analysed the hopelessness of the Jewish situation in Europe, to which the only remedy, according to him, was a mass-evacuation of Jews from Poland and other countries of the Diaspora to Palestine. (How that was to be achieved in practice and how the British were to be persuaded to open the gates of Palestine were questions left aside for the time being.) Such a thesis was, of course, grist to the mill of the Polish nationalists and rightwingers who wanted to be rid of the Jews at any price. They were delighted to claim Jabotinsky as a new ally and quoted him in support of their slogans. He should have foreseen that such abuse of his thesis would follow, and that to enter the public arena with a programme for evacuation in those circumstances was an act of criminal irresponsibility. But Jabotinsky's prediction that Jews in Europe faced a terminal threat of physical extinction proved all too tragically accurate.

Jabotinsky visited Kraków from time to time and spoke at public meetings, four hours at a stretch. As an orator he had no equal, he was inspired and cooly calculating at the same time, in the tradition of true people's tribunes.

From Kraków he would make forays into neighbouring towns –

that was the way Zionist propaganda was organised, speakers did their rounds of local meetings, as I did. But a visit from Jabotinsky was an event which was talked about long before and long after. Often, when he arrived at a railway station and got into his *droschke*, his supporters would unharness the horse and pull the carriage to the hotel. There was a cult of Jabotinsky such as no other Zionist leader enjoyed.

A friend of mine who survived the war in exile in the depth of Russia described to me a little incident which throws some light on what the name of Jabotinsky meant to some people. In the Siberian twilight a long, bedraggled column of deportees moves slowly. On the horizon another one appears, moving towards them. When they come within shouting distance of each other a voice floats across: 'Jabotinsky lebt?' In that remote, snowy desert, at the extremity of the human condition, someone is concerned with that one thing – is Jabotinsky alive? If he were, then the world would be redeemed and it was worthwhile trying to survive.

At that time – it must have been in 1941 – these poor wretches in Siberia had no way of knowing that Jabotinsky was no more. He had died in America in 1940, aged 60.

His place in history remains contentious. He was wilful, could not work in harness and gave free rein to his own, grandiose ideas. In 1935 he did great damage to the cause he meant to serve; he broke away from the World Zionist Organisation and founded his own New Zionist Organisation, causing a huge loss of resources and energy through fratricidal quarrels. Rabid partisanship in the community was rife – it persisted even at the most tragic moment in history, the Warsaw ghetto uprising. The Revisionists would not submit to the unified command of the Jewish Fighting Organisation under Anielewicz of the Hashomer Hatzair. They fought separately, on their own section of the front. They all perished without trace.

Mutual hatred did not cool down in Palestine, nor even after the creation of the State of Israel – on the contrary. The fight continues to the present day. I am inclined to the view that only Jews can hate each other so. But I remember the Irish. Also the Poles.

* * *

Where does this exposition or meditation lead me? It leads me to the conclusion that my Motherland is not territorial, that it does not depend on this or that scrap of territory, on a border, a banner or an emblem. It is not Poland or Kraków where I was born, where the birth certificate was issued and where I spent my childhood and my early youth. It is not England where I have spent my whole adult life, where my naturalisation papers were registered and where I feel more or less at home. It is not Israel and Jerusalem which I love but where I am only a casual guest, not deserving special consideration. One could surmise from this that I am a 'rootless cosmopolitan', an appellation which at certain times and in certain countries was deeply defamatory and dangerous. It was simply a cryptonim replacing the word 'Jew', at a time when official doctrine negated antisemitism but, in fact, the system was rabidly antisemitic.

I would be ready to rehabilitate this epithet. I place true cosmopolitanism high on the scale of human values, in direct opposition to chauvinism which I hate – whether in England, in Poland or in Israel. It is an ideal worth striving for. It is not easily achievable, it calls for shedding many prejudices and bad mental habits. The climate for it is, for the time, unfavourable. After the dark night of communism, in many countries there is the deadly ferment of primitive nationalism which has been in the past and could again become the ruin of Europe.

As for the designation 'rootless', I answer – following George Steiner – that trees have roots and stand immobile in one spot; humans have legs and can move around this earth where the spirit moves them (and the frontier guard allows passage – a cynic might add, but that's another matter). Life's elixir should be drawn from universal, all-embracing sources. Above all, I would like to be able to say, after Lamartine, 'Ma patrie c'est la vérité.' The distance which separates one from being able to say this without some vast distortion is the measure, in my eyes, of one's success or failure in life's long journey.

2 • *What shall we tell Miriam?*

I HAVE given my little piece a title which might strike you as quaint. I call it 'What shall we tell Miriam?' It is thus entitled on the assumption that there must be many Miriams and Sarahs and Shulamiths and Samuels and Josephs and Daniels everywhere in the world where Jews have set foot (which means virtually everywhere) who are or very soon now will be asking their parents and grandparents questions to which hitherto they have seemed strangely indifferent: what was life really like in that country where you were born, in that incredibly distant past, before the Second, before the First World War? What were these people like, the grandparents and the great-grandparents, how did they live, what did they do, what did they think, what did the places look like, what did they smell of... In the words of the historian Ranke: *Wie es wirklich gewesen.* Posing such questions is part of a natural cyclical process: indifference – then curiosity.

I think it is important to tell them – for our sake and for their sake. Who will, if we won't? Ours is the last and vanishing generation of living witness. The point arises how to do it, the young have little patience, their concentration span is short. Of course it would be simple enough to use the precept of the Sage Hillel – *tseh ul'mad* – go to the library, read and learn, there is no shortage of sources. But that, I fear, is a counsel of perfection, rarely followed.

There is another, more personal way, and I would like to give an example how this might be done, bringing it home through the story of one's own family. I am somewhat reticent about introducing an autobiographical note – the personal pronoun is the most suspect part of speech – but I think in the event it is justified, since my family, in its mainstream and offshoots, serves as a not-untypical illustration of the many aspects of Jewish life in Western Galicia, that is the 'Austrian' part of Poland, in and around Kraków at the end of the nineteenth and the first decades of the twentieth century.

I am descended on my Father's side from a long line of rabbis, or the less snobbish would say, *melameds* – religious teachers, who would surely be horrified at what has happened to their issue. My Father was

What shall we tell Miriam?

the youngest of 15 children. They did not all have the same mother and, of course, did not all survive to adulthood. To give a thumbnail sketch of the family one would need a very large thumb indeed.

The grandfather, a white-bearded patriarch, by trade an innkeeper, in his youth reputedly an oak of a man, with proof of virility for all the world to see, as I remember him was already a shadow of himself, bent in half, toothless, shrunken with incessant toil, worry and the blows of fortune; he died at a then good age, certainly less than 'three-score-years and ten'; and the saying at the time was: *a yingerer zol nysh shtarben* – let never a man younger than him die – and this tells its own story.

As can easily be calculated, the Scharfs were so thick on the ground in that part of the land, in the villages, townlets like Chrzanów (the headquarters), Kalwaria, Alwernia, Żywiec, Bochnia and the environs of Kraków, that it is a wonder there was room for anybody else. (Incidentally, if you are interested in statistics, the great majority of the Jewish population inhabited localities of less than 20,000 people.)

This vast clan was seething with activity and appeared to be in a state of perpetual motion, travelling with trunks, cases, parcels, by train or horsedrawn carts in feverish pursuit of their affairs big and small, and also to family gatherings – the weddings, the circumcisions, the funerals. I remember the colourful, noisy crowd passing at various times through our house in Kraków, en route to their next port of call, to rest awhile, to exchange family news, to seek advice from my Mother or a loan from my Father and refreshing themselves with a cup of tea – but no more. My Mother's kitchen was suspect to them, rightly so. Even though the meat was kosher and ham was never eaten inside the house, the dessert after goose could well be wild strawberries and cream, in defiance of the ritual command.

The spectrum of religious orthodoxy, belief and practice was wide. There was my oldest uncle, Motl, almost 40 years my Father's senior, an ascetic and forbidding figure, a follower to distraction of the Rebbe of Belz, and not on speaking terms with his younger brother Saul, who was not – God forbid – an 'anti-Hassid' but, ridiculously, a follower of another 'wonder-rabbi' not nearly as holy. As a boy, I firmly refused to visit him after the day when he pinched my cheek, in a supposed sign of affection, but, as I well knew, in retribution for the fact that, as he discovered to his disgust, I was not wearing *tsitsit* – the four-cornered garment which a Jew is enjoined to wear through the waking hours.

Poland, what have I to do with Thee ...

There was Cousin Hymie, a dreamer and a schemer, frantically engaged in projects which, if successful, would shed enormous benefits on the whole family, but in the meantime required continuous injections of cash, a figure modelled to a t, in the way life imitates or rather parodies art, on Shalom Aleichem's Menachem Mendl.

There was Aunt Rachel, an early widow, with as many children as there had been years in her happy marriage, making a living in an otherwise male provenance as a marriage broker. Since that involved continuous travel in search of information, developing connections, soothing anxieties and supervising *bekucks* (the preview to which the couple was entitled) – a subtle and sophisticated pursuit – she was also a ministering angel to the sick in the family wherever she found them (and she found them aplenty) applying her uncanny knowledge of folk remedies and deep psychological insights. Long before the name was invented she understood the nature of psychosomatic illness, which featured in her sources as *anredinish is arger wi a krenk* – meaning that you can talk yourself into an imaginary illness, worse than a real one.

There was, before my time, deeply secreted in the tribe's common memory, the allegedly beautiful Auntie Rosa, her yellowing photograph buried in my Mother's knick-knacks drawer, safe – but not from my probing hands – who, I can only piece the story together, eloped with an 'Austrian' officer, and after he had had enough of her (as he would) finished up in the gutter as a street-walker. There is no evidence for this, but it was felt that the story could not have ended otherwise. Her parents, of course, cast her out and went through the ritual of mourning the dead and were till their dying day, which came all the sooner for it, consumed by grief and shame.

This motif, which with slight variations recurs frequently in Yiddish and also Polish literature until it becomes a stereotype, is proof enough that such skeletons rattled in many families' cupboards. Traumas of this kind tore the guts out of the community; no worse thing was conceivable. Yet in the limited interaction of the group with the surrounding world, menacing yet alluring, an occasional crossing of the barrier was inevitable. Revulsion against what was seen as suffocating obscurantism also played its part. But the convert remained in the eyes of his contemporaries an abhorrent and despised figure. No Jew could believe that the change of faith was genuine (a suspicion shared widely, I think, by the receiving side). How *could* it

What shall we tell Miriam?

be? It was generally considered that, with miniscule exceptions, the convert – indifferent to the old religion and dissimulating the new – was in it merely for personal advantage of one sort or another.

A case less dramatic than that of Auntie Rosa, but probably no less typical, revolved around my Uncle Joshua. His, and my mother's, stepmother decided that the parental home was no longer the place for him, and he was packed off, just like that, to go to America. This, as we know, was not an uncommon practice in those days, and that migration, as a whole, proved to be the most timely and beneficial of all. But Joshua – what would he have been? 14, 15 years of age? – was not concerned with History, other than his own – a lost, castaway boy. What were the mechanics of these journeys? I presume he had a *Schiffskarte* sewn into his pocket and was supposed to sail from Liverpool; how he was to get there in the first place I do not know. In the event, he didn't make it – first time round. En route, it transpired, he met fellow-travellers who knew the family and considered it wicked of them to send the boy away thus, depriving him of his 'portion' of the inheritance (of which, no doubt, they had a vastly exaggerated notion). He turned back and on his return journey, I gather he must have been spotted by some members of a missionary society, in whose eyes (mistakenly I think) the conversion of the Jews must precede the Coming (Second Coming, if one accepts their reckoning) of the Messiah, and they decided that Joshua's destiny was to speed Him on his way. Anyway, a hot meal and a few kind words could – then as now – do wonders. I can still sense the horror with which my Mother related the story – half-a-century on – how people, neighbours and friends, came rushing into the house, utterly scandalized, to tell his father and stepmother and the other children that Joshua was standing in the central square selling missionary tracts! There was heartbreak, remorse and dread of scandal. In the end – by bribery, persuasion or force – the boy was despatched again, this time effectively, to reach the Other Shore. Virtually nothing was heard of him after that – until shortly before the last war some members of the family started digging for his address to write to him to plead for 'an affidavit'. It was too late.

My Father was an early rebel. Feeling constrained by the life in the *shtetl* he cut his jacket 'short' and changed his hat from the round black velvety kind, part of the Orthodox uniform, for one of lighter colour, fashionable but not very. This declaration required probably more courage than we imagine. He arrived in Kraków in search of wife and fortune – and soon succeeded in his first objective beyond his wildest dreams. The second became somehow less important. He retained, of course, a total attachment to Judaism. He knew nothing else, felt not the slightest need for anything else.

I see him on a Saturday afternoon, reaching for a volume of the Talmud, and from the way he handled it, the caress, one knew the book was holy. Bending over an open folio he would slowly turn the pages, as if feeling his way through an embarrassment of riches, and then, with a familiarity that breeds contentment, he would settle down to the study of a chosen passage. He was no scholar – he had the mandatory few years of 'cheder' behind him and was quite unable to make his own way through the undergrowth of commentaries, sprinkled with the poppyseed of glosses. But no matter, he was not looking for solutions to problems or rulings of law, but seeking to wash away the triviality and harshness of everyday existence in the waves of the eternal. He believed, simply, that the book contained the truth and that it was good to touch it.

He wished to persuade me to share his outlook but we did not know how to talk to each other, and he realized that an argument with a precocious know-all only led to an aggravation of spirit. Only once, I remember, he exploded when I asked him: 'What is all this for?' 'What is this *for*, fool? The whole of life is for *this*!'

He saw his role at home as that of the breadwinner, and even though he genuinely believed that all he had aspired to was for our sake, the bringing up of children would not have been part of his conscious concern. What little modicum of success he had as a merchant and small-time manufacturer was brought about by ceaseless hustle and total immersion in the task at hand. He would provide for all our needs – and be the sole judge of how these were defined. While spending money on books was grudgingly approved, there was much pursing of lips and shaking of the head. Novels, in his eyes, were *narishkeiten*, foolishness and frivolity. How could adult men and women give serious attention to the imaginary misfortunes of nonexistent people! I argued that they nourish the sources of feeling and imagination, open the door to experience beyond one's personal orbit and give a glimpse of the many faces of truth. Where else could knowledge of the ways of the world come from? Were not the scandalous infidelities of Mrs G. next door made comprehensible through the reading of Madame Bovary?

My Father understood perhaps more of these matters than he

What shall we tell Miriam?

thought fit to concede. He and I maintained a brittle truce which lasted till just before the outbreak of war, when I left home and hearth for a foreign land. I never saw him again: he died in 1942, felling trees in the Arctic Circle, a task for which he was ill prepared.

There was, in those days, a yawning, unbridgeable 'generation gap' by comparison with which our contemporary conflicts are puny. The rebellion against the old order was gathering momentum. The tribe was bursting at the seams and moving in all directions. It proliferated into a human landscape of great diversity. Some young members of the family became communists, cardcarrying members. Now, that was serious business, illegal and dangerous. It could and often did end badly. Police searches at home, to the dreadful distress of parents; arrests, prison sentences. In spite of that, or rather because of that, this attracted some very good people indeed. The idea was irresistible – it was offering a solution not only to the Jewish question, which seemed trivial by comparison, but to all other questions of social injustice and exploitation, in the trail of its historically inevitable victory of the proletariat. The brotherhood of nations would come naturally, as a bonus. This idea deserved sacrifices – and there were many, including the ultimate, and massive, under Stalin's execution wall. My favourite cousin Moishe, later Misha, a brilliant linguist and chess-player, perished thus.

Some of the clan gave their allegiance to the Jewish Workers Movement, the Bund, but the large majority was swept by the liberating wind of Zionism, in all its hues. You could say that by the late 1920s and early 1930s the *shtetl*, the Jewish townlet, had been left behind, and most of the members of the family had migrated to larger towns, mainly Kraków, where they embraced and penetrated and intermingled with other families, to the extent that virtually everybody was or became a relative: the black-bearded Schwarzbarts and the red-bearded Rotbarts, the ubiquitous Landaus, Grosses and Kleins, Schusters and Schneiders, Wolfs and Schaffs, Sperlings and Spatzes, Spiras, Schapiras, Kohns and Kahans and Kohens (here also belong the Loewys), Sonntags, Montags, Freitags and Sonnabends, Zuckers and Pfeffers, Gruens and Brauns, Golds and Silvers, Nussbaums, Gruenbaums, Rosenbaums, all the other -baums, and Aschkenase and Gumplowicz. I have named only those of whom I have direct knowledge of a bond with the Scharfs.

It was an interesting community, of a mixed profile. I was told a story which describes it nicely. A man goes to Kraków and on return tells his friend: 'The Jews of Kraków are remarkable people. I saw a Jew who spends all his nights dreaming and all his days planning the revolution. I saw a Jew who spends all his time studying the Talmud. I saw a Jew who chases every skirt he sees. I saw a Jew who didn't want anything to do with women. I saw a Jew who is full of schemes how to get rich quick.' The other man says: 'I don't know why you are astonished: Kraków is a big city and there are many Jews, all sorts of people.' 'No' – says the first – 'it was the same Jew.'

But I also want to draw another profile of a Jew of those days. It comes from a little verse called *Avi* (My Father) by Itzhak Katzenelson, the author of what is possibly the greatest poem written during and about the Shoah: 'The Song of the Murdered Jewish People.' He writes: 'When did he (my father) learn the Bible by heart? The translations of Onkelos and Luther? The Talmud, Codes, Midrash, Shakespeare and Heine? When did he read Gogol, Thucydides and Plutarch? When did he study the Holy Zohar? When did he sleep?'

If not for the fact that all these people lived, and soon after died, in apocalyptic times, some of that profusion of humanity would have overspilled into other streams, all over the map, and with their diverse talents, energy and purposefulness they would have enriched the world. As it is, from my closest family (and that, as has been said, included hundreds of individuals) – there was not a single survivor except, blissfully, my Mother.

When talking about Polish Jewry before the War, before the Wars, it is important to steer a clear course between nostalgia and reality. In mourning the past it would be wrong to idealise it. The literature of that time, the only authentic descriptive record, in Yiddish and Hebrew, is sharply and mercilessly critical, even though the criticism is tempered by compassion, as behoves the prophetic tradition. Mendele, Shalom Aleichem, Peretz, Opatoshu, portray the sordid conditions – the poverty, the powerlessness, the oppression, the obscurantism – and lash out against it; that is the function, or the mission, of literature. If you want to know, for instance, what was the position of women in that society, a short passage from the book *Debora* by Esther Kreitman, the sister of the Singer brothers (and brushed by the talent so prodigiously bestowed on them) will tell you more than a dozen learned tracts.

Once, when she overheard her father saying proudly of Joshua: 'One day he will be a brilliant Talmudic scholar' she asked: 'And Father, what am *I* going to be one day?' Her father looked as if he didn't quite understand the question. 'What are *you* going to be one day? Nothing, of course!' Do you need to know any more?

It is true to say that poverty was dire and widespread. But it is well to remember that it was not a specifically Jewish poverty, which contrasted with non-Jewish well-being. On the contrary, urban squalor knew no boundaries and the Gentile unemployed workman suffered the same, if not worse, hardship and degradation. The countryside could be harsher still: the small-holder and landless peasant led, in a bad year, a pitiful existence.

On the other hand, the idea that Jewish life in Poland was always one of unredeemed gloom and oppression is ill-founded. There were lights as well as shadows: the rich fabric of Jewish existence is woven of many strands, and some of its brightest and most life-enhancing manifestations took place on Polish soil. When faced with the bleakness of the picture one can well ask the question: if it was so bad, why was it so good?

The structure of what somebody has called 'The Jewish Nation in Poland' was diverse. It had its urban proletariat with its industrial workers, tradesmen and craftsmen (mainly tailors and shoemakers), its *Luftmenschen* with no visible means of support, a large and amorphous middle class of shopkeepers and business people of all categories, its free professions – doctors, lawyers, scholars – and its plutocracy of manufacturers, bankers, big industrialists.

The community's religious administration lay in the hands of the *kahal*, with considerable autonomy and a wide range of competence. There were Jewish and Hebrew schools of all grades; *yeshivoth* and high schools, scholarly institutes – among them the famous YIVO in Vilna and the Institute of Jewish Studies in Warsaw, which had university status. A Jewish press flourished, in Yiddish, Polish and Hebrew (in 1939, according to a recent study, there were 30 Jewish daily newspapers and 130 periodicals of all kinds). There were innumerable trade and professional associations, of writers, journalists, doctors, lawyers, engineers, merchants, homeowners (in the late 1930s 40% of town property was in Jewish hands).

There was a network of charitable institutions, hospitals, orphanages, provident funds and summer camps to help the disadvantaged. There were sport clubs giving scope to aspiring and actual record-holders in all disciplines. Above all, there were the political parties, with their affiliated youth organisations, with a vision of a better future. Jewish deputies represented the whole spectrum of political life in both chambers of the Polish Parliament.

Poland, what have I to do with Thee ...

The community was fragmented and torn by internal strife, but there was one unifying factor – a sense of sharing a common fate which transcended social and political differences. There was a marked spirituality, even among the non-religious, an instinctive allegiance and response to what was felt to be the Jewish ethos: a deeply ingrained, universal conviction that, beyond the mundane, man had to aspire to higher things, however defined.

It is also important to remember that there existed a considerable area where the division between the Polish and the Jewish world was blurred and the long cohabitation resulted in mutual acceptance, tolerance and harmony. This produced a cross-fertilisation with an untold enrichment of both cultures. Polish literature of the time glitters with illustrious names – Leśmian, Tuwim, Slonimski, Wittlin, Bruno Schulz, to name but a few. A civilization flourished here with its traditions, language, folklore, literature and music, and with roots deeper than Polish civilization. Did it ever occur to a Pole that, in the neighbouring town or for that matter on the very same street, something was happening that could engage his attention and deserved his interest? With a few notable exceptions, the answer is no. The Jewish population was commonly regarded as a 'dark continent', backward and primitive, evoking feelings of aversion and repugnance. The Poles automatically regarded themselves as infinitely superior – each Pole superior to each Jew, be he a rabbi, a writer, a merchant, a shoemaker. The Jews requited it with a shrug of their shoulders: what could you expect of 'them'?

To complete the picture, here are three snapshots from memory, which illustrate the pressures of growing up and living as a Jew in a country where Catholicism dominated and filled the atmosphere like ether.

Once, a very long time ago, our housemaid, out of affection for me and genuine concern for my soul, took me with her to church and confronted me with that huge human figure stretched on His cross, nails piercing hands and legs, droplets of blood oozing from open wounds. She whispered urgently: 'This is God Jesus and He loves you, though you are a Jew and your forefathers crucifed Him – and you mustn't tell your mother about it!' I was struck with terror and nausea. On coming home I sobbed inconsolably but would not let on why. (Perhaps this experience left me with my lifelong interest in theology. Many years and many learned books later, with the clock ticking ever faster, I remain an unregenerate agnostic, thank God. This

What shall we tell Miriam?

serves me reasonably well by day, if not so well by night.)

When the street urchin from next door where we lived wanted to chase me and harm me, it was not with a stick or with a stone (that also, sometimes) but with what he felt was a much more potent weapon: he used to make his index fingers into a sign of the cross – I was supposed to cower in the face of it and run. I did, too.

I think that in this image alone, in the small example of *Ecclesiae Militans*, there is enough food for thought to make one ponder what happened, no, what was bound to happen in the future to the generation of both boys – the one making the sign of the cross and the one who was made to run away from it.

On returning to Kraków for the first time after the war, I avoided the street where we used to live. But in time, it seemed, the wounds partly healed and I was overcome by an irrepressible impulse to cast a glance over the place where we lived – was the old furniture there, my bookcase, the paintings on the walls?

The house stood facing the Planty, the park around the old city centre, in a district which was then respectable, reasonably prosperous, and later – like most buildings – fell into neglect, decay, nobody's property.

I entered the familiar entrance hall. I struck a match to discover from the list of tenants the name of the owner of flat 4.

As I was gathering courage and composing my thoughts on how to explain my ghostly visit, the doors opened on the ground floor, and a man – menacing, cross and angry, as is the habit of the land – came close to me: 'What are you looking for? There is nothing here for you!' Indeed, I thought. How well he put it. There is nothing here for me.

Finally, a scene from my recent visit to Kraków. Usually, as dusk falls, I am in the habit of leaving my favourite seat in the Cafe Noworolski, under the arcades of the Sukiennice, to stroll across the square, the Rynek, into the Church of the Holy Virgin Mary, from whose tower, the taller of the two, there sounds the famous, hourly trumpet-call. I spend there a quiet hour or so, contemplating the altarpiece by Wit Stwosz, a magnificent example of religious art. I also listen to the quiet evening service.

On my last visit some months ago, my neighbour in the pew happened to be a youngish man of fine face, who prayed silently with great concentration. At the end of the service, as we were leaving the church together, we got talking, with growing sympathy and openness – two authentic Krakówians, spanning two generations.

Poland, what have I to do with Thee ...

After complimenting me on my Polish, which oddly has not gone rusty after half-a-century away from the country, he confided in me thus: 'I am a believer, as you see, and a practising Catholic. I am also a student of ancient history. I know, and it no longer causes me any difficulty to accept this, that Our Lord Jesus was a Jew. But in no way am I able to accept that Our Holy Virgin Mary, the Queen of the Crown of Poland, as we like to call her, was a Jewess...'

I didn't know what to say. To understand these things, on a level which does justice to the depth and complexity of these predicaments, is too difficult for me, for most of us.

The Jews in Poland,
Jagiellonian University, Kraków 1992

3 • Kraków – blessed its memory

IT DOES not take much to set an old Krakówian musing, by the waters of the Thames, about his old city: – an odd word, somebody's name, an echo of a melody, a taste of a madeleine. The photographs of Stanislaw Markowski open the floodgates of memory. But I have no desire to let the stream flow; on the contrary, my impulse is to get out of its way. It was all a long time ago, before the Flood, the other side of the nightmare. Continuity was suddenly, brutally, irrevocably disrupted. People with whom I shared that past have dispersed all over the world (mainly to the other!). I want to run away – yet something is holding me back.

I have been an eyewitness to that period of history which remains tattooed on my consciousness. There is a duty to bear witness, every piece of evidence counts. There is not a great deal of it left, and it will be all that will remain after we are gone.

For me, Poland of those days meant, almost exclusively, Kraków. I did not go to 'Kutno or Sieradz', I did not visit Warsaw; whatever for? After holidays in nearby Zakopane, Zawoja or Rabka, the return to Kraków was always joyful. I presume that those less privileged who lived in Lwow, Lodz or Warsaw had similar local patriotism, but I find it hard to imagine. The town must have had a singular charm which endeared it to its inhabitants, since true old Krakówians, wherever you find them (not all that often in Kraków itself!) speak of it with such warmth and affection (even those who appear quite indifferent to the rest of the country).

It was small and beautiful. Smallness is a quality more and more appreciated. My longest walk (excluding Lasek Wolski, Wola Justowska or 'Sikornik') was from the periphery of Blonia; skirting the park named after Dr Jordan, the football pitch of the Kraków sports club, along Wolska Street, past the University, then along Szewska Street, the Market Place, Sienna and Starowislna Street, crossing the 'Third Bridge' to Podgorze, to the front door of the house where my girlfriend lived – a daily walk, not long enough to say to each other everything that needed to be said.

Some while ago I met in London an elderly gentleman who now

lives in Mexico. It transpired that he was born in Kraków, hence an immediate bond of mutual attraction (as if that alone guaranteed quality). Somehow we had not bumped into each other before the war. Where did you live? In Sebastiana Street. Isn't that odd, so did I. What number? Thirty-three. Ah, I lived at number six. That was a long way away, no wonder we did not know each other.

Kraków was beautiful. Surrounded by tree-lined paths, in springtime brimming with jasmin and lilac, with enchanting little byways, a 'swan lake', statues of Copernicus, Grottger, Balucki. There was Wawel Castle with its cathedral, the great bell of King Sigismund, the 'Dragon's Cave', the monument to Thaddeus Kosciuszko, views over the River Vistula.

When you stood under the arcades of the Clothiers' Hall looking towards the Market Place, the monument of Adam Mickiewicz, the Church of the Virgin Mary, and the little chapel of St. Adalbert, you had in front of your eyes an urban vista beyond compare. (I catch myself using the past tense, but why? All this, blissfully, stands now as it stood then, virtually unchanged, and only for me does it seem to be placed in the very distant past.)

Go down Grodzka Street and Stradom, here is the Warszawa cinema hall, where crowds gathered to listen to Vladimir Jabotinsky on his visits to Kraków. Cross Dietla Street, and you find yourself in the heart of what was the Jewish Quarter of Kazimierz. Here was the tavern of Mr Thorn, here the tenement house of Mr Süsser, whose huge courtyard could well have served as an inspiration to the famous poem 'El Mole Rachmim' by Wiktor Gomulicki. That courtyard was the habitual scene of public demonstrations. There were no microphones – the speakers, addressing the crowds from the balcony, were shouting their hearts out, rousing the crowds against the injustices of this world; against the British Government's White Paper limiting the immigration quota to Palestine, against Mrs Prystor's proposal to abolish ritual slaughter of animals, against the pogrom in Przytyk – such causes abounded.

Penetrate this labyrinth of lanes, alleyways and *cul-de-sacs*. Where else in the Diaspora were streets named after figures of the Old Testament – Jacob, Isaac, Joseph, Esther? Here, on the square at Szeroka Street was a flea-market, you could call it 'the mother of all flea-markets'. Here also stands the famous 'Remu' synagogue, called after the great Cracovian rabbi and scholar Moses Isserles. Nearby is the great, old 'Alterschul' synagogue.

Kracow – blessed its memory

The corner of Brzozowa and Podbrzezie streets is the site of the Hebrew School (primary and secondary, the so-called 'Gimnazjum'). The names of the streets suggest birch trees, but there were none – the prevailing aroma was that of freshly baked bread from the bakery of the aptly named Mr Beigel. Some years ago it fell to me to unveil two memorial tablets – one in Polish, one in Hebrew – on the facade of that building, to remind the passer-by of the former Jewish presence within those walls.

That school had a state-approved secular curriculum, which entitled those who passed the matriculation exam to enter the University. But over and above that there was a comprehensive syllabus taught in Hebrew – Bible, Jewish history and literature. Pupils came from far and wide, from Debniki, Pradnik, Krowodrza, even from Wieliczka. Fees were modest, most pupils had them reduced, nobody was barred from admission for lack of funds. The school was held in great affection by the pupils. It was a kind of oasis, where one felt free and on home ground, had the illusion that the world was and would remain benevolent. One could also – if one was so inclined – acquire a little learning.

In Miodowa Street stood the 'Temple', the 'progressive' synagogue. Its rabbi and preacher was the estimable Dr Joshua Thon, a member of Parliament and a Zionist leader. Nearby were other synagogues: Popper's, Kupa, Ajzyk's, Wysoka. At Orzeszkowa Street No. 7 were the editorial offices and printing-house of *Nowy Dziennik*, a Jewish daily newspaper in Polish. That was, for many readers, the main and irreplaceable source of information about events in Poland, in Palestine, around the world. Its circulation grew when there was something which gave cause for particular concern. In 1924/25, for example, there was, in Lwow, a court case against a Jew, by the name of Steiger, for an alleged attempt on the life of the President of the Republic. He was defended by many eminent advocates, among them Natan Lewenstein and Lejb Landau (also Szurlej and Grek, non-Jews). Their arguments, cross-examinations and speeches kept readers in a state of feverish excitement. In the event – despite the plotting of the authorities – Steiger was acquitted, to the great relief of the Jewish community, which felt slandered and threatened by the whole affair.

On Bochenska street there was a Jewish Theatre at which repertory companies from all over Poland, including the famous 'Vilna Troupe' of Jonas Turkow, performed the classic Yiddish repertoire: plays by Perec, Shalom Aleichem, Goldfaden, Anski.

Around the corner, on Skawinska Street, was the seat of the 'Kahal' – the Council of the Jewish Community.

One of the centres of Jewish life in Kraków was the stadium of the Makkabi sports club – a football field in summer, a skating ring in winter. (One glorious year the soccer team beat the champions, Cracovia, 1:0. That happened only once, a long time ago – but who would ever forget it!) Women in the field-events notched up some remarkable records and the water-polo team were the national champions of Poland. On state holidays and the Jewish feast of 'Lag Be'omer' the orchestra of the Hebrew school (my elder brother was its first drum-major and I, playing the euphonium, basked in his reflected glory), with its blue-and-white flag, led the entire school to the stadium, where there were exhibitions of gymnastics and other sport events for boys and girls.

Not far from the stadium were the premises of the youth organisation, the Hashomer Hatzair – on the far left, close (some thought too close) to communism. Other rooms in various parts of Kazimierz housed a variety of youth organisations – Hashachar, Akiba, Gordonia, Massada, Betar.

While some youngsters were engaged in high-minded, ideological pursuits, others spent their time in bars and cafés (I recall finding time for both). My favourite café was the famous Jama Michalika, at one time the seat of the Zielony Balonik cabaret (The Green Baloon), immortalised by Boy-Zelenski in his incomparable *Slowka*. I misspent there many an hour in the days of yore. Even now, when I happen to recline there on the old sofa, I have the impression that the velvet is still moist from the tears of my then girlfriend (I was unkind to her, I regret it).

It behoves me to mention Szpitalna Street which, although outside the perimeter of Kazimierz, was, in a way, a Jewish street. Not only because it had a synagogue, but because it was the scene of a second-hand book market. Familiar names, Taffets, Seidens, carried on a long family tradition in that trade, which – like shoemaking and watch-repairing – was almost entirely in Jewish hands. At the beginning of each school year that street provided a background to a veritable carnival – crowds of students of all ages milled around the pavements and shops, buying, selling and bartering old books for new, having a great deal of fun on the way.

Dietla Street, with its hundred houses, ran from the Vistula to the railway viaduct in 'Grzegorzki'. These houses were inhabited mainly by Jewish families, in their thousands (my own lived there for a time). When I walk down that street now, I seem to remember them all, their faces, their names – Einhorns, Johaneses, Luftglasses, Lipschitzs, Bloeders, Sonntags, Fallmanns, Ohrensteins, Rakowers, Weisbrods, Holzers, not forgetting the Schneiders, a family of nine brothers, mighty sportsmen and soda water manufacturers.

At a certain time my family lived in a house on the corner of Saint Sebastian and Berek Joselewicz (a Jewish colonel during the Kosciuszko uprising), so close to the school that when I heard the bell at home it was enough for me to quicken my pace and reach the classroom ahead of the teacher. The street named after Berek Joselewicz is referred to, obliquely, by Boy-Zelenski, as one 'having, in Kraków, a peculiar destination'. He pokes gentle fun at Professor Wilhelm Feldman, his origin and accent, who might one day also have a street named after him, where gentlemen might arrive in hansom-cabs to visit a bordello. (A social historian could deduce from this that Kraków was not well endowed with houses of ill-repute if gentlemen had to be driven, in search of pleasure, as far as Jewish Kazimierz.)

For me the association with Berek Joselewicz Street was of a different nature. At number 5 there lived Mordechai Gebirtig, a carpenter. I remember his slight, inconspicuous figure. Nobody paid much attention to him, no-one would have predicted that he would achieve, posthumously, international fame. Gebirtig was an authentic folk singer, the bard of the Jewish street. He set his own words to music and these Yiddish songs gained wide popularity. One of his best known songs is the one written in 1936 after the pogrom in Przytyk, 'Dos shtetl brent' (Our town's on fire), calling for action – in later years often sung in the ghettoes. In another of his poems, as he is forced to leave his home, he says: 'Farewell, Kraków, farewell – A horse-drawn cart is waiting for me out in the street – I'm driven out of here like a dog – Will I ever see you again? – This place is so close to me – I've wept my heart out on my Mother's grave and shed my last tear on my Father's tombstone – this hallowed ground ...' Another poem written in 1940, entitled 'S'tut vey' (This hurts), Gebirtig addresses to 'those Polish sons and daughters, who bring shame on their country', who sneer at the suffering of the Jews inflicted on them by their common foe. Anna Kamienska wrote a beautiful ballad about the 'Jewish carpenter and poet from Kraków'.

Gebirtig had two lovely daughters. He wrote a song about one of them: a boy stands on the pavement opposite and whistles, a signal for her to come down. Her mother warns her – don't go, this must be some non-Jewish good-for-nothing, Jewish boys don't behave like that. She was wrong – that boy might well have been me. Many a time did I stand there waiting for Reisele to come down.

Gebirtig was murdered, with his daughters, by the Germans in 1942. After the war his songs were collected, published and recorded; they are widely performed – a part of the Jewish, Cracovian heritage.

We had a neighbour, a shoemaker, by the name of Fischer. He had his workshop on the ground floor, giving on to the street; one could see him, bent over his last, till the early hours. He lived with his family in a tiny flat, one room and kitchen, at the back of the house, on top of a spiral staircase. He proclaimed that he would continue to father children until he was blessed with a daughter, so first came Jankiel, then Hesiek, Josek, Berek, Shmulik, Mojshe and only then, blissfully, Sabcia.

Of them all there was one survivor – the wily Shmulik, my contemporary. When I met him in Kraków soon after the liberation, he told me his story. He had played a squeeze-box on the steps of St. Catherine's church, humming Hassidic tunes, the only ones he knew. He was in rags, had a dirty face, kept his eyes shut, feigning blindness (but what he did see would fill volumes). He slept in some cellar, in a cardboard box stuffed with old newspapers, plagued by rats. Throughout that time he never opened his mouth to speak to anybody. Good people would throw him a coin, a crust of bread. At night he would search dustbins for scraps, would steal food when he could. At the first opportunity after the war he went to Palestine. He fell in the War of Independence, in 1948, from an Egyptian bullet. A child of our times, you might say, a Jewish child of our times.

A snapshot from memory: I remember the last stage of Marshal Pilsudski's funeral, in May 1935 – the hearse driven through the town to the Cathedral in Wawel Castle. I watched the procession from the windows of an office in the centre of town belonging to 'Brothers Safir, Agents for the National Lottery' (trading under the slogan: 'Looking for luck? – Just drop in for a moment').

In the *cortège* behind the hearse, among the dignitaries from all over Europe, marched Marshal Herman Goering, resplendent in his uniform, dripping with medals. The local contingent was represented by the town's president, Kapellner-Kaplicki, a former fighter in Pilsudski's Brigade (reaping, as was the custom, his dividend for loyalty to his old leader) and the garrison commander, General Bernard Mond (the only Jew of that rank). Cracovians were used to seeing, on state occasions, an odd trinity: Archbishop Sapieha supported by the two Jews – Kaplicki and Mond.

The country was gripped by mourning – sincere and feigned. It would have been foolhardy to belittle the tragic loss, and not display sorrow. The praises and eulogies in the press and from the public platform knew no bounds. But there was, undoubtedly, a widespread and genuine grief – the 'Grandad', the real one and the mythical one, was greatly loved. Many people felt that the fate of the nation had rested in safe hands.

I remember that my Father, usually wrapped up completely in his daily cares, cried on hearing the news of the Marshal's death. I was startled by this reaction; I was not used to seeing my Father moved to tears by matters of that sort. He must have shared a perception common among Jews in Poland that Pilsudski, a sworn adversary of Dmowski, would protect them against the wilder excesses of the Endeks and that with his passing away history would take a more threatening, dangerous course. That premonition proved accurate all too soon.

Cracovians were proud of their town, boasted of its culture and tradition. The citizens of Warsaw, Lodz or Lwow looked down on us, provincial and miserly, with gentle mockery. It was true that by 10 pm the town would be deserted, its burghers scurrying home before the house gates were shut – the concierge would demand 20 grosh for letting them in after 10. It was said that a typical Cracovian invitation was: 'Come and visit us after supper – there will be tea freshly brewed this morning.'

Society, Polish as well as Jewish, was sharply stratified; one was supposed to adhere to one's place on the social ladder. The pecking order was well established and ideas above one's station were discouraged.

The following picture springs to mind. On the corner of Starowislna and Dietla Street used to sit a beggar. I use the word 'sit' but that is an exaggeration. He had no legs, only stumps wrapped in rags. He moved along the pavement by raising his trunk, yard by yard, with some wooden handgrips. It is not easy to visualise that mode of locomotion. When there was mud on the street (as there frequently was and of a quality seldom found these days) the rags splashed about leaving a smudge of dirt in the beggar's wake. It was a gruesome sight, but familiarity bred composure – one used to throw, in passing, a coin into a cup dangling from his neck.

One day it came to my knowledge that this beggar had offspring. I was startled out of my wits – how does he do it? I found out about this because he applied for his son to be admitted to our school – my Father was on the committee adjudicating exemptions from fees. This became the subject of a heated argument over the dinner table. My Father thought such ambition arrogant and presumptuous, whereas my brother and I argued that the beggar's son had an entitlement equal to ours, if not better. 'Better?!' – my Father nearly had an apoplectic fit, fearing that he had fathered a couple of imbeciles.

* * *

'There is a multitude of them – nowhere' says Jerzy Ficowski. That crowded, eternal absence is far more tangible here than anywhere else in the world. How is one to settle down to the normal business of living when one knows that all the people whom one then knew – family, friends, neighbours, teachers, shopkeepers, beggars – have perished, from hunger, by the bullet, from gas, in torment; and that oneself, just through some odd twist of fortune, did not perish with them? I find it difficult to express this in words. I think such words do not exist.

That human landscape which Markowski records in his photographs did not, at that time, appear to us to be attractive. On the contrary – I am ashamed to admit – many of us looked on these people with a sense of embarrassment. Those beards, sidelocks, crooked noses, misty eyes, what do our non-Jewish fellow citizens make of this?

It is now clear that those faces, lined with care and wisdom, glowing with some inner light, as if they had stepped down from portraits by Rembrandt, were beautiful. We realise that now, when they are no more.

4 • *Cum ira et studio*

PRESS reports, letters and conversations demonstrate that the Oxford Conference gained the approval of the participants and also of those whom news of it reached. As was the intention of the organisers, an opportunity was given for an exchange of views and for a study into what life was really like for Jews in Poland. It is hoped that further serious discussion will follow and will serve, also, as a sort of therapy.

The theme is wide, complicated and – in most of its aspects – unpleasant; both sides approach it with a heavy heart. I believe that Poles who want to talk and think about these matters (maybe only a handful of them), feel somewhat ill at ease with the subject, as if expecting that something will come up that they will find difficult to cope with. No one likes to be censured, least of all justly.

Amongst the Jews themselves there are many who have no wish to return to these matters, nor open up old wounds; they want to forget about the past in Poland, turn their backs on it for ever. They regard conferences, symposia, discourses on these matters as drawing-room games. Who needs this now? they ask.

The extermination of the Jews in Poland (I purposely avoid the term holocaust, because it is ill-chosen and remote, even in those languages where its constant use has made it into a household word, and in Polish it is certainly totally artificial) has left scars on the psyche of the survivors so deep and crippling that their reactions are not always finely balanced. One must bear in mind that we will not talk about the subject 'objectively' – objectivity, in other words distance, calm, equilibrium would be out of place here.

The fabric of Polish–Jewish cohabitation on Polish soil has been irreversibly destroyed. No one is under any illusion that the few thousand Jews remaining in Poland, who openly consider themselves to be such and who, as it were, apologise for being alive, are not physically and spiritually a community in terminal decline. They have no schools, no synagogues, no rabbis, no contact with Israel, no leadership, no future. It has to be admitted, albeit regrettably, that world Jewry has ceased to care for them, they have been written off as lost. Therefore, from the Jewish point of view, we are talking not about current affairs but exclusively about history.

For the Poles, however, it is, I believe, a subject of primary importance. A millenium of Jewish presence on Polish lands and their sudden and final absence, are facts without which Poles are not able to understand their past and, therefore, their present. The history of Poland in the version taught and presented to the nation is full of falsehoods, as happens everywhere where an official version has a monopoly fitting the current dogma and where the researcher is hampered by censorship and lack of access to sources. Moral regeneration calls for an authentic dialogue with the past. The way other people see us must serve as a corrective to the way we see ourselves in the mirror. In the case of Poles gaining self-knowledge, the Jews appear as a witness who must be listened to carefully and who can, of course, be questioned.

If a means has been found for Poles and Jews to meet on neutral ground, it is important that they should tell each other what most concerns them, not for the sake of recrimination and rhetoric, but in order to come closer to the truth. There was a time when the Poles could say publicly what they liked (or more usually what they did not like) about the Jews. The Jews had to swallow it or resort, in debate, to codes or euphemisms. It is a relief to be able to talk about it all openly and frankly. All too often Poles, among themselves, speak of Jews differently from the way they speak in public (especially as, for the time being, antisemitism is not deemed respectable), and so do Jews with regard to Poles. It is time we freed ourselves of this double-think and double-talk and abandoned the stereotypes.

The Jewish stereotype in Polish eyes was radically transformed after Israel's Six-day War (but immediately a new one took its place, equally distorted). Jews, in turn, commonly take it for granted that a Pole is an antisemite, and call for special proof when it is claimed that one or another of them is not – he is then seen as an exception.

Thus the augury for an honest and productive discussion is not all that propitious. One ought to begin by agreeing some historical facts, but what constitutes a historical fact is also subject to question.

Take this vast, if now somewhat enveloped in mist, subject of Polish–Jewish relations in inter-war Poland. If the question were asked whether Poland was a country where antisemitism grew and was rampant, the answer for every Polish Jew, every eyewitness, would be so obvious and unequivocal that he would be angered and resentful

Cum ira et studio

of anybody doubting it. As soon as Poland regained independence after World War I, the framework of an anti-Jewish movement began to take shape. It grew in strength and came to be for us an ever-present force, filling the atmosphere like ether. The fact that the Poles were and are not aware of this – at least this is what many claim – is for us hard to believe and understand. They have either forgotten how it was or have been seeing life from an altogether different perspective. The young have been told nothing and have nowhere where they can find out.

Is it undue prickliness which makes us remember the 'Endecja' (National Democratic Party), the 'Chadecja' (Christian Democratic Party), the ONR (the National Radical Camp) – political parties whose main programme was a more or less brutal battle against their fellow Jewish citizens? Was it a figment of our imagination that there was an officially approved boycott, discrimination in all areas of state service, daily incitement in the press, the programmatic and primitive anti-Judaism of the Church, sporadic pogroms. In the universities, in some faculties, there was a *numerus clausus* and, often, 'ghetto-benches'. (Maria Dabrowska called it 'the annual shame' – it is good to remember her for this.)

At the end of the 1930s the dominant party was OZON (the Camp of National Unity), which vied with other parties in their antisemitism, and it is very probable that but for the outbreak of war, a variant of the Nuremberg Laws would have been presented to the Sejm (a project was ready). These were the political realities of inter-war Poland – some kind of anti-Jewish obsession, one might say, which diverted attention from other problems, infinitely more important.

It behoves us, however, to give due weight also to the other side of the picture. Someone asked very pertinently: if it was so bad, why was it so good? Because despite the fact that the climate was severe (and maybe thanks to it, who knows?) on these lands there blossomed a full, rich, varied and creative Jewish life. There was total freedom of worship, an autonomy in religious matters, rabbis of all types from the ultra-orthodox to the so-called progressives (and like today, everywhere, in perpetual strife); there were many Hassidim with their 'courts' of faithful; there were schools where instruction was held in Hebrew and Yeshivoths for Talmudic studies; there were newspapers printed in Polish, Yiddish and Hebrew (according to Marian Fuchs of the Jewish Historical Institute in Warsaw, there were 30 dailies and 130

Poland, what have I to do with Thee ...

periodicals in Poland in 1939). There were political parties – Zionist, religious, workers, assimilationist; there were Jewish members of the Sejm and Senate; there were men of science and men of letters. There were theatres, charitable and educational associations, sports clubs. A specific civilisation flourished.

Painful and difficult though it is for both sides, we must face up to the time of Occupation. Here is the source of the most acute friction in Polish–Jewish relations – I am not sure that much can be done about this. The problem has been bitterly aggravated by the fact that this has never been openly discussed and written about in Poland. The whole subject of the extermination of the Jews has been treated grudgingly and half-heartedly, and only in accordance with the official line. This was, that a large majority of Poles sympathised with the Jews, and helped and saved them where they could, and that the sporadic incidents (about which so much noise is made in the world) of blackmail and informing and of Jews being handed over to the Germans, were isolated cases perpetrated by 'the scum of society' whom the underground was sentencing to death. It is held that the Polish community as a whole came through this unprecedented trial with moral credit and with their honour unstained.

I well understand that the Poles want to, that they *must* believe this. Władysław Bartoszewski, an eyewitness, and one of the organisers of help for the Jews, therefore well qualified to express an opinion worthy of a hearing, believes this. I myself would give a great deal to be able to believe this.

Unfortunately – and this is the heart of the whole matter – the opinion of Jews, in other words those who know best, those who lived through it or who were given first hand evidence, is overwhelmingly that this thesis is contrary to their experience; that the Poles, with a few exceptions – for them great and eternal praise – did not show any sympathy, did not help or save, that a Jew in hiding or in disguise lived in fear not so much of the Germans but of his neighbours or passers-by, with their acute Polish sensitivity for Jewish features, manner of speaking or fear in their eyes. If the Jews could have depended not on active help, which called for heroism, but neutrality, causing the Pole to look the other way – the chances of survival would have increased a hundredfold. And if they could have joined partisan units, how many could have been saved (it cost many who thought this was their chance, their lives).

Let us consider an interesting document – the report of Jan Karski,

Cum ira et studio

daredevil and hero, who has gone down in history as an eyewitness of the extermination of the Jews at the Bełżec death camp. He was the first person to bring out to the West an authentic account of the gas chambers and crematoria. Previously, Karski as one of the first couriers from occupied Poland, had arrived in Angers in France, the seat of the Polish Government in Exile, in February 1940.

Karski was, as he was to prove, very well acquainted with all aspects of the situation in Poland. The Minister of Home Affairs, Stanisław Kot, avid for every minute detail of all that was happening in Poland, asked Karski to write, among other things, a report on the situation of the Jews.

Karski gives an acute and far-sighted account, full of pertinent observations. He declares in it that many Poles are openly hostile to the Jews and in principle sympathise with the objective of the Germans to 'solve' the Jewish question in the occupied territories. Here are a few excerpts:

> The solution of the 'Jewish Question' by the Germans – I must state this with a full sense of responsibility for what I am saying – represents a very dangerous tool in the hands of the Germans, leading toward the 'moral pacification' of a broad section of Polish society ... Although the nation loathes them (the Germans) mortally, this question creates a kind of a narrow bridge, upon which the Germans and a large part of Polish society find themselves in agreement ... This situation threatens to demoralise broad segments of the populace and this, in turn, may present many problems to the future authorities endeavouring to reconstruct the Polish State ... Hitler's lesson is well taken ... Might it not be possible in some way, taking the existence of three adversaries (if, of course, one should currently regard the Jews as an adversary), for the two weaker partners to form something of a common front against the third more powerful and deadly enemy, leaving the accounts between the other two to be settled later? ... The establishment of such common front would be beset with very many difficulties, for a wide segment of the Polish population remains as antisemitic as ever ... [1]

There is a good deal more of it. This is not just Jewish invective and slander – this is Karski's report.

And a further turn of the screw: members of the government (it is clear from the annotations that the report was available only to a selected few), Mikołajczyk, Stroński, Kot, realised that this was dynamite. If the extent and persistence of antisemitism among the Polish population, even during the war against Hitler, became public knowledge, Poland's cause would have been discredited in the eyes of her Allies. What was to be done? Another version of the report was prepared, in which the whole Polish population was portrayed as being united to a man in their condemnation of German anti-Jewish activities: *Sapienti sat*.

A few years ago, in a discussion with Andrzej Szczypiorski in the Paris monthly *Kultura*, I wrote that, when the crematoria were being stoked, when the trains were rolling night and day to Chełmno, Sobibor, Bełżec, Treblinka, Majdanek and Auschwitz, and for months smoke bellowed from the chimneys, if it had been known that it was not the Jews who were being incinerated but Polish fathers, husbands, mothers, wives and children, the explosion of wrath and revenge would have been uncontrollable, even if it came to – I used the expression – 'tearing up the rails with bare teeth'.

Szczypiorski argued fiercely with me at the time, emphasising the impotence of the Poles in the face of such actions as the 'pacification' of Zamojszczyzna, street round-ups and transportations to concentration camps, public executions, the systematic decimation of the Polish intelligentsia, and later the crushing of Warsaw, whose victims were Polish flesh and blood. Even then – Szczypiorski pointed out – no one 'tore up rails with their teeth'. Therefore my objections on that point were ill-founded and unjust.

Thinking further about these things, as I do always, I fear that I am unable to alter my judgement. The fact that the gassing and burning of Jews, which went on for years, was never interrupted by a single external act of blind rage has strengthened my conviction that the Poles, although they may have observed it all with compassion, did not feel sufficiently moved and enraged to intervene individually or collectively, with 'their bare teeth' or by whatever means, regardless of consequences. What the Germans did in the death-camps could only have been done to the Jews.

It is true that in their bitterness Jews often were and are insensitive to the predicament and misery of the Poles. They do not remember that attempts to help a Jew threatened death; they tend to think that the attitude to Jewry is the only important matter, to the exclusion of all other matters; they brood over the dark side of things, because, as the poet says, 'wrong is engraved in stone, and kindness in sand.' As long as Polish apologetics stick unwaveringly to the official version and Jewish opinion on this matter is considered libellous, we shall be engaged in a 'dialogue of the deaf'. It is the tragedy of the Poles that

Cum ira et studio

in the midst of the cruel visitations of fate, they were exposed to an unprecedented moral trial. They did not come through it victorious. It can be argued that nobody would have come through it any better, but that is little comfort for the Jews.

A few words about the role of the Church. Bartoszewski absolves the Polish Church too lightly, methinks. In any honest balance-sheet the debit will look differently. If at some stage the Church has the inner need and the courage to carry out a self-examination, it will see with horror and contrition what role its immemorial and relentless anti-Judaism played in the extermination of the Jews – *in capite* and *in membris*. The record of the Polish Church with regard to the Jews is disgraceful – the sowing of hate does not yield a harvest of mercy. Michael Borwicz has discussed the attitude of clergy with regard to pogroms and murders of Jews after the war. One sentence from the statement of Bishop Wyszynski (as he then was) haunts me and undermines my faith in the effectiveness of dialogue: 'At the trial of Beilis many old and contemporary books were brought forth, but the question of the use of blood by the Jews was not determined decisively.' If the question whether the Jews use blood for matzoth is not clear to Wyszynski, what do his priests believe and what does the flock believe? And if so, with whom are we to engage in a dialogue and on what subject?

There is yet another ironical thread: Poland's newest saint, Father Kolbe, was in theory and practice an ardent antisemite, and although his heroic martyr's death calls for admiration and respect, it cannot alter the assessment of his anti-Jewish activities over many years, which, to put it mildly, were no qualification for sainthood.

In his heart-rending lament *My, Żydzi polscy* (We, Polish Jews) which Julian Tuwim wrote in America, where he learnt of the death-camps, there is the following passage:

> ... On the armbands worn in the ghettoes, the Star of David was painted. I believe in a future Poland, in which that star, the one from the armband, will be one of the highest decorations awarded to the most gallant Polish soldiers and officers. They will wear it proudly on their breasts, next to the Virtuti Militari. There will also be a Cross of the Ghetto, a deeply symbolic title. There will be the Order of the Yellow Patch, more honourable than many a previous trinket ... With pride, mournful pride we shall count ourselves of that glorious rank which will outshine all others, the rank of the Polish Jew, we, who by a miracle or by chance remained alive ...

Poland, what have I to do with Thee ...

Sancta simplicitas. Poor Tuwim – endowed with genius (which deserted him in post-war Poland), naive and 'not of this world', lived long enough to see that the yellow patch remained a yellow patch. It was decided to turn one's back on all matters Jewish, as if nothing of any consequence had happened. A shroud of forgetfulness was thrown over this awesome breach in society's fabric. People tried hard not to notice this great absence (although the Jews recruited for the Department of Security were scrupulously counted). Even in Auschwitz, for years, the Jews were passed over in silence. 'Babi Yar'-style. Information on the Jewish section could only be obtained by persistent questioning, and then the key had to be searched for. All this was supposedly in line with the principle that although only Jews were gassed and incinerated and many more of them died than all the others put together, no distinction should be made among the victims according to nationality.

There was a widespread feeling of relief among the Poles, that the 'Jewish problem' had been 'solved' in a manner for which they could not be blamed, and that Poland could now be rebuilt without the Jews – and all the better for it. The Jewish survivors who came out of the camps and hiding places often heard the opinion, that like it or not, Hitler had done a good job on the Jews. Hitler's lesson – as Karski foresaw – found adept pupils.

The majority of the few who survived due to 'Aryan documents' realised that in the existing climate it was safer to continue the masquerade, often not betraying their real identity, not even to their own children. Those returning from Russia soon took note of the climate and, whenever possible, assumed some sort of protective cover. It appeared that these latter-day 'marranos' would somehow get by, but – as it turned out – their ugly origin had been duly marked in their files, for future use. And the future, as is its wont, was not long in coming.

In the baneful period of 1967 and the following years, when the authorities again unleashed a wave of antisemitism (trusting that this would always be well received), the former Jewish names, to the surprise of their owners, were recalled and heralded, as a stigma which automatically disqualified (thus, dear Tuwim, goes your 'rank which outshines all others'). This infamy needs separate discussion, but whatever interpretation one puts on it, it was the final signal for the Jews that Poland had no place for them.

In the consciousness of the Jews who left Poland and settled in various parts of the world, there is a deeply embedded feeling of wrong suffered – during the pre-war years, during the Occupation and during the post-war period. Let Poles who complain that Jews damage Poland's reputation in the world ask themselves to what extent this distant and recent past could breed ambassadors of goodwill.

And finally, let it be mentioned, the trauma of unreciprocated love. Many Jews of this last generation, nearing its close, cannot erase from their hearts this country where 'they were born and grew up', where – as Tuwim wrote – 'in Polish they confessed the disquiet of their first love and in Polish they stammered of its rapture and tempests'; where they loved the landscape, the language, the poetry; where they were ready to shed their blood for Poland and be her true sons. That this was, evidently, not enough leaves them broken-hearted.

The paths of 'two of the saddest nations on this earth' have parted for ever. I wonder how far the Poles are aware of the fact that with the Jews an authentic part of *their* Poland was obliterated. The question begs to be asked: Will that Poland one day be better, richer in spiritual and material goods, without the Jews?

Lecture at the International Conference
in Oxford 1984

NOTE

1. The original documents are in the Hoover Institution Archives Stanford, California: 'Polish Government Documents Collection' set 921, a second copy is in the Stanisław Mikołajczyk file, labelled 'Jews in occupied Poland'. I am indebted for this information to David Engel; viz. his article in *Jewish Social Studies*, Vol.XLV, No.1.

5 • *Let us talk ...*

I AM LIMITED by time, by the Chairman's tolerance and what is more important, the audience's patience – those are narrow boundaries. I have, therefore, prepared only loose pages, which can easily be shuffled and, if necessary, omitted. I shall raise, at random, a few problems which I consider to be fundamental. Perhaps these fragments will join up, in some way, to form a more coherent account.

When I was thinking what title to give to my talk, various ideas came to mind. At one time, I thought to call it: 'To My Polish Friends', but this echo of Mickiewicz ('Do Przyjaciół-Moskali') could have sounded, in my mouth, a bit pretentious. I played with the title, 'At the Crossroads', imitating the famous 'Al Parashat Derakhim' of Ahad-Ha'am, an excellent heading, universally applicable (are we not eternally at some sort of crossroad?) – I discarded it as too general. I thought of calling it, 'Very Difficult Accounts' – but that would give the impression of a contest and it is my intention to get away from the 'settling' of accounts. I tried to call it 'Not all is Black and White', which does define my approach, but in the end I brought it down to the simple, 'Let us Talk – With Whom and About What?'

With whom, then? If there is to be a dialogue, one must have a clear profile of one's interlocutor. I take here a model which one might define as 'elitist'. I want to sit down to the table with the best and not the worst. Not with those who hated the Jews before the war, who were betraying them to the Germans during the war and who drove them out of Poland after the war. Not with the Poland of 'Grunwald', the Poland of the Moczars, not with those who sell copies of the Protocols of the Elders of Zion, nor with those who at every opportunity spout virulent rubbish about Israel or write that Korczak ill-treated Christian children, and not with those who, like that journalist in the paper *Ład* in Warsaw, declare that 'if the Jews don't change their ways the time will come when we shall have to hide them again in cellars' (it is easy to guess how many he would hide). Nor yet with those whom I often overhear in London, declaring 'No matter what we say, the Jews shout us down anyway'. There is no

Let us talk ...

shortage of dimwits, cranks and bigots anywhere, sadly also amongst us, the Jews. I quite understand that a Pole cannot enter into a dialogue with those who hold that every Pole is an antisemite; who have seen and continue to see in Poland nothing but antisemitism; who maintain that the extermination camps were located in Poland because the Germans could count on the passivity of the Poles and that there is no point in discussing these things any further.

I want to speak with Poles about a Poland which gave birth to Kochanowski, Mickiewicz, and Norwid, Konopnicka, Prus, Orzeszkowa, Gomulicki, Dąbrowska, Nałkowska, and also Turowicz, Błoński, Bartoszewski, Kołakowski, Anna Kamieńska, Wisława Szymborska, Miłosz, Ficowski. About a Poland where there flourished, and died, a Jewish civilization, unique and unrepeatable.

In one of my earlier addresses I remarked that the culture which existed cheek by jowl, nay, right in the middle of the Polish community, remained totally unknown and uninteresting to the Poles, indeed, they would have been staggered to be told that something was taking place here which deserved to be called culture.

It is worth considering here how the Poles, generally, saw their Jewish fellow citizens, as that view, after all, would have formed their opinions and attitudes. In the first place, then, they saw the dark, motley crowd, Jews in their traditional garb, with beards and sidelocks, in 'kaftans', in skull-caps, in black hats; in the small towns, in market places, jabbering, noisy, uncouth, poor, though their poverty was somehow different from the Polish poverty. They saw the petty merchants, the small shopkeepers with whom they traded and from whom they bought, often on credit, in spite of the slogans 'Buy from Your Own' and the officially sponsored boycott. The Jewish shopkeepers were competitive, the more so as Poles very often regarded trade as being beneath their dignity. The Poles saw the artisans, watchmakers, cobblers, tailors, unsurpassed in their skills. They saw the middle classes in the larger towns, who in their dress and behaviour differed little from the Poles, although their lifestyle was somewhat different. They saw 'landlords', owners of tenement houses – bricks and mortar being the preferred Jewish investment – the proportion of Jewish owners was substantial. They saw, at school, fellow students who, if they differed at all, differed by their diligence and ability. They saw colleagues at university who often (let it be said – not always and not everywhere) were forced to sit on separate benches. They saw the Jewish professional classes, the doctors and

Poland, what have I to do with Thee ...

lawyers, amongst them doubtless some of the best. They saw a few (and even those seemed too many) Jews in high positions, probably converts. On the literary scene they saw great luminaries of contemporary literature – Leśmian, Tuwim, Słonimski, Wittlin, writing often for that excellent paper *Wiadomości Literackie,* owned and edited by Grycendler-Grydzewski (and Borman). This illustrated a process of osmosis at the boundaries between the two communities, and it comprised that part of the Jewish community which identified with Polish national aspirations to a degree only possible under the regime of Piłsudski. The process of assimilation became increasingly difficult and unrewarding, and this, it so happens, was in keeping with the instinctive stance of the overwhelming majority of the Jewish community. That majority was separated from the Polish community and all the more effectively as both sides favoured separation. To give you a small example: at the time when I lived in Poland in the inter-war years, not once did I go into a Polish house or flat, unless you count a peasant's cottage rented for the holidays in Zakopane or Zawoja. What is more, I did not look upon this as a deprivation, I took it to be the most natural thing in the world. I had many non-Jewish friends at university, we also had many such clients in our legal practice, but as a rule there were no social contacts.

The reasons for this were many, but the main one was that the Poles did not consider the Jews to be their equals as human beings. They looked down on us from a position of natural superiority. Regardless of their social position, Poles, as a rule, considered themselves to be better and superior to Jews, any Pole to any Jew; superior, as it were, by definition. This lack of a feeling of any common bond, the result of existing conditions, comes closest to explaining the fact that the greater part of the Polish community was insensitive to the fate of the Jews under the Occupation. Quite apart from 'the scum on the periphery of society' (the term commonly used in Poland); apart, also, from that section of the political and moral spectrum which openly welcomed the destruction of the Jews by foreign hands; granting also that there must have been vast numbers of good, ordinary people who were deeply shocked by the monstrous spectacle enacted in front of their own eyes and who had genuine compassion for its victims, it is an undeniable fact that the majority of the Poles remained indifferent.

We know that active help was risky and demanded courage and altruism. It was simply not to be expected that general attitudes,

Let us talk ...

developed over the generations would change overnight. Teresa Prekierowa, on the data available to her, estimated that 1–2½ per cent of the population actively participated in helping the Jews. (This includes a considerable number who did this for money, but that is a mere detail.)

One can argue the accuracy of statistics and round off a percentage here and there (I do not decry the value of work done in this field, I value it highly), but the Jews have no need of statistics, *they know how it was*. Poles, generally, do not know, they cannot know, perhaps they do not want to know. The Jews are bitterly resentful, but no one would claim that they were expecting it to be different – and that alone provides a tragic commentary. The rancour, which they are not slow to express, sometimes noisily, is not only against the Poles, but against the world in which such things were possible and tolerated. And in the last instance, against the Almighty who, also, did not cover Himself in glory (but this is a separate theme).

A question occurs: are we to judge human behaviour by the absolute standards of ethics and morality, or are we to deem these concepts utopian and unattainable and resign ourselves soberly, not to say cynically, to the fact that dark and primitive instincts effectively dominate human nature and cause humans to be base and cruel?

And further: if, in our weakness or understandable concern for our own lives and the lives of those close to us, we are unable to behave morally and measure up to those high principles which we know from religion and philosophy and which we approve in theory, do we in such a situation consider our behaviour blameless and justified by rational requirements; or rather, are we left with a sense of shame that we did not live up to the call of conscience, shame increased by the knowledge that someone else – true, not many, but somebody, somewhere – did live up to it? I am putting these thoughts for consideration to those who sleep peacefully since, as they say, 'nothing could be done'.

Błoński's example, the moral tone of his utterance, prompts me to raise the discussion above a mere settling of scores, recrimination, verbal squabbles and rhetorical victories. That sort of contest might have been in order in the past, nay, it has been unavoidable; blunt speaking helped to clear the air of accumulated poison. At that stage I was myself an active participant in that debate. We are nearing a time when there will not be a single eyewitness, no one who themselves went through that inferno, there will no longer be survivors from the camps and from the bunkers, those who owe their life to 'Aryan papers', those whose salvation proved to be exile in Siberia. There will be no one from Gomulka's Fifth Column, no Jews from the security apparatus and none from the expellees of 1968; gone will be those who have never recovered from their love of Poland, those who on the banks of the River Thames dream of their Vistula, and those, who like myself – and forgive me if it sounds precious – after 50 years away from Poland put themselves to sleep with lines from the 'Crimean Sonnets' or the 'Grave of Agamemnon'. I believe that then the historical perspective and the parameters of these issues will change. With the passage of time it will become clear that the agenda is not about us alone; that our debate and controversy is merely incidental to something bigger and more comprehensive. What is at issue here is a great, common cause of universal significance. The extermination of the Jews on Polish territory was a crucial event in history, marking the crisis of Christianity and the crisis of our civilization (some people regard those concepts as synonymous, but fortunately that is not so). Those events cannot be forgotten or ignored, they will weigh upon future generations for all time.

What lessons will human beings draw from this? How will they face up to it, conscious of the enormity of evil which they are capable of perpetrating? How will they renew their faith in the basic moral values in a world of which, in Adorno's words, 'we cannot be too much afraid' and where there exist instruments of destruction which put even the gas chambers in shadow? On answers to these questions hang all our tomorrows.

I revert to my title: what shall we talk about? Someone might say that there is nothing to be added to what has already been said in the context of Polish–Jewish discourse. Let me answer with the sentence from the Hagada which begins: *Af im kulanu hakhamim* (Even if we were all wise ...) which in free translation might be taken to mean that although we have learned from many sources and have absorbed a great deal of wisdom, nonetheless it is incumbent upon us to tell this story ...

I know not everybody will agree with me that there is plenty to talk about. Many of my friends both in Israel and in England say, 'Why bother yourself, and us, with these matters, what good will it do? Everything connected with that time is so sad and painful, why rub salt into open wounds?' I take the point but am not persuaded by it. To turn one's mind away from these topics would be, in my view, an

Let us talk ...

impoverishment, and I suspect that those who want to distance themselves from them would distance themselves from other serious topics as well.

I believe that the more things concern us the better. Surely there is plenty to talk about; our history – the part which is common and the part which is separate; about how things really went between us, at close quarters and at a distance; about the climate that nurtured us, the conditions which formed us; about mutual influences, good and bad; about the wrongs endured and the benefits received, about that which united and that which divided us, about all of that, as long as it is not superficial but serious and with concern for the truth. This does not mean that we shall see the truth in the same way, because the truth is complicated and has many dimensions; we are sensitive to some of its aspects, blind to others; only some segments of it are accessible to each of us. The sheer awareness that this is so seems to be a step in the right direction.

We, who form a link in the chain of the 1000 years of Jewish presence on Polish soil, does it not behove us to remember that part of our heritage is to cultivate it and pass it on? Every brick, every stone, every graveyard, every footprint, each document, each scrap of paper, each trace in whatever form, is valuable beyond measure for a nation whose roots give sense to its history and whose memory of the past vouchsafes the continuity of its existence. The history of the Jews did not begin in 1948 with the creation of the State of Israel. A large part of the history was enacted on Polish lands. Should one, could one, turn one's back on it, bury it, forget it? Surely not, surely the very opposite must be the case.

I learn from the papers and friends in Poland that there is, mainly among the young, a growing and lively interest in things Jewish; history, literature, monuments, and relics. One of them wrote to me thus: 'Are we, the Poles, not a strange nation? For forty years all these matters were hidden under a shroud of forgetfulness, a shamefaced silence, a programmatic taboo – as if the Jews never existed. And now, suddenly, this seemingly spontaneous outburst of interest, curiosity, desire to know. Is this salutary? Where will this lead to?' What shall I answer him? Better late than never? If such interest has been awakened and if it is genuine and not merely morbid or psychopathic, then I applaud it and I think that there is a helpful role for us to play in this pursuit. I am not afraid, as my correspondent seems to be, of the possible undesirable consequences, that the pendulum will once again swing in the opposite direction – we are by now beyond reach of any malevolence threatening from that side.

I think that when this new generation become acquainted with that part of their history and discover how it was with the Jews in Poland and what sort of community it was, this will not only open their eyes but will be good for their souls. They will need to ponder about the past and face up to it squarely. I want to believe that a generation of Poles is coming into its own, which is not poisoned by the virus of antisemitism and anti-Judaism. That is, however, not our problem but theirs, because we shall never again, as a community, find ourselves physically in close proximity.

I read Błoński's article, for the first time, with growing excitement and quickened pulse. At one point he makes reference to one of the speakers at the conference in Oxford in 1984, whose words, he said, inspired him to ponder these matters. From the words quoted by him it was clear that he was referring to me. I was startled and also moved to see how one word, a sentence, a thought can strike another man's mind, can germinate there and bear fruit beyond expectation. I was talking then, at least that is how Błoński understood it, to the effect that we Jews no longer expected anything from the Poles but the admission that they have been, in some way, at fault. For many years we listened, waited for a sign – but we heard no voices. In the end, I had thought we would be straining our ears in vain. But now, at last – we hear the voice of Błoński.

Many people in Poland say that Błoński is fouling his own nest and that even if what he has to say is true, he should not be saying it in public as this brings succour to Poland's enemies. That is an old argument – 'Do not rock the boat.' We know it particularly well in Israel where there is a widespread tendency to merciless self-criticism, but also great concern that this should remain in the family – a slippery path.

More than a year has passed since Błoński's voice sounded. I would like to assure all those who feared that it would have a harmful effect on Poland, that quite the opposite has occurred. His article is seen, in itself, as a certain rehabilitation of sorts. When, paradoxically and undeservedly, I am put in the role of an *advocatus Poloniae* I myself, in many instances, recall this article and those which followed. I maintain that one can no longer speak loosely about the Poles' opinion on the subject without taking into consideration these new voices, which save the reputation of Poland.

Let us talk ...

That reputation is a source of considerable difficulty. It rebounds on every Pole abroad, particularly in America, where in a foreign forum he has continually to explain – and not always knowing the facts – that not every Pole is and was an antisemite. That 'foreign forum' is very often not well informed in the matter, but always knows one thing and that is enough: that in Poland life for the Jews was bad.

Poles often complain that it is the Jews who influence this unflattering opinion, by spreading falsehoods, greatly exaggerating their past misfortunes and generally blackening the good name of the country of their birth.

If that were true, the question arises why should these Jews (I am talking of those at whom the reproaches are directed) want to do such things? Is it pure malice, is it because they are naturally nasty people? Does this ring true? Or is it perhaps, if such is their perception, that it is the result of their experience, their ordeals, their feelings of injury? I am putting it thus in order to illustrate how quickly, if we are not careful, we can find ourselves back to square one: seeing one's own side of the picture alone.

All the more, it seems to me, that the public reckoning of Błoński offers a different model and calls for a new climate of relationship. It deserves an adequate response. It behoves us to remember that antisemitism is not a peculiarly Polish invention. It is an age-old sociological, theological, and political phenomenon which, to a greater or lesser degree, is always with us, which defines us and in the absence of which (but there is no danger of that) we would feel strange. We would certainly be a different nation, a different community, different people – it is doubtful that we would be better. That does not mean that one should accept antisemitism complacently and turn the other cheek. Quite the opposite, one must fight it by all possible means – I think that our meeting here in Jerusalem, the capital of the Jewish state, is a significant act in that struggle.

At the source of Błoński's discourse are poems of Czesław Miłosz. This is understandable. Poetry touches the essence of our being, our thoughts and feelings and brings forth resources which we ourselves are often not aware of. Joseph Brodsky, in his Nobel Prize acceptance speech, said: 'It is more difficult to break a man who reads poetry than one who does not.' I am thinking at this moment of Max Boruchowicz – Michał Borwicz, who, sadly, is no longer with us, missed as no other. In his book *Literatura w obozie (Literature in the Camp,* Kraków, 1946) he

Poland, what have I to do with Thee ...

describes how fragments of poetry known by heart were a kind of life-belt, which in the most atrocious conditions of human degradation helped him, and others, to survive. I am thinking of that scene in the Janowski camp when a 'selection' was taking place, when his comrade, on the point of collapse, begged him with his eyes for a word of solace, and how Borwicz then spoke aloud a couple of lines of poetry (some banal verses of his own, he says) and how these words, somehow, renewed his friend's failing strength and will to live.

My Polish of 50 years ago is no match for Błoński. But in order to remain in stylistic harmony with him I seek recourse to someone else's words and want to end these remarks with an excerpt from a poem by my friend Jerzy Ficowski, entitled fittingly 'The Way to Yerushalaim':

>   through woodlands rivers
>   through an autumn of bowed candlesticks
>   through gas chambers
>   graveyards of air
>   they went to Yerushalaim
>   both the dead and the living
>   into their returning olden time
>   and that far they smuggled
>   a handful of willow pears
>   and for a keepsake
>   a herring bone
>   that sticks to this day

Lecture delivered at the International Conference
in Jerusalem, February 1988

6 • *As in a dream*

SOME OF you may wonder why it has fallen to me of all people to speak on this important occasion – in truth, I am wondering myself. I confess that I consider this to be no mean honour and that I am moved by it. It is due not to any special merit – I am not conscious of any – but to the accident of birth which makes me appear in this context a sort of museum specimen: an authentic, pre-war Homo Cracoviensis – and a Jew, to boot. A Cracovian Jew who is ready to rush to Kraków, in weather fair or foul, to respond to every call from there.

I dreamt one night, a short while ago, that I saw on a television screen the Prime Minister of Israel Itzhak Rabin, shaking the hand of Yasser Arafat, and those two creased their faces in a semblance of a smile. All this, it seemed, was taking place on the steps of The White House in Washington and, as happens in dreams, there were some familiar faces in the background: President Carter, Bush, Clinton, Kissinger ... Voices were coming at me from all sides, that we were witnessing the dawn of a new era, that there would be peace in the Middle East, in Israel ... It is a pity to wake up from such a dream.

Another night I dreamt that in Kraków, in Kazimierz, there arose a beautiful building which called itself The Centre of Jewish Culture, that the privilege of opening that Institution fell to me, and that I stood in front of a big and distinguished audience and – which does not happen to me often – I was at a loss for words.

It seems to me that this ceremony marks for me a long and tortuous journey. I left my Kraków, family and friends more than 50 years ago, before the outbreak of World War II. Why I left Kraków – on that theme one could write a tract about Polish–Jewish relations in the 1930s; now is not the time to mull over this.

But it would be insincere and not in the spirit in which we want to lead this Centre, not to call things by their name. Suffice it to say that I, and many like me, could not find our place in Poland at that time. I got offended, turned my back on it, wanted to forget it, to 'convert' from my Polishness – but the vaccine, as it were, did not take. I realised that were I, in some way, to shed my Polishness, be stripped of it – I would be damaged, impoverished, incomplete. Moreover,

Poland, what have I to do with Thee ...

when I am thinking of those times, as I often do, the idea occurs to me – when it was so bad, why was it so good?

And so I come back here, after 'years stormy and turbulent', to cast an eye over the landscape of my youth and my childhood, where every stone is laden with sweet memories, to walk through the streets where our fates intermingled, where the Street of Corpus Christi crossed with the Street of Rabbi Meisels, and the Street of Saint Sebastian with that of Berek Joselewicz; to trample through the alleyways named after Esther, Jacob and Isaac – where else in the Diaspora were streets named after the biblical patriarchs? To walk again down Koletek Street towards the sportsground of the Maccabi club, Orzeszkowa Street to *Nowy Dziennik*, Miodowa Street to the 'Tempel' prayer-house, Brzozowa Street to the Hebrew School. To pause in front of the synagogues – 'Altershul', 'Popper', 'Kupa', 'Remu' – one could deduce from the number of synagogues that the Jews of Kraków were singularly pious. Well – many were; but there were also those who – as described by Isaac Deutscher, the son of a Kraków printer and a famous biographer of Lenin, Stalin and Trotsky – there were those who, like himself, on Yom Kippur, the Day of Atonement, went to the grave of the holy Rabbi Isserles and ate a ham sandwich – to spite him and their parents.

One could say that Kraków was wonderfully overflowing with Jews. This was a community whose tone was set by Dr Osias Thon, the preacher in the liberal synagogue and a member of Parliament, Dr Ignacy Schwarzbart, a Zionist leader (during the war a member of the National Council of the Polish Government in Exile), Dr Chaim Hilfstein after whom the Hebrew School was named; teachers of that school – Scherer, Haber, Mifelew, Rapaport, Katz, Szmulewicz, Feldhorn, Stendig, Waldman, Metalman, Mrs Goldwasser – many others, each of them deserving an epitaph of their own; lawyers – Susskind, Hoffman, Feldblum, Goldblat, Bader, Schechter; the orthodox Rabbi Kornitzer, the assimilated chairman of the 'Kahal' Dr Landau; Wilhelm Berkelhammer, Moses Kanfer, David Lazer of the *Nowy Dziennik*; Rywek Wolf from the students' home, Rosa Rock of the orphanage. Here were active the Przedświt – Hashachar youth organisation, Hashomer Hatzair, Gordonia, Akiba, Massada; Maccabi and Jutrzenka sports clubs; here flourished the worthy, middle class families of Tigner, Einhorn, Fallman, Lipschutz, Leser, Selinger, Bester, Rosthal, Stoeger, Freiwald, Herzig, Aleksandrowicz, Karmel, Freilich, Monderer, Ehrlich ...

As in a dream

This sounds like a grey list of tenants, but for me it is anything but grey – every single name evokes, with poignant clarity, a distinctive face, movements, gestures, expressions, as if it was yesterday. I think of them with unfading affection. I could find my way to their dwellings with my eyes shut, touching, to be sure, the cavity on the side of the door where there used to be the 'mezuza'.

That human landscape is etched in my heart, my memory. I cannot forget for a single moment that the majority of them, family, friends, acquaintances – none of them was a stranger to me – were hounded to death in the ghettoes, in the labour camps, the death-factories, the gas chambers. We have got used to talking about this, using words derived from ordinary, everyday discourse, but nobody is able to take in the real meaning of that loss.

I love that Jewish Poland which is no more. I love it with a love which is different from the one I nurture for the State of Israel. I know that my feeling is filtered through the memories of my youth and my childhood and smacks of a Proustian 'Remembering of things past'. But there is more to it. I see and feel that it was a world of authentic, uniquely Jewish experience – in a sense in which this is not recreated in a normal country like Israel. Zionism, which brought about the State of Israel, was, in its basic assumptions, a protest against the life in the Diaspora and one must be eternally grateful to its Founding Fathers that their vision was realised at the time of Jewry's greatest catastrophe and despair. Due to this alone the Jewish Nation lived on to be reborn.

But the result of these events, its side-effects, intended and accidental, was the irrevocable loss of those forms and values which were the essence of Jewish life in the Diaspora. One of its hallmarks was the conviction that – irrespective of the poor living conditions and the daily struggle – man must aspire to things above the mundane, strive for a realisation of some high ideal, however defined. There was a deeply ingrained perception that decent behaviour towards fellow human beings, religious practise, the observance of ethical norms, respect for the scholar, pursuit of learning would speed the Messiah on his way and would initiate an era of universal justice.

We are witnessing today an astonishing event. In the year 1993, and the year of 5754 according to the Jewish calendar, in the heart of old Kazimierz, like the phoenix from the ashes, there arises a structure calling itself the Centre of Jewish Culture. That such a thing can happen in Kraków today, at this juncture of this country's history, is little short of miraculous.

Poland, what have I to do with Thee ...

Like all miracles, this would not and could not have come about without human aid. It is, in truth, due to the vision, enthusiasm and hard work of a few dedicated people whom I hestitate to single out, but it is no secret that the merit lies mainly (not to say solely) with our devoted friend Mark Talisman from Washington, Professor Gierowski and Joachim Russek. I congratulate them on this realisation of their vision and express to them our gratitude.

I see in this enterprise a sort of new beginning. Maybe it will be seen – a future historian will utter a verdict – to mark a turning point on our way to reconciliation and alliance in the common cause: the point at which Poland emerges at last from the sickness of antisemitism which had addled her brain and done so much harm; the point at which we begin to see in each other the best and not the worst; the point at which old wounds start to heal and a new generation grows up free from bigotry and prejudice. It may be that Poland and the State of Israel, which to a large extent was fashioned by Polish Jews, will now enter into the best of relations and serve, perhaps, on the international forum as an example of civilised behaviour. There is a saying in Yiddish expressing a pious wish: 'Fun dein mojl ins Gotts oyren' – let this go from your mouth into God's ears.

The creation of this Centre is deeply symbolic. But it would not accord with our wishes and it would not deserve the enormous effort and money that have gone into it if it were to remain a symbol only. A symbol on the one hand – but solid, daily labour on the other.

The walls, the roof over our heads – this is something tangible. It is a frame, a shell which will be filled with rich and vibrant contents. It is an address which was lacking until today, an address to which visitors from near and far will direct their steps on arrival in Kraków, where they will find a friendly face behind the desk, books and information of every kind, where they will rest awhile and lose themselves in thought, where they will meet like-minded people, where they will feel at home.

It is here, in this place, that we shall cherish and cultivate the memory of Polish Jews. We shall be proclaiming the truth of their existence. In this quarrelsome world of ours, riven by fratricidal wars, in Yugoslavia, Ireland, in Russia and South Africa, we will be able to point out that here, for centuries, despite everything, there existed a model of co-existence, of a common life, of a symbiosis of two cultures resulting in mutual enrichment.

As in a dream

There is an expression in Hebrew: 'Ir wa'em be' Yisrael' – 'city and mother in Israel'. Not many places on earth are graced with this epithet but Kraków, our Kraków of blessed memory is one of them. Let me finish with the prayer of thanksgiving that we have lived to see this day – 'She hechejanu we' kijmanu la zman haze.'

Opening speech at the inauguration of the Centre of Jewish Culture in Kraków,
24 November 1993

7 • *From the abyss*

MY THEME is 'Literature from the ghetto in the Polish language' – I give it the title 'Z otchłani' (From the Abyss), for such was the title of a collection of poems published in the Warsaw ghetto in 1944. Considering the circumstances in which these poems were written and came to light, I have no hesitation in calling that little volume an event unique in the history of literature.

The volume was smuggled to London and then to New York, where it appeared in print in 1945, with an introduction by Jakób Apenszlak. The poems were reprinted and their story told for the first time after the war in a volume edited and prefaced by Michał Borwicz, otherwise known as Max Boruchowicz, my colleague from the Hebrew High School in Kraków, himself a survivor (of whom more later). In 1947, it appeared under the imprint of the Central Jewish Committee in Poland, entitled 'Pieśń ujdzie cało' (The song will survive). (This phrase, as every reader of Polish poetry will know, comes from a poem by Adam Mickiewicz, wherein he predicts that when all other monuments lie in ruins, the song, the poetry will continue to be heard; he likens it to a nightingale which escapes from a burning building, rests for a while on the roof and when the building collapses flies away to the forest to continue to sing its mournful song.)

I cannot speak on the subject without referring, in the first place, to the book by Frieda Aaron 'Bearing the Unbearable', published in 1990 by the State of New York Press. Frieda Aaron has analysed some of the most significant poems written in the ghetto. She was there at the time and her personal memoir in that book is one of the most moving I have ever read. I myself am not a survivor *sensu stricto* but only one of the millions of the walking wounded who lost members of their families and friends in the Shoah.

A debt is also owed to Irena Maciejewska who edited a comprehensive anthology of writing in the Polish language on the subject of Jewish martyrdom and destruction under the title 'Męczeństwo i Zagłada Żydów w zapisach literatury polskiej'. I confess that I am having a number of difficulties in addressing this

From the abyss

subject here – whether and how I shall overcome them I myself am waiting to see.

The first is that I must assume that Polish is not the language of the majority of my audience and so I am unable to quote the poems in the original and thus convey their full power and meaning (Robert Frost said that poetry is what gets left out in a translation). I can only talk about them, around them, show through a glass darkly, as it were.

The second difficulty is that the texts I am to speak of should, like a dangerous potion, carry a health warning. Through continuous reading – and for the purpose of this paper re-reading of them – I have become a casualty; I have abused and damaged, not irreversibly I hope, my literary sensibility. I do not want to sound like that proverbial nurse who was known to complain that she had a terrible night because her patient tossed and turned and would not let her sleep, but the truth is that a total immersion in this material makes one unfit for reading other literature.

What is facing us here makes other matters appear trivial and artificial. Kochanowski grieving in his Threnody over the loss of his Ursula; Słowacki's 'Ojciec Zadżumionych', a father losing through pestilence members of his family one by one; Dante's Ugolino gnawing at the head of his son who died from hunger; Jeremiah lamenting the Fall of Jerusalem; Job tested by Satan to the limits of endurance and beyond – superb works of literature one and all – what are they in the face of the gradual murder of a whole people and real suffering on a scale which defies comprehension? When the true human condition is, for all the world to see, manifested in the ghettoes, the camps, the death-factories, isn't literature which brings catharsis and solace a cruel mockery? And writing, which is an act of faith in man, an impermissible self-indulgence? It is that which made Adorno say that 'writing poetry after Auschwitz is barbarous'. By normal standards many of these poems would appear crude, amateurish, some outright bad.

The trite phrase that they were verses 'written in blood' acquires here a fresh, literal meaning. They were written by people on the edge of an open mass grave, in haste, before the bullet. They are like messages scratched on the walls of the death cells. Despair dictates phrases which are cruel, accusations which may be unjust, curses on the perpetrators, bystanders, the world.

They are voices of men and women outside the law – man's law and God's law; they speak of suffering, of pain, of hope and the loss thereof, of loneliness and helplessness, of utter darkness of the soul. They bear witness to courage, tenacity, a will to live in conditions of terminal agony, of death, one's own and that of everyone one loved. They are also the instrument of resistance. They proved one's humanity – against all the efforts of the Germans to reduce Jews to a sub-human level. Writing or merely listening to poetry offered a breath of air, a momentary escape from the reality around. It was a kind of healing magic.

Borwicz describes a moment when, in Janowski camp in Lwow, one of the more advanced places of slow torture and murder, his companion in the ranks of prisoners on the 'Appelplatz' is at the end of his endurance, visibly sinking, and how he, Borwicz, recites to him two lines of poetry which came to his head. His companion somehow felt re-invigorated and seemed to regain his strength and the will to live. Examples like that abound. Joseph Brodsky says that it is harder to break a man who reads poetry than one who does not.

For a small illustration of how such poetry came to be written I go again to Borwicz. Remembering that writing of any kind was forbidden in the camps on the pain of death, it was done between one beating and another, between one execution and the next one.

'An icy January in 1943', writes Borwicz in an essay called 'The baccillus of literature'. 'For sixteen hours every day, without respite, exposure to piercing frost, turning a man into an icicle. We hack ice and clear snow in Zamarstynowska Street in Lwow. During this activity I feel, ever more clearly, the pressure of words, unprompted, forming in my mind a poem. Having become conscious of it, without interrupting the physical work, I try to smooth out and improve certain lines. When the first stanza appears to be ready, I begin to think of noting it down. Pushing the wheelbarrow with ice towards the canal I find on the rubbish heap a dirty sheet of paper. With a pencil stub which I had secreted, at a suitable moment, using the dust-cart as my desk, with fingers numb with cold, I scribble the lines on paper and put it in my pocket. The next line begins to sprout in my mind...' Where is the room here for comparison with 'writing' as we know it?

In one respect at least the Germans were unlucky in their choice of victim. 'The People of the Book' were literate and had faith in the written word. The compulsion to record, to leave a trace in writing, was widespread and overwhelming. The fear that the incredible events of which they were the witness and victim might not become known or would not be believed was greater than concern for their own survival. The last words in one of the most searing documents of that time, the diary of Chaim Kaplan, before his deportation to Treblinka, were: 'If I die, what will happen to my diary?'

In the Warsaw ghetto alone, between June 1940 and July 1942, there appeared 56 different publications – 26 in Yiddish, 20 in Polish, 10 in Hebrew. What has reached us, by a chain of miracles, is merely the tip of the iceberg – but even that makes the Shoah the best documented period in history. I think, therefore, that the so-called 'revisionists', both those who are evil and those who are merely demented, are irritating but not really dangerous.

One of the most desolate and heartrending scenes imaginable was the sight of the ghettoes after an *Aktion* – the empty flats from which people were dragged away, feathers flying from bedding ripped open to disclose hidden treasures, odd articles of clothing lost or abandoned, corpses of those who were not able to keep pace, and papers, single sheets or sheaves of pages, copy-books strewn over staircases or flying in the wind – the writing, choked half-way. What flowering of human thought and feeling, what possible masterpieces...

From the general to the particular. Undoubtedly the most significant poet writing in the ghetto in the Polish language was Wladyslaw Szlengel, who was born in 1914 in Warsaw and died in 1943 in a bunker, during the Warsaw ghetto uprising. He lived in the ghetto from its formation till the end. He was little known before the war, although he had some lighthearted satirical texts published in *Nasz Przegląd* – the Jewish paper in the Polish language appearing in Warsaw, also in the famous humorous journal *Szpilki*.

In the ghetto he grew in stature and had, as it were, greatness thrust upon him. He observed and recorded the life in the ghetto in all its aspects. The facts are well known and have been described many times. Hunger was rampant, typhus took its daily toll, at times too fast for the corpses to be cleared from the streets. Nobody knew when he would be awakened by the sound of the *Aktion*, whether he would be murdered in his bed, or whether he would return from the street to the quarters which had to pass for home.

Every night Szlengel appeared in a sort of cabaret in cafe *Sztuka* in the Leszno district. He was the moving spirit, the announcer, the main provider of texts, which varied from the merely amusing, to divert the audience for a short moment from the grim reality around, to poems

Poland, what have I to do with Thee ...

tugging at the heart-strings by bringing back memories of life before the nightmare. Then there were those dealing with daily life in the ghetto with its new, sinister vocabulary, bitter tirades against the oppressors, sallies against his own brethren and co-victims and those beyond the wall, those free spirits in the far-away wide world, who didn't know or didn't want to know how tragic human fate can be. He had forebodings of the approaching end – forebodings all too soon fulfilled.

After the so-called *Grossaktion* of July to September 1942, when 300,000 Jews were murdered by bullet or gas, Szlengel, astonishingly, reaches the peak of his creativity, expressed in some of his most potent poems. He himself described them as 'pages written in a U-Boat which will not surface'. Like the entries in the diary of Czerniakow or Janusz Korczak or the Notes of Ringelblum, these verse-documents recorded the history of people condemned to death.

These verses, those that survived – we have knowledge of other of his poems that have not reached us and never will – were published after the war in a collection called *Co czytałem umarłym* (What I read to the dead), Szlengel's own title.

I must restrict myself to only a brief summary of some of these poems.

In the early verse 'Klucz u stróża' (Key with the concierge) he makes light of the fact that his former doorman now parades in his, Szlengel's, fur coat which he looted, and is clearly content with the new social order which has been created.

Szlengel's flat happens to have 'an impudent Jewish window' ('Okno na tamtą stronę') through which he takes a forbidden look over the sleeping city beyond the wall, now totally unattainable, paradise lost.

In the verse 'Telefon' (the same in all languages) he has a sudden impulse to phone somebody outside the wall (remarkably, this was for a while possible) and realises, with a shock, that there is no one there to receive his call, that in 1939 there was a parting of the ways, lifelong friendships were severed, there is no one, no one to speak to... He dials a familiar number – the time-clock; and now every stanza in which he recollects the golden times of yore, the cafés, the cinemas, ends with the sound: ten fifty three... ten fifty six...

Szlengel had contact with Janusz Korczak. He wrote the invitation for the performance in the orphanage of Rabindranath Tagore's play 'The Post', in which an Indian boy is shown on his death-bed –

From the abyss

Korczak's idea of familiarising the children with death. The sight of Korczak's march through the ghetto with the children to the Umschlagplatz in August 1942 during the *Grossaktion* has entered the folk memory as one of the symbolic images of that time, contrasting mindless German barbarism with the children and the noblest human spirit. Szlengel was a witness of that scene and he was the first to describe it in a poem 'Kartka z dziennika "akcji"' (A page from the diary of the *Aktion*) where he stresses the spiritual significance of Korczak's unswerving devotion to his children, unto death.

In another poem entitled 'Pomnik' (A monument) he reverts to mundane, everyday things. He describes an ordinary woman, a very ordinary woman, a wife and mother, who by her mere presence spread comfort around her. One day she was taken away, while she was cooking supper. Her husband, her son, will come home, will find it empty, no fire in the hearth. A cold pot staring at them – her monument...

One of the most original and artful poems is called 'Rzeczy' (Things). It traces the path Jews were forced to take from the streets where there was still room to breathe, stage by stage, to the ever more constricted space until all life is extinguished. In Szlengel's imagination it is not people who walk that path but the inanimate Jewish possessions of which their owners were gradually stripped: tables, chairs, trunks, bundles, suitcases and bedding, dresses and pictures, pots, pans and carpets, jars and kettles, books and knick-knacks. As they are driven from place to place the possessions get fewer and fewer and fewer, until all that remains is a little poison-pill. In later days, slowly, order is resumed in the empty, abandoned houses, things are put where they stood before, new, non-Jewish inhabitants lead their normal, ordinary lives. But, one day, when all has seemingly been forgotten, Szlengel has a surrealist vision: all the former Jewish possessions, the things, the tables and chairs, trunks and bundles, the suits and kettles, everything will jump out of the windows and will march down the streets and will gather on the highways, along the black railway tracks and will disappear, and no one will know what the meaning of all this is – only the little poison-pill will bear evidence.

During the first days of armed resistance in the ghetto in January 1943 Szlengel wrote a poem entitled 'Dwie śmierci' (Two Deaths) where he compares the way it is given to a Pole to die in battle with the way the Jew is killed like a dog. The first death, face to face with the enemy, in a great cause, praised and honoured; the second – in an attic or a cellar, wholesale, anonymous, meaningless; an ugly death, fit for a dustheap. When those two deaths meet each other – they bicker, as Life, the same Life, mean, cunning and evil looks on, mockingly...

On learning about the gas chambers in Treblinka – and from the factual details he cites there is no doubt he knew by then the unspeakable truth – Szlengel bursts into full blooded blasphemy. I hesitated to include it in my selection here, but the picture would remain incomplete without it. Besides, sitting in judgement upon God's inscrutable ways is well within the Hassidic and kabbalistic tradition, like that group of rabbis in the Vilna ghetto, who reportedly put God on trial, adjudged him guilty and – minding the time of day – adjourned to say the evening prayers. Szlengel in his terrifying poem entitled 'Już Czas' (It Is High Time) is more rational, severe and unforgiving. God's guilt is clear and calls for revenge. He has delivered us into the hands of the killers. Through the millennia we have been His loyal children, dying with His name on our lips, on the crosses of the Romans, on the pyres of Spain, at the hands of the Cossacks and now in Treblinka – we shall pay Him back for all this. We shall bring Him to that place of torture to die a Jewish death. The poem ends with this stanza:

> And when the executioner will chase and force You
> Drive and push You onto the steam floor,
> And seal behind You the hermetic door,
> Hot vapours will choke You...
> And You will scream and weep and want to flee –
> And when Your death agony comes to an end,
> You'll be dragged, and in a monstrous pit land,
> Then they will tear out Your stars – the gold teeth from your
> jaws –
> Then they will burn You.
>   And You'll be ash.
>
> *(Translation by Frieda W. Aaron)*

Echoes of puzzlement with the ways of God are frequent enough in the poetry of the ghetto. 'God, have you ever been hungry?' asks Joseph Bau. Izabela Gelbard-Czajka tells of Abram Gepner, a merchant, Czerniakow's deputy in the Judenrat and a man above reproach, who is greatly troubled that the balance sheet of God's justice seems grossly deficient. Stefania Ney tells of a little boy, Herszek, in a poem of that name, who prays to God to let him return safely from yet another smuggling escapade, but 'God has at that time other weighty matters on His mind anyway, it is difficult to reach Him all the way from the ghetto' and Herszek is killed. The theme of the boy-smuggler is taken up also by Henryka Łazowert. Born in 1910, died in 1942 in the ghetto, Henryka Łazowert was established and respected as a poetess before the war. In the poem left to us she speaks of the cunning little boy who knows that each escapade may be his last and has only one worry – if I don't make it who, mother dear, will bring you bread tomorrow?

A few words about some poets who wrote outside the ghetto, on 'Aryan papers'. Zuzanna Ginczanka, a beautiful Jewish girl, of legendary charm, had many pre-war admirers in the literary milieu. She was discovered in her hiding place in Kraków, was imprisoned and killed in autumn 1944. The poem which reached us entitled 'Non omnis moriar', on which her fame rests, is a paraphrase of one of the best known poems by Juliusz Słowacki 'Testament mój'. She invites her friends to gather around and drink to her memory, whilst her enemies share out her worldly goods. In a memorable image she visualises how the feathers from the bedding which they ripped open in search of hidden gold and diamonds cling to their outstretched arms, stuck together by her blood and form the wings of angels, giving shape to Słowacki's vision of turning ordinary men, by the force of his poetry, into angels.

Mieczysław Jastrun, who survived the war and continued his literary activity in Poland, was born in 1903; his real name was Agatstein. He already had a considerable reputation before the war. He wrote poetry on the 'Aryan side' in Warsaw, published immediately after the liberation in a small collection 'Godzina Strzeżona' (The Guarded Hour). One of the most moving of his poems which appeared during the war in the volume 'From the Abyss' is one called 'Tu także jak w Jeruzalem' (Here too as in Jerusalem), where he dwells on the motif of the abandonment and isolation of those dying: 'No one cast the good earth – onto that mass grave – greeted by silence, free of treacherous words – When with mouths like wounds – parched, you called for water – No one brought water – to the sealed trains.'

Like Jastrun, Stanisław Jerzy Lec was writing poetry outside the ghetto walls and he speaks openly of his Jewishness. The situation of those on 'Ayran papers' has been described many times and took many forms, the common feature being a sense of terrible isolation and omnipresent, marrow-chilling fear. We know of many cases of people who risked their all to find a hiding place outside the walls and, unable to take the strain, returned to the ghetto to share the fate of their own people. Lec speaks of feeling like a hunted beast, of fearing that he will be unable to disguise his pain in front of the shopkeeper, the neighbour, his companion, nay, himself – the death of his people is writ large, indelibly, on his face.

One cannot speak of poetry arising from and concerning the ghetto without referring to that Righteous Gentile Czesław Miłosz, whose poem 'Campo di Flori' written during the Warsaw ghetto uprising and printed for the first time in the volume 'From the Abyss' is one of the finest in all his opus – and that is saying a great deal.

The tragedy which Miłosz describes acquires a historical perspective and is universal: a man, Giordano Bruno, is burnt at the stake for his convictions – people remain indifferent to what goes on under their very eyes, the passing crowd is paying little attention, is laughing, trading, playing. Before the ash of the pyre cools down – the man is already forgotten. Miłosz likens this scene to the famous carousel and swings near the wall of the ghetto, which on a bright Sunday morning attracted merry crowds. Hot wind from the burning ghetto was bellowing girl's skirts, the playful melody drowned the salvoes from behind the wall. Those consumed by flames, dying their lonely death, were already sinking into oblivion...

Miłosz's poem is passionate, but it is written from the outside; it is controlled, polished and balanced, as behoves a mature thinker and poet. It is a far cry from the cries of anguish from the heart of the ghetto.

I have restricted myself – as was my brief – to some of the more important poems of that time and place, which have reached us by various routes. Since then, of course, writings in the Polish language on that subjest have been massive. Slonimski, Tuwim, Wittlin, Broniewski, Wierzynski, Borowski, Kamienska, Szymborska, Ficowski, Nalkowska, Newerly, Rudnicki, Wygodzki, Wojdowski, Grynberg – their work forms a lasting testimony to this most tragic period of our times and leaves an indelible trace, as only artists can, on the consciousness of mankind. Whether all this writing will feed our hope or deepen our despair is quite beyond me, beyond any of us to judge.

I would like to finish with a few simple words – and they could not be simpler – not my own. They are the words of some children,

From the abyss

overheard by somebody who, later, put them down on paper.

'Daddy,' says a Jewish boy, 'Daddy, when I grow up, I want to be a German.'

A child's voice heard in Belzec: 'Mummy, I have tried to be good – it is so dark here, so dark...'

Another: 'Mummy, when they kill us, will it hurt?' 'No, my dearest, it will not hurt. It will only take a minute.'

It only took a minute – but it is enough to keep us awake till the end of time.

Lecture delivered at a Conference
in the Yeshiva University in New York in 1993

8 • The lesson of Auschwitz

I AM HUMBLED by the task thrust upon me – who wouldn't be? – of addressing this distinguished audience, at this solemn time, when people in all parts of the world gather together in assembly-halls and houses of prayer, to mourn the dead and ponder the meaning of Auschwitz, on the 50th anniversary of its liberation. It is particularly poignant for us here, in the physical proximity of the camp-site, within its sinister shadow.

I must explain why this heavy duty falls on me, even though I am not a survivor *sensu stricto*, but only one of the millions of walking wounded who lost their families and friends in the Shoah.

My Father's family came from that innocent 'shtetl' called Oświęcim, which had its name forcibly changed and gained posthumous fame as Auschwitz – the most accursed sound in the language. My Father was one of fifteen children, so you can reckon that in Oświęcim, there were, literally, hundreds of Scharfs, of all ages, shapes and sizes, from the 90-year-old patriarch Elias to the 4-year-old Chanele. There were no survivors. They did not have far to go.

But I have yet another title. We are assembled here, in the heart of Kazimierz, the former Jewish quarter of Kraków, the city of my birth, which makes me a true Krakówian: and the city which I love – which makes me even more so. I am familiar with every street, every house, every nook and cranny – its doorways seem to be haunted, the windows stare at me like empty eye-sockets. I want to cry out with Jeremiah: 'How lonely sits the city that was full of people – How like a widow has she become – She that was great among the nations … '

Kraków, and within it Kazimierz ('ir va'em be'yisrael'), was the place where, for generations, Jewish life thrived and Jewish culture flourished. Singular, authentic Jewish life and culture – which was brought to an abrupt, violent end and the like of which will not be seen again. Kraków stands for the life that was. When we think of the numbing statistics of Auschwitz, Kraków, as it were, gives a face to those who perished there, makes us think of what it was that we mourn.

Paradoxically, the inter-war years, despite the growing impoverishment and the rising tide of antisemitism, could be seen as

The lesson of Auschwitz

a sort of golden age of Polish Jewry. Jews were born, grew up, had families, studied, earned their livelihood through craft and trade and the practice of professions, maintained 'cheders' and 'yeshivas', secular schools and institutions of higher learning, built synagogues and theatres, played and danced and enjoyed themselves, wrote books sacred and profane, pursued their manifold and diverse interests and – above all – (and therefore I call it the golden age) died in their own beds and were buried in ordinary cemeteries.

They lived, on the whole peaceably, among their Polish neighbours, separately yet together, and made an enormous contribution to industry and commerce, to Polish literature and culture. The nations among whom Jews dwelt have always greatly benefited by their presence.

Were one to specify a single, dominant feature in this rich and diverse tapestry of Jewish life, one could say that it was a degree of spirituality. No matter how poor, humble or oppressed, or – conversely – how prosperous and successful, Jews, in their majority, knew that 'man lives not by bread alone' that he has to rise above the mundane and has to strive for the fulfilment of some ideal, however defined.

It is well-nigh impossible to sustain a rational discourse about Auschwitz. The very word lacerates a raw nerve. It means many things. It is not only a physical place in Poland. It is also an abstract notion which fills us with awe and profound unease. It is a symbol – holding different meanings for different people.

To Jews, Auschwitz is the symbol of the Holocaust. They are surprised and outraged at any attempt to invest it with a different meaning. But for Poles it is a symbol of the German rape of their country and the persecution of their nation – and they have their very good reasons for perceiving it thus.

Similarly, to Christians, the Cross is a sign of love and hope: how are they to be made to understand that to most Jews it symbolises oppression, persecution, the Church's triumphalism, the intention to convert 'the stray brothers'? Can they see that the Cross, in what is perceived as the greatest Jewish cemetery of all times, offends the deepest Jewish sensibilities?

I am going to say something which may be resented by my non-Jewish friends, but this is no time for equivocation. What prompted this thought was my first visit to Auschwitz. I am sorry to admit that, through the years, I could not bring myself to go there, but

Poland, what have I to do with Thee ...

some two years ago I participated in an international conference in Kraków, with speakers from many countries and many denominations, and a visit to the site could not be avoided. On return, when we all sat together, huddled deep in thought, I felt impelled to say that a Jewish perception and response to Auschwitz is different from that of a non-Jew, no matter how sensitive, compassionate and well-intentioned. One of my Polish friends, a man for whom I have the highest regard, told me afterwards that he was hurt and offended by my remark: 'Does my pulse beat in a different rhythm to yours?' he asked. 'My feelings, my emotions, my reason – are they essentially different from yours, somehow less human? Am I less capable than you of grasping the magnitude and the universality of the tragedy?' No, I certainly did not mean to give offence or to exclude. On the contrary, I think that our thoughts and our concern about Auschwitz bring us together and in the face of Auschwitz we are all, in the most profound way, equal. But Jews have been marked as people apart, selected to die, and die they did by the million. Others would get over it (sometimes all too quickly). Jews have not, nor will they. The sense of loss and the pain are always present. In my journeys in all parts of the world I have not come across a single family that did not have near or more distant relatives perish in the Shoah. The Jewish national psyche has been shaped by this experience. Every Jewish reflex, individual, communal or national, is conditioned by the memory of Auschwitz. Am I wrong to hold that for Jews Auschwitz means something more and something different than for non-Jews?

When we want to talk about Auschwitz, we face an intractable dilemma. We are only capable of comprehending the world through words, of communicating through language. Yet in this instance we feel that words are not adequate. By talking about it we trivialise. Adorno said: 'Poetry after Auschwitz is an act of barbarity', meaning that what Auschwitz was and what it truly means should not, in all decency, be used as raw material for literature. When the true human condition is, for all the world to see, manifested in the ghettoes, the camps, the death factories, is not literature which brings catharsis and solace a cruel mockery? And writing, which is an act of faith, an impermissible self-indulgence? By the same token it should not be used for rhetoric, for speechifying, for effect.

Yet this view would set limits on our deepest needs – to share, to instruct, to warn, to transmit. By talking we trivialise and thus falsify, yet by keeping silent we betray.

The lesson of Auschwitz

We have not kept silent. A massive literature exists – memoirs, reports, histories, documents, analyses – considering and illuminating every aspect and detail, and the end is not in sight. (Therefore the efforts of the 'revisionists' and those who deny that it all happened are not dangerous but merely ridiculous.)

The problems are so baffling – we read and study and write and discuss and have come no nearer to understanding the basic questions.

How did a seemingly civilised nation, in the twentieth century, in the heart of Europe, allow itself to be seduced by a gang of perverts and in the course of a few years to be brought down to a state of barbarity? How was it possible to conceive and carry out a plan to build gas chambers and crematoria and, in cold blood, exterminate human beings, by the million? It took so many 'ordinary' people to do it and so many more to allow it to be done – the bystanders, both individual and nations; the accepted order was so easily and so totally subverted.

How did it happen that a great and ancient civilisation could be extirpated and wiped out in the course of four years, so that we have to scrape around for its traces in the land where it flourished? And, most importantly, how are we, the survivors of Polish Jewry, to carry on with our daily lives, burdened with the memory of what happened to our people and how it happened?

What are we to do? How do we conceive our duty towards the new generation, towards the world? What are we to transmit and how?

In the Jewish tradition there is a strong command to teach the young about the past ('ve shinantam le 'vanecha').

I want to share with you a little instructive tale told me by a woman who knows a great deal about these things and who, like myself, gives them serious thought.

Some years ago – she tells me – she went with her son, then a precocious ten-year-old, on holiday to Spain. It so happened that in the place she rented there was a severe plague of flies and insects, which became intolerable, tending to spoil the holiday. One day she undertook a radical measure: she shut tightly all doors and windows and sprayed the space and every corner with a strong disinfectant, whereupon she went with her son for a long walk. When she came back and opened the door – she was taken aback by a macabre sight. The walls and the floor were covered by layers of dead half-dead

Poland, what have I to do with Thee ...

insects, some still crawling heavily. The boy, looking at this for a while, asked her: 'Mummy, is that how Jews were dying in gas chambers?'

What must she have told her son once, that such an image got stuck in his little head? Did she have the right to tell him such a thing? Did she have the right not to tell him? Are we telling our children and grandchildren enough? At the right time?

Surely, there are lessons to be drawn from Auschwitz. How corruptible the creature homo-so-called-sapiens is, how thin the veneer of civilisation. Fifty years on, as I speak, a hundred different wars are being fought around the world, some in distant places of which we know nothing, some in nearby places of which we want to know nothing. The most terrifying lesson of Auschwitz seems to be that it will be easier next time round.

One must try not to give way to despair. Excessive mourning is discouraged in orthodox Jewish teaching (as it is supposed to imply that 'the mourner is possessed of more compassion than the Almighty'). Surely, life must go on (in some ways it has gone on as if nothing happened). The spiritual resources have not dried up, there is rebirth, renewal, the march of generations. Above all, for us, there is the State of Israel, a source of strength and pride and fulfilment.

For sanity's sake we must cling to the notion that somehow, ultimately, there is on this earth a balance of justice (though not easily seen with the naked eye), that our philosophical, theological assumptions are not without foundation.

The Holocaust throws into relief both the worst that human beings can do to each other and the best of which the human spirit is capable. This brings us to the crucial conviction that there is always a choice between the best and the worst; and that there may be times in a person's life where he or she is called upon to make that choice, perhaps at great risk – 'all that is necessary for evil to flourish is that good men do nothing.'

Custom and good manners require one not to end an utterance like this on an entirely bleak note. Not much optimism, as you will have gathered, can be expected of me. I am too far gone, have spent too much time wandering in that ungodly territory. Nonetheless – Hope Dies Last.

Speech on the 50th Anniversary of the camp's liberation,
in the Centre of Jewish Culture in Kraków, 1995

9 • On the 50th anniversary of the Warsaw Ghetto Uprising

I TAKE PLEASURE in the fact that Polish circles in London have taken the initiative in commemorating the anniversary of the Warsaw Ghetto Uprising, and although I am not sure why I of all people have been asked to say a few words on this occasion, I confess I feel honoured.

Perhaps my title to speak out on this subject, should someone question it, lies in this – that the majority of my family on my Father's side came from Oświęcim, an innocent townlet, which later under its accursed pseudonym entered history and covered itself in sinister, posthumous fame. Jews formed the great majority in that townlet and among them the Scharf family was thick on the ground.

Polish–Jewish dialogue has often been, somehow, halfhearted, not open and sincere. One has the impression that many Poles, when speaking about Jews among themselves in private, express views different from those they utter in public – and Jews do the same (I try to fight this – on both fronts). Often when Poles touch upon these Jewish themes, the war, the occupation, they show some disquiet, as if they fear that they will be put on the defensive, will be asked about things difficult to explain, will find themselves, generally, on unfamiliar ground. Few Poles had real knowledge of Jewish life, their writing, internal politics, views and concerns, what made them tick – these matters were simply of no interest to the average Pole. In England we would often recriminate and argue until we were blue in the face. Our views on Polish–Jewish relations in the inter-war years and, above all, under the German occupation, differ.

The anniversary which we now commemorate serves as a good example. When Jews speak of 'The Uprising' they refer to the uprising in the Warsaw ghetto; when Poles speak of 'The Uprising' they mean, naturally, the Warsaw Uprising, that memorable and tragic episode in Polish history.

In Poland the Ghetto Uprising used to be commemorated at regular intervals. On occasion I observed these ceremonies at close quarters. One invariably had the impression that their true purpose was not to pay sincere homage to the heroes and their memory but to

Poland, what have I to do with Thee ...

prove some official thesis, to demonstrate, for instance, how the powers-that-be cared for their Jews or how wrong it was to accuse the regime of antisemitism (which no longer existed in Poland). On other occasions the stress was on the help which the People's Army brought to the ghetto fighters – a list of arms and ammunition to the last bullet (it amounted to precious little even by their own reckoning). At other times the so-called commemoration gave a chance to declaim about the German–Zionist conspiracy threatening Polish independence – of which the sole true protector was Soviet Russia.

The Warsaw Ghetto Uprising was a hopeless, desperate, suicidal gesture, the outcome of which could only spell death to the heroes. Such a typical Polish gesture – I use this adjective advisedly, for Poles and Jews, seemingly so different, in many ways resemble each other (particularly in their tendencies to internal discord). In the history of underground resistance it occupies a unique place. It has become a symbol, on a world scale.

The Ghetto Uprising is sometimes regarded as some partial rehabilitation of a Jewish community often accused of passivity, of going like sheep to the slaughter, without resistance. I disagree with the view that Jews could have shown more will to fight. One must bear in mind the total disproportion of forces: on the one side a population exhausted by disease and hunger, terrorised and defenceless – on the other a mighty, victorious army and the whole apparatus of a police state. In Auschwitz for instance there was a group of 13,000 Russian prisoners of war, young, strong, disciplined. When Auschwitz was liberated there were only 92 of them left alive. If they could not offer any resistance, what could be expected of the rest?

Moreover, the Germans conducted their policy of extermination with extreme perfidy and cunning. The prisoners were isolated from the outside world, unaware of what was in store for them, always with a flicker of hope of survival. The slightest sign of resistance was instantaneously and brutally suppressed, including measures of collective punishment. Despite that, there were attempts at armed uprising in the ghettoes in Częstochowa and Białystok and in the death camps of Treblinka and Sobibor.

It is well to bear in mind that resistance means not only a desperate shot from a pistol, the throwing of a hand grenade or petrol bomb. Resistance is also the underground teaching of adults and children; resistance means a network of charitable organisations; resistance

On the 50th anniversary of the Warsaw Ghetto Uprising

means collecting reports and documents ('The Ringelblum Archives' are our main source knowledge about those days); resistance is artistic activity, concerts, satirical songs, verses written on scraps of paper; resistance is the underground press, bulletins, the spreading of information from received broadcasts. Resistance is Janusz Korczak, a model of human dignity, staying with his children to the last.

Resistance means, above all, every good deed which restores faith in man, a sign that in that flood of barbarity all is not irretrievably lost.

In retrospect, no-one other than those who fought and strove in the ghetto emerges from the story with credit. Not the Allied governments who turned a deaf ear to the heartrending appeals from the ghetto, including the personal appeal of that audacious hero Jan Karski, or the suicide of Szmul Zygielbojm. Roosevelt held on to the thesis that 'the defeat of Germany will bring with it the rescue of Jews.' The vast majority of Europe's Jews did not live to see the defeat of Germany.

Little credit attaches to the Polish Underground. The Home Army, which reflected accurately the profile of the Polish nation, was – with few exceptions – indifferent to the fate of the Jews and in many cases was downright hostile. The commander-in-chief, General Grot-Rowecki, in a radio-telegram to the Polish Government-in-exile reports thus: 'Various Jewish groupings, including communists, have turned to us lately requesting arms, as if we had plenty. As an experiment I gave them a few pistols. I am not sure they will make use of them. I shall not give them any more, you know that we have not a great deal ourselves ... '

Also one must not overlook the part played by the so-called 'Narodowe Siły Zbrojne' – 'The National Armed Forces'. Contemporary historians are not always honest when dealing with this subject but it remains an incontrovertible fact that in collaboration with the Germans and in accordance with their programme these groups themselves murdered thousands of Jews.

During the Warsaw Ghetto Uprising the Polish Government-in-exile was suddenly confronted with the revelations of Katyn and the rupture of relations with Russia – these matters left little time for anything else.

Among those who did not cover themselves with glory were the leaders and activists of American Jewry. The spokesmen for the Uprising called upon them to lie down on the steps of the White House, if necessary, and not budge until the American Government promised to undertake some moves towards rescue or retaliation. It is possible that Nahum Goldman or Stephen Wise approached Roosevelt by the back door, but no one lay down on the steps of the White House, no one stirred public opinion, no one achieved anything to any effect. The inhabitants of the ghetto – and that was the most painful aspect of their existence – felt abandoned by God and men.

The possibility of rendering help, and the nature and extent of it, differed of course, enormously. One thing could be expected from Roosevelt, another from Churchill, yet another from Nahum Goldman. No one, no one beside the fighters themselves, emerged from this with credit; some with eternal shame.

Whoever wants to form a view on these matters must remember that those were truly apocalyptic times, without precedent in history, when all basic concepts, mental habits, normal reflexes ceased to function. There were situations so monstrous, so – literally – inhuman, that passing judgement on them in retrospect, applying ordinary standards, would be totally misleading. How do you divide your bread ration among members of your family when there is not enough to go round? How does a mother decide which of her two children to save when there is a chance to save only one? What do you do when a Jew pursued by the Gestapo knocks at your door when you know that offering him shelter can result in your own and your family's death? You might have heard of the case of one Adina Szwajger, who died not long ago in Łódź and whose obituary notices appeared in 'The Times' and 'The Independent'.

She was a doctor in the children's hospital in the ghetto. When the hospital was being evacuated for transport to Treblinka, Adina Szwajger, to save the children the torment of that journey to the gas chamber, went from bed to bed and gave the children a lethal injection. By what categories can you judge such an action? Read the following extract from a diary written in the ghetto by one Jan Mawult:

'Think of this, a handful of people decide to defend themselves. They have no arms, they cannot erect barricades, they cannot collect ammunition, every pistol has to be bought, smuggled in with great effort. They've decided to die, one and all. Fine. But what to do with the old people, their mothers and fathers, the children? Wives will fight with their menfolk, shoulder to shoulder, but what about the rest? Leave them to their fate? Their fate by now would mean to be

On the 50th anniversary of the Warsaw Ghetto Uprising

burnt alive, not even being poisoned by gas. To leave them to that fate? Impossible. So what is there to be done? It would seem that we have to kill them ourselves. But even that is not simple. The few bullets we possess are precious, must not be wasted, each is destined for a German. To poison them then, but how? The gas is cut off. Cyanide is not available in sufficient quantities. And when, at what precise moment, is this to be done?'

Since it is difficult to talk about these things I thought to escape the inadequacy of common words and resort to poetry, for poetry sometimes manages to deal with the otherwise inexpressible. I am thinking, for instance, of that famous poem by Czesław Miłosz 'Campo dei Fiori' which Miłosz wrote in Warsaw, at Easter 1943. He speaks there of the loneliness of those who die, like Giordano Bruno, at the stake and how the crowd passes by, indifferent, how people 'trade, play, love' and 'forget before the ashes have cooled down.' He likens it to the famous fairground near the Warsaw ghetto walls which, when the ghetto was burning, was attracting local citizenry. I quote some stanzas:

> The bright melody drowned
> the salvos from the ghetto wall
> and couples were flying
> High in the blue sky.
>
> At times wind from the burning
> would drift dark kites along
> and riders on the carousel
> caught petals in midair.
> That same hot wind
> blew open the skirts of the girls
> and the crowds were laughing
> on the beautiful Warsaw Sunday.
>
> Those dying here, the lonely
> forgotten by the world,
> our tongue becomes for them
> the language of an ancient planet ...

The uprising in the Warsaw ghetto is undoubtedly the last chapter in the history of the Jews on Polish soil. The Warsaw ghetto was razed to the ground and became not only the grave of that last group of fighters but also a symbolic tombstone of Jewish civilisation in Eastern

Europe. It was there, on Polish soil, in that raw climate, that there flourished the most creative, resilient, life-enhancing branch of the Jewish nation in the diaspora.

One third of the Jewish people perished, were gassed, extirpated, turned into ashes. In those ashes how many potential Einsteins and Freuds, Heines and Mendelsohns, Gottliebs and Chagalls, Tuwims and Korczaks – people burdened with that genetic endowment which gives rise to genius.

A thousand years of Jewish civilisation in Poland, that which was shared and that which was separate, were destroyed in the course of four years of Teutonic barbarism. This is a fact which the mind cannot encompass and from the enormity of which thought and imagination recoil.

The Jewish people have emerged from this war not only physically truncated but also mentally damaged, in the sense that all other evil in the world appears, by comparison with what happened to us, trivial. Our sensitivity to other people's suffering has been diminished.

It is customary on occasions like this for the speaker to end on an uplifting note, with an accent on hope and optimism, as if to say that despite it all – and so on ... You must forgive me – I cannot rise to that. I stand helpless, orphaned, with a sense of an enormous, irreparable wrong.

There is not a day in my life but that I think of this. I cannot forget, must not forget, don't want to forget. The world should also be made to remember.

Speech in the Polish Cultural Centre in London,
19th April 1995

10 • Rumkowski of the Łódź ghetto

CHAIM Mordechai Rumkowski is one of those figures – complex, grotesque, tragi-comic – worthy of the pen of Balzac or Dostoyevsky – a figure which could come into existence only in demented circumstances when time was out of joint.

To begin with he was an ordinary 'Lodzermensch', an individual of limited education but great native intelligence and iron will, who had once made a fortune and then lost it, a not uncommon case of the rise and fall of that type in the 'Promised Land' which was Łódź at the turn of the century. He took an active part in the life of the community, was a philanthropist. In the interwar years he built, from funds raised by himself, a great orphanage in Helenowek, which was named 'Little Palestine', as the wards were taught agriculture in preparation for their emigration to the Holy Land.

When the Germans occupied Łódź, they called together the Jewish councillors, in order to set up the 'Judenrat'. They nominated Rumkowski as Chairman (*der Aelteste der Juden*); it is not clear why – probably merely because he had bushy white hair and stood out – after all it was all the same to them who was to carry out their orders, one little worm passing orders to other little worms.

The Germans could not have foreseen how lucky they were in their choice. In Rumkowski they found a functionary of demonic energy and outstanding organisational talent. It looked as if his whole life so far had been a preparation for this role, to become in the full flowering of his sixty years, to the joy of his masters, 'The King of the Ghetto'.

Behind the barbed wire, in the district of Baluty, without a sewage system, six people to a room, Rumkowski created a self-governing territory, a mini-state, with its own administration, courts, currency – the notes carried his portrait – and, of course, its own police and prisons.

Food rations, principally bread, were a visible instrument of absolute power and a sufficient sanction to enforce obedience.

Rumkowski organised factories, workshops, hospitals, soup-kitchens, schools – there was a time when people still gave thought to the education of children. From his office Rumkowski directed the whole network of enterprises. He was the sole link with the Germans, the only conduit of their orders.

It is clear, in retrospect, that he was not evil, like some who collaborated with the Germans for their own gain and did their dirty work for them to save their own skins. He was undoubtedly a man of good intentions, convinced that he was acting in the interest of the community. He surrounded himself with a number of able people whose hands remained clean. He carried one idea in his head which guided him like a lodestar: if the Jews proved useful, if they worked, worked, worked till they wore themselves to the bone – they would justify their existence and survive.

It is easy to see today how utterly senseless this idea was. Neither Rumkowski nor anyone else could have then known nor foreseen in their darkest nightmares that the Germans were planning the total extermination of the Jewish people, and that this plan took priority over all other commitments. Nothing, but nothing that Rumkowski did or omitted to do could have had any influence on the fate of the Jews.

Although he was no more than a puppet in the Germans' hands, the role he played turned him into a megalomaniac. He used to speak of 'my factories, my hospitals, my doctors, my Jews', addressed 'his' population, haranguing them continually in the manner of Goebbels. In exchange he expected, and received, paeans of praise: 'Our great Chairman, our wise Chairman ... ' How little real power he had and how his German masters did not even pretend that they owed him anything for his sterling services was shown, when one day he went courageously to the Gestapo to intervene on behalf of his arrested colleague from the Judenrat, he was beaten and thrown out like any other Jew.

Whether Rumkowski was deceiving himself or whether he was striking attitudes in order to impress his fellow creatures is hard to know. He acquired the manners of a despot and this semblance of power turned his head.

Czerniakow, the Chairman of the Judenrat in Warsaw, who in similarly tragic circumstances also played an ambiguous role carrying out German orders, when it came to signing the edict about 'resettlement' at the time when he knew already that the terminal stations of 'resettlement' were the death camps, refused to sign and committed suicide. This act also, of course, had no influence on the fate of the Jews, but Czerniakow did thus rehabilitate himself in the eyes of posterity. Not so Rumkowski – till the last he countersigned the orders put in front of him, until he himself, with his young wife (whom he married in the ghetto), his adopted son and other members of his family, was dispatched to Auschwitz. It is said that the true ruler of the ghetto, Max Biebow, the merchant from Bremen, for whom Rumkowski was ceaselessly amassing a fortune, on 23 August 1944 despatched Rumkowski to Auschwitz not in a cattle-truck, like other Jews, but in a first class carriage.

Was Rumkowski a monster, a benefactor, a fool, a leader? It is impossible to form a balanced view. It is worthwhile to quote his speech to the population on 4th September 1942, after he received an order to deliver for 'resettlement' 20,000 people from among the children and the old:

'Terrible tragedy has befallen the ghetto. We are asked to give up what is most precious to us – our children and our old people. I have not been fortunate enough to have children of my own, therefore I gave the best years of my life to other people's children. I never thought that it would be my lot to have to sacrifice children. It has fallen to me to stretch my arms out to you and implore you: brothers and sisters, fathers and mothers – give up your children to me' (sobbing then convulsed the crowd).

Rumkowski went on: 'I had a foreboding of some terrible threat. I was awaiting some blow, I kept vigil, day and night in case it were in my power to avert it.

'I failed to do so, I did not know what was in store for us. I did not foresee that they would even carry out the sick from the hospitals – but of this you have the best proof, my nearest and dearest were among them and I could do nothing for them. I thought after that that we shall have peace for a while. And now a new threat emerges. Such is the Jewish fate – ever new and more dire suffering.

'Yesterday afternoon we received an order to deport 20,000 people from the ghetto. 'If you do not do it' – we were told – 'we shall do it ourselves.' We were given the choice: to do it or let them do it. With that in mind – not how many will die but how many we shall be able to save – I and my closest aides have taken the decision that, however ghastly the task is for us, we must take the responsibility for carrying out this decree. I cannot escape from having to carry out this bloody operation. I must sunder the limbs in order to save the body. I must take the children from you, else others will die with them.

Poland, what have I to do with Thee ...

'I have not come to bring you solace, I have not come to lighten your hearts – I am here to share the awesome burden of your grief. I come like a thief to steal what is most precious to you. I have not spared myself to have this decree annulled. When that proved impossible, I tried to blunt its severity. I made a register of the children of nine years and older, to get at least those reprieved – they would not have it. I succeeded in one respect – those ten years old and above will not fall victim to the decree. Let this be some consolation.

'We have in the ghetto a great number of people infected with TB, who have only a few days, maybe a few weeks to live. I do not know, maybe this idea is diabolical, but I am asking you: should we not give up those sick people in order to save the healthy? I know that every family takes particular care of their sick. But in the face of this threat we must weigh this up and decide: who can, who should be saved? Common sense dictates that we try to save those who have a chance of survival and not those who will die anyway. We exist in circumstances where there is not enough food to sustain those in good health, let alone the sick. Every one of us keeps a sick person going at the cost of our own health, giving them our own crust of bread, our own lump of sugar, our own mouthful of meat – but this is not enough to save them and we ourselves fall ill. I understand that such sacrifices are noble. But if I am faced with the choice whether to save the sick ones or the healthy ones I cannot hesitate for long. I ordered the doctors to give up all those incurably sick, to save in their place those who can live (wailing and weeping shakes the crowd).

'I do understand you, mothers, I see your tears. I feel for you, fathers, who, tomorrow, when your children will have been taken away, will have to go to work as usual. I know all this and my heart breaks.

'Since 4 o'clock yesterday afternoon, when the decree was brought to my knowledge, I have been a broken man, I share your pain with you, I don't know how to gather strength to continue living. I tell you one thing – the demand was for 24,000 deportees, 3000 per day for 8 days, I managed to bring it down to 20,000, but only on condition that all children under 10 must go. Because these children and the old people add up to only 13,000, we must make up the quota by giving up the sick. I appeal to you, help me to carry out this task. I shudder to think that, God forbid, it will be left to others to carry it out.

'You have in front of you a wreck of a man. This is the most terrible moment of my life. I stretch my arms to you and implore you: make

Rumkowski of the Łódź ghetto

this sacrifice to spare us from having to make even greater sacrifices, in order to protect the remaining Jewish community of 100,000 ... '

It seems to me that nobody who was not there has the right to form a judgement on Rumkowski and on those who found themselves in a similar situation.

Jehoshuah Sobol, an Israeli playwright, wrote a play about the Vilna ghetto, where one of the protagonists is Jakub Gens, the chief of the Jewish police, and later – like Rumkowski – the Chairman of the Judenrat. Gens is faced with the same dilemmas – he is 'serving' the Germans, supplies the workforce, prepares lists of those to be transported to the death camps – always with the thought that he might be able to save somebody. Sobol puts into Gens' mouth the following speech:

'Many of you consider me a traitor. And wonder how I still exist among you, the pure, the innocent, the incorruptible ones. I, Jakub Gens, who uncovers your hideouts, who delivers you to the Germans, am the same Jakub Gens who is plotting day and night how to save Jewish lives. I weigh up Jewish blood, not Jewish dignity. When they ask of me one thousand Jews, I deliver to them one thousand Jews, otherwise they will come to fetch not one but ten thousand. You and your tender consciences! Where there is villainy and filth you avert your eyes. If any of you survives, he will have clean hands, whereas mine are dripping from slime, soaked in blood. I shall appear in front of Jewish judges, shall submit to their verdict. I shall say to them – whatever I did, I did to save Jews, as many as possible, to lead them to freedom. In order to do so I had to lead others to death, yes, with my own hands. So that you should keep your conscience clean, I had to sink in filth. I could not afford the luxury of a good conscience ... '

I don't know whether it serves any good purpose talking about this further. What is there left to say? How much can human sensitivity endure and reason grasp? I confess that even though I have spent the greater part of my life thinking about these things, I am no nearer to understanding how this could have happened, no nearer to grasping the dimensions of the catastrophe and the extent of its consequences. The mind refuses to act – it is better thus, not to look into the very bottom of the pit.

But of this one must be constantly aware: that the extermination of Jews on Polish soil is a critical event in history, concerning not only Germans, Poles and Jews, but the whole of humanity. It marks the crisis of Christianity and the crisis of our civilisation (there are those who would consider those two notions synonymous, but fortunately this is not so).

What lesson humanity will draw from that cataclysm; how it will cope with the awareness of the depth to which man showed himself capable of sinking; how man will renew belief in basic moral values, in a world possessing means of destruction, by comparison with which even the gas chambers pale into insignificance: on answers to these questions depends the future of humankind.

11 • *Janusz Korczak and his time*

THE FOLK memory works in mysterious ways. From the huge mass of events, words and images which leave their imprint on the common consciousness, it selects and fastens onto some quintessential image or figure or a set of words which iron out the complexities and symbolise the whole epoch. Thousands perished at Inquisitional stakes to affirm freedom of thought – it is Giordano Bruno burning in Campo dei Fiori who illuminates the age. The self immolating torch of Jan Palach glows over Prague. Yevtushenko's *Babi Yar* has an impact stronger than all the efforts to drain the event of its true meaning. The prolonged 'S'hema' of Rabbi Akiba reverberates with all the voices of Jewish saints. Of the countless photographs of Nazi brutality, in and outside the camps – the one that haunts us through sleepless nights is of the boy in the Warsaw ghetto, in the oversize peaked cap, with raised arms, the big eyes looking at us, knowing too much.

Thus also Janusz Korczak is a legend of our time. The story which makes him so is simple – but it stands at the heart of the Holocaust and it illustrates perhaps more than any other the horror and the pity of it. On the 5th of August 1942, as part of the liquidation of the Warsaw ghetto, the Germans ordered Korczak's orphanage to be emptied and the children transported to their death in Treblinka. Korczak arranged his 200 wards in orderly ranks and marched quietly ahead of the column to the 'Umschlagplatz' on the corner of Stawki and Dzika Streets, where he and his children were packed into the trucks and despatched to the ovens.

This march through the streets of the ghetto, seen at the time by a mere few hundred people, has cast a long shadow ahead and the small figure of Korczak, on his road to Calvary, unconscious of heroics, wretched with grief, doing what was natural to him, has captured man's imagination. The news of it spread like a bush fire, stories began to be told, filling out the details. How Korczak carried two little ones in his arms – improbably, since he was so sick that he could hardly drag himself along; how – due to the last moment intervention of the *Judenrat* – a messenger caught up with the column with a German warrant to set Korczak free and how he, disdainfully, pushed the messenger aside; how the guard in charge of the trucks, just before sealing the door, offered to leave Korczak out – and how Korczak mounted the steps without a backward glance. How to spare the children anxiety he told them that they were going for a joyride in the countryside and how they trustingly followed him without a tear or murmur. The story in its stark outline wants no embellishment and nothing need be added to make it more telling. The antithesis of spirit and force or, if you like, of the Jew and the Nazi, is pinpointed and fixed. The learned, selfless, caring, man *in excelsis* against the mindless, malevolent barbarian, here at his fiendish worst.

Among the million anonymous deaths, Korczak's death acquired a meaning. As the news spread through the camps and the ghettoes, it provided an inspiration at the time when the greatest single help to survival was the stubborn residual belief, in the teeth of all the evidence to the contrary, that human dignity could still have its triumph.

The underground literature in the camps and on the 'other side' bears witness to the comfort and pride which Korczak's finest hour gave to his contemporaries. Since then his fame has spread and a cult developed. The world was not slow to recognise the moral symbolism of Korczak. Articles, books and plays are written about him, stamps are issued, statues are erected, institutions are given his name, prizes are given to commemorate him.

* * *

It behoves us to see to it that the manner of his death does not overshadow the manner of his life. Henryk Goldschmit, to use for once his real name – Janusz Korczak being a pseudonym which he picked from an obscure novel – was born in Warsaw a hundred years ago, into a well-to-do family. The fact that his father was a fashionable lawyer and his grandfather a doctor illustrates the degree to which this particular milieu was assimilated. He had a sheltered and solitary childhood and grew up hardly conscious of his Jewish origin or what that meant. When still a schoolboy he lost his father, who fell prey to a mental illness, as a result of which the family fell from relative affluence to utter penury. As soon as he was able he took it upon himself to support his mother and sister and he knew years of near starvation and of hard struggle while he studied medicine. Only when he became a doctor did success begin to smile upon him, partly due to his growing reputation as a writer – but then, moved by some inner compulsion, he took deliberate steps to alter the course of his life.

From the moment when at the age of 34 he abandoned his career as a practising doctor and took up residence at the 'Orphans' Home' which till the end remained connected with his name, he was like a man possessed of a magnificent monomania – to live his life in the service of the child. He was no starry-eyed idealist but he was endowed with an uncanny empathy with children and had a sober and steely concern for children's rights in a world ruled by adults. He had a mistrust of the adult world but, like every true reformer, he believed that it is better to light a candle than deplore the darkness. His insights were unclouded by sentimentality, but were based on a continuous clinical observation and meticulous listing and shifting of data. He was wise, loving and utterly single-minded, without a thought for such needs as affect other mortals – money, fame, home or family.

The orphanage, an institution built and supported entirely by private charity, was at the service of the most deprived, the children of the poorest quarters of Warsaw. The raising of money for good causes, then as now, has its vulgar side which tends to irk those depending on it. Korczak shook his head over 'the cost of the wax to polish the dance floor for the charity ball' and begrudged the time spent showing visitors round the home. However, by the force of his personality he established a proper respect for his work, and donors came to understand the privilege of supporting it.

He was an original and pragmatic thinker in the field of child psychology and education and he pioneered concepts which became models of their kind. He continually sought to perfect a system which was based on understanding of the child's deepest needs. Korczak exercised his influence through his close presence and also through his writing for the house newspaper, which was produced for and by the children and the communal reading of which was an important weekly event. It is said that in 30 years of pressing activity Korczak never failed to deliver his weekly contribution. Part of the system of self-government was the administration of justice, according to a Code, with its dreaded paragraph 1000 – the ultimate sanction of expulsion from the home. Every child with a grievance had the right to summon the offender to face the court of his peers – Korczak

Poland, what have I to do with Thee ...

himself had to appear when called upon and had to submit to its judgement. At the end of his day, after the last inspection of the dormitories, Korczak would retire to his small room in the attic, the only 'home' he had all his adult life, to compile his notes and to write his books.

He was a prolific writer in his professional field, but above all of stories for and about children. Deceptively simple in form and content, with a blend of melancholy and humour which reflected his own inner disposition, often sharply satirical of society, always heart-warming and perceptive – they left an indelible trace in the memory of readers young and old.

In the mid-1930s Korczak visited Palestine twice, staying in the Kibbutz Ein Harod. He felt spiritually refreshed and moved by what he saw. Prompted and encouraged by his many friends and former pupils, he began to think seriously about moving to Palestine for good. The obstacles he saw were many. It troubled him greatly that he could not find a suitable successor to fill his place and carry on his work in Warsaw. The thought of tearing up his roots from his native soil was unendurable. In letters to friends explaining the delay he speaks movingly of 'my Vistula', 'my beloved Warsaw', the parting from which, he knew, would leave him disconsolate. Also – he was penniless and feared that he might become a burden.

But the rising tide of antisemitism in Poland was sweeping the essential decencies aside and Korczak could stand it no more. He was ousted from the radio, he had to resign from the non-Jewish orphanage of which he was the founder. The year was 1939. He decided to pack and go.

Stefa Wilczynska, a woman of great heart and shining courage, who over many years was Korczak's close colleague and twin pillar of the venture, had already gone to Palestine a year or two before. Knowing Korczak's helplessness in worldly matters she now returned to help him wind up his affairs and make the journey. The outbreak of war caught her in the trap. She naturally took up again her post in the orphanage, at Korczak's side.

When the Germans ordered the Jews of Warsaw to move into the ghetto, the orphanage lost its home in Krochmalna Street which was on the 'Aryan' side and had to move to makeshift accommodation within the walls. By then Korczak saw more clearly than most people that the screw would continue to be turned pitilessly till all life expired. But he would not give up his inalienable right to relieve suffering. Himself in deepest despair and ailing, he gathered his remaining strength, day after desperate day, in an effort to replenish the essential stock of food and medicine. He steadfastly went on his begging missions for stores and money, at times quite futile, often yielding only a pittance. He felt no constraints in appealing, begging, shaming people into support of this best of all causes. On days when nothing else availed he would go to plead with the execrable ringleaders of the Jewish gang of smugglers and extortionists.

While hunger was growing and disease spreading, he tried to maintain inside the home the pretence of normalcy – teaching, playing, caring, as ever. Into the woefully congested quarters he frequently brought in a new boy or girl, whom he picked up from the street with life ebbing away and for whom being taken, for the moment, under Korczak's wing was the only salvation.

In this extremity of the human condition, such as in saner times is beyond imagining, we have in Korczak, in his daily round, a witness to what a single true man can do out of love.

His was an exemplary life – and it is tempting to see in him, in the frail figure in a janitor's apron, which was his habitual uniform and which is how most people remember him – an epitome of the whole generation, the archetypal 'Child of our Time'. His greatness, which lay in the pursuit of his worldly task, was of a kind potentially within everybody's grasp and even the high drama of his death became ordinary, where martyrdom was commonplace. Insofar as a single individual, through the strands which make up the pattern of his life, expresses the authentic pitch of history at a particular junction, it would be hard to find a figure who more pertinently than Korczak embodies what was significant and particular of his time and place.

Korczak grew up feeling Polish to the core. In his attachment to the Polish soil, history, literature and language nobody could be more so. In this he was typical of a segment of Jewish society in love with the *idea of Poland*. It was only by a gradual and painful process, in the cooling moral climate, that he was forced to recognise that his case was one of love unrequited, and no matter how pure and worthy his devotion he would stay condemned by the sheer fact of his origin. The unhealed wound of this rejection never ceased to plague him.

To understand this fully one must look at the issues in the context of Jewish life as it was, the world of yesterday which came to an abrupt end.

It has been observed, acutely, that Poland has always been a country with a great deal of history but little geography. Constantly imperilled, frequently occupied and ruled by its big and rapacious neighbours, it had few opportunities to develop into an independent, balanced entity. The heavy and ubiquitous hand of the Catholic Church, the ethnic fragmentation, the divisive legacy of the partitions, the impoverished peasantry and the general economic backwardness did not favour conditions wherein liberalism could flourish. During the spell of independence between the wars, the neighbouring states, with the brief notable exception of Masaryk's Czechoslovakia, hardly provided models to follow. Indeed, by comparison with the Germany and Russia of the 1930s one could wax nostalgic over the conditions of relative freedom which did prevail.

One likes to think that the treatment of Jews provides a standard for gauging the moral temperature of a country. This may well be so, but one must not think of it as the only measure. Minorities, particularly if they are substantial, distinctive and competitive, do give rise to acute problems. The will, the wisdom and the means to solve or assuage them are precious commodities, in short supply, and the love of one's neighbour is, sadly, not a universal fact of life. Whether one sees it as a virtue or a fault, the fact is that the Jews of Poland, in their mass, *were* inassimilable – and in that sense remained 'foreign'. It is regrettable but not surprising that the ultimate advantage of diversity and the enrichment of the living fabric of a pluralistic society was not apparent to the Polish 'nationalists' – as it is not even now to many other people the world over.

The Jews were subject to their historic condition of Dispersion and foreignness, a condition which the Poles did not invent and did not know how to deal with. It is now idle to speculate how the problem would have developed without Hitler. It certainly was heading with increasing momentum towards the sharpest conflict. But that was still the time before the word 'solution' was conceived as a synonym for extermination by poison and fire.

Jewish life in Poland moved in its own orbit. In the tightly knit, inward looking urban community the Jewish trader or artisan or worker went about his business almost exclusively among his co-religionists, with only a sporadic and superficial contact with the local population, separated from it by force of reciprocal prejudice, suspicion and profound ignorance of what the man across the street was really like. The Jews lived, in the main, in tenement houses, where – as likely as not – the only non-Jewish occupant was the *concierge* in the basement. Even the intelligentsia of the middle classes, where contacts were more frequent, stayed effectively at double-arm's length, not ever seeing the inside of each other's homes, the doctors tending their Jewish patients, the lawyers their Jewish clients, the teachers teaching mainly in Jewish schools. The occasional Jewish civil servant, university professor or judge had the rarity value of a freak and made people wonder how surpassingly good, or well connected, he had to be to have got there. Charitable, social and political organisations proliferated and displayed the community's diverse concerns, sometimes parallel but seldom identical with those of the local population.

The pattern of such assimilation as there was in Poland followed the familiar general forms, but it also had its specificity. With their ears cocked to the stirrings of emancipation in the West, the rebels and innovators were given to their own visions. The *haskalah* having effected the first breach from the inside, the magnet of the new passwords, *freedom for mankind – equality for the Jews* exercised a mighty pull. The Polish struggle against the foreign yoke and the fight for independence forged bonds of common understanding, of *our freedom and yours*. The thrust was reinforced by growing revulsion against the old Jewish milieu, its claustrophobia and separatism and its antiquated forms – religious and social. By comparison, the attractions of the greener grass on the other side of the hill appeared irresistible.

A new breed of Polish patriots sprang from the midst of the Jewish community. With the zeal of the novice they embraced the dominant culture, so exciting and so different from their own or their parents'. They felt genuine attachment to the land where their ancestors had dwelt for generations, with its language and literature. Within that schizophrenic situation, the dilemmas of divided loyalties, the pull and recoil of the old and the new which always attends the process of assimilation, there were those who remained with a foot in both camps; those who fell between the two proverbial stools and also some who achieved, particularly among the left-wing groupings and intelligentsia, a degree of acceptance as genuine and complete as anywhere in Europe.

There were, of course, also those who for quite unsentimental reasons joined the stream because it offered better career prospects and, as they saw it, a more attractive future. Some of them went the whole hog and got baptised – the Church welcomed converts and the act often revealed a road to social and professional advancement otherwise inaccessible. Their numbers do not seem to have been significant. The atavistic odium which stigmatised a convert remained potent even among those whose links with the Jewish religion had atrophied or were consciously rejected. Excepting the case of a genuine religious conversion, which is as rare as it is mysterious – apostasy for self-advancement carried the penalty of the contempt of the old side and the suspicion of the new. When the end of that era was being acted out in war-time ghettoes, in the depth of misery, this group was the most wretched – alienated from its origins, not at ease among the Jews, uncomprehending why it should be joined with them in death – they suffered the ultimate isolation without the comfort of fellowship.

Despite the fact that entry into the surrounding element was being made increasingly more prickly, assimilation would have continued to grow in scope and numbers but for the emergence of Zionism, which aimed at the physical and moral rehabilitation of Jewry, offered new ideals and hope for the future and successfully contested the leadership of Jewish life in Poland. Though fragmented into parties of every possible hue in conflict with each other, it was united in blocking the road to assimilation. On the other side the *Bund*, whilst fiercely opposing Zionism, proved, among the working class, an influential centre of its own distinct group consciousness.

Whilst the input from the Jewish side into the various aspects of Polish cultural life has been considerable, one need not distort it by exaggeration. The contribution to Polish writings is not comparable, for example, with its German counterpart. Apart from Julian Tuwim, who was in a class apart and undoubtedly the greatest Polish poet of our time, one could list perhaps no more than a dozen names of above average importance – Słonimski, Leśmian and Ważyk among the poets, Wittlin, Rudnicki, Schulz and Brandys among novelists, Klaczko, Feldman, Kleiner among the critics, Askenazy and Handelsman among the historians.

It is also interesting to note that in some of the finest examples of Polish literature, in the works of Mickiewicz, Lenartowicz or Norwid, Orzeszkowa or Konopnicka, the figure of the Jew is portrayed with sympathy and compassion.

A potent process of osmosis, of mutual influences transcending the conscious will of the protagonists, was incessantly at work.

The time has come to face the obstinate fact that the stage for the extermination of the Jews proved to be conveniently chosen. It is clear that the genocide could not have been carried out with the same implacable thoroughness and efficiency, down to the last child, if it had not been correctly assumed that the victims would be considered strangers in their own land, with whose fate their co-citizens would not identify. The searching out, the assembly, the transport, the poisoning and the burning would not have been possible if the local population had felt that this was being done to their own flesh and blood. They would not have looked on, indifferently, or perhaps with a pious sigh, month after month, on the passing cattle trains and on the rising smoke of the ovens – but at whatever cost and risk would have disrupted the process. Moreover, the Germans, moving in an element foreign to them, could not distinguish, on sight, who was and who was not a Jew; the Poles were unfailingly sensitive to every Jewish peculiarity. They could tell by a twist in the hair, by the colouring, by a mannerism, by voice inflection, by word usage, by a look in the eye. Above all, if the victims had known that they would find a hiding place among their fellow citizens, that they would meet enough compassion and solidarity against their common enemy, countless numbers would have saved themselves, aided or unaided, over the vast tracts of the country. But the opposite was known to be desperately true – that the Poles in their overwhelming majority would not hide or help, but would seek out, denounce and deliver.

Why this should be so is, like so many 'whys' which cry to heaven, an unanswerable question, of the same order of mystery as why a nation with the proudest cultural tradition and achievement suddenly and quickly sank to the lowest depth of depravity. Beyond the partial answers of politics, economics and psychology one has to look for further (partial) answers into the unplumbed darkness of the human soul.

Louder than the volumes which have and will be written on the subject speaks a brief Yiddish poem by Mordechai Gebirtig, *S'tut Vey!* (It hurts!). Gebirtig, a poor carpenter in Kraków, the centenary of whose birth, like Korczak's, ought to be fittingly commemorated this year (1978), was a true folk singer and poet, whose simple words and melodies circulated among the people. His life and work epitomise the character, the spirit and the ways of a whole generation. He became the troubadour of the ghetto, where his few songs written before he was murdered with his wife and two daughters in 1942, although unbearably poignant, brought solace to those who heard them, the way only true poetry can. *S'tut Vey!* speaks of young Poles making fun of the blows and humiliation inflicted on the Jews by the common enemy and the pain and puzzlement which this causes. To Gebirtig's sensibility the injury is greater than the one due to the outright German beatings. You do not expect compassion from a beast, you do from a fellow-sufferer ... It is significant that in some of the most evocative Polish writing about that time, in the works of, say, Andrzejewski, Rudnicki, Wygodzki, Grynberg, this motive of hostility of the Poles and the danger which they presented to the hunted Jew is also seen as causing the greater anguish.

Now, it must not be forgotten that active efforts to help and to save, as the screw tightened, often incurred mortal risks and called for qualities of character bordering on the heroic – rare in any circumstances and especially so in an environment of shattered values and rampant evil. In no other occupied country was the crime of aiding a Jew punishable by death. In spite of that, there were many hundreds of well-attested cases of surpassing goodness, self-sacrifice and nobility in the name of friendship and common humanity. And, no doubt, thousands more deeds of kindness, unsung and unrecorded, other than in the memory of those who received them, if they but lived to tell the tale. But it is quite beyond question which was the rule and which the exception.

Hitler brought the history of the Jews in Poland to an end. And with whatever degree of abhorrence and pity the Polish population watched – or turned their heads away from – the process of extermination, the vast majority, it must be admitted, were not displeased with the outcome. They would not and could not have done it themselves. As it turned out, the deed was done and cannot be undone and Hitler is to blame.

The lesson he gave was not lost. With the Germans gone, with the country liberated, the Jews who emerged from the bunkers and from the forests into the sunlight were often hunted and murdered. Remember Kielce, where 200 survivors tried to re-establish a semblance of a community. In July 1946 a group of Polish 'nationalists' staged a pogrom and slaughtered 42 people.

The ironical twist of history is that Poland, having got rid of its Jews, has its 'Jewish' past cling like Deianeira's tunic. Poland's modern history is often seen in the West through the prism of the discrimination against the Jews, as if that was the predominant and distinguishing mark and as if nothing else mattered. The world remembers it as the scene of the extermination of the Jews by their millions and the unhinging dimensions of the drama have largely obscured Poland's own position. Mention, for instance, the Warsaw rising and, as likely as not, the reference will be widely understood to be the rising in the ghetto and not Poland's own heroic insurrection. Poland's destruction and sacrifices, loss of life and territory are found to pall into insignificance by comparison with what is thought the larger tragedy. She commands no great store of sympathy and goodwill and her voice carries little moral authority.

The future will pass its verdict upon what, in the historical balance sheet, is Poland's profit and loss on this account. It is permissible to surmise that the excision of the Jewish genetic pool from the grain of national life, the severance of the creative strain, the stimulant and the catalyst must lead to an impoverishment rather than enrichment of the national fabric.

But for the Jews, let there be no mistake, the loss of Poland is incalculable. For despite the chequered fortunes, despite the vicissitudes, or perhaps because of them, the Jews in Poland through generations formed the most energetic, resilient and productive, the most 'Jewish' part of the Diaspora. Deep roots were struck and they nourished abundant growth.

One must not idealise the picture or view it through a haze of nostalgia. There was squalor aplenty, material and spiritual – often ruthlessly castigated and ridiculed by Jewish writers in the midst of it. There were features of character and mentality which mark a society in a distressed condition.

But the total scene was not, as is sometimes assumed, bleak and forlorn. In the unique historical and social situation of the Jews in Poland the inner strength which vouchsafed survival came from many sources. There was the religious life of intense spirituality, centred around local leaders. There was the family life of great warmth and cohesion. There was the total absence of serious crime. There was a feeling of responsibility for all members of the community, which resulted in a widely cast net of private charity and communal institutions. There was a reservoir of human material, talented and dynamic, on offer to every progressive movement.

This was the heartland of the Yiddish language, a potent unifying force, which gave rise to a flourishing literature. Indeed, there was a living culture – rich and many-faceted, one which drew on its own ancient tradition but was also sensitive to the surrounding influences; a culture which produced Nahum Sokolov and the Gaon of Vilna,

Yizhok Leib Peretz and Scholem Asch, I. M. Weissenberg and the brothers Singer, and a great many of the major Yiddish writers who emigrated to the United States and laid the foundation for the American Yiddish literature that developed there. (Also, for that matter, Julian Tuwim, who wanted to be known as a Jew *doloris causa*.) But the loss goes beyond the list of illustrious names, however long. It concerns a social organism, a dense, complex and fertile human mixture of sharply distinctive character and spirit. The ingredients and the chemistry which gave rise to that amalgam can never be repeated and the world will remain the poorer for its passing.

It is hard to know what the current grassroot Polish perception of the Jew is, what new image is formed in the common psyche. It is an eerie thought that a generation has now grown up in Poland which has never come across a living specimen of the ancient race. The new vestigial Maranos have now fully merged with their surroundings, while those who openly cling to their roots and faith live out their days in a muted, twilight existence. The clerics have lost their target – and a good deal of their power. The anti-Russian sentiments which unify the nation can no longer be focused and vented on the Jews in the Communist Party. On the contrary, some of the bitter recriminations which flared up after the 1967 Israeli–Arab war were due to the fact that part of the population openly cheered the Israeli feat of arms, acclaiming it as a victory of 'our Jews' over 'their allies'. One suspects that in that unseemly joy, which incurred the government's wrath, there was more of a *Schadenfreude*, tinged with envy, over the humbling of the big bully than genuine affection for the victors. All the same a new picture, a Jew no longer pushed around and trampled upon, but defiant and victorious in his own war, has emerged and the word 'żydek', a partly contemptuous, partly endearing diminutive, has lost its place in the vocabulary.

What contemporary scribes and authors of schoolbooks are allowed or instructed to say in the matter is another story. Orwellian 'newspeak' and rewriting of history to serve the latest twist of policy is common practice and affects not only the Jewish aspects but also the relationship with Russia, which calls for massive 'reinterpretation' of traditional and well-established Polish views. How effective and long-lasting such made-to-measure agit-prop can be, remains to be seen.

The spectre of Korczak holds up a mirror to the rulers of present-day Poland – and the reflection is grim. Whilst they are keen to take credit and bask in his posthumous fame, not a word must be breathed in public that he was a Jew. The obsession with the Jew haunts them beyond the grave; it has survived Hitler; it survives the absence of Jews.

Published in *The Jewish Quarterly*, Summer Issue 1977

12 • *Warsaw ghetto*

WHEN THE German army entered Warsaw on 20 September 1939, nearly 400,000 Jews were living in the city, roughly a third of the population. Immediately, they became the target of mounting repression – subjected to forced labour, prohibited from using railways and other public transport, made to wear the Star of David, stripped of their possessions. Virtually without protection of the law, they fell to the mercy of hooligans, sadists, and robbers, of whom there was no shortage. The daily food ration for Warsaw's Jews became 184 calories compared with 669 for a Pole and 2,613 for a German.

On October 2 1940, the Germans established an area into which all Warsaw Jews – roughly 138,000 people – along with persons of Jewish origin and Jewish refugees from the provinces were herded; some 113,000 'Aryans' living in that area had to leave. The Germans then declared the district a 'plague-infested' zone, and the Jews were required to build a wall around it.

The Germans did not like the word 'ghetto' and forbade its use; they referred to it as the 'Jewish residential district' (*Wohnbezirk*). Indeed, the comparison with a medieval ghetto is totally inappropriate, as it implies a degree of normalcy, where people were born, pursued their interests, died in their beds. In that 'district', surrounded by a ten-foot-high wall and a parapet of barbed wire, in a space of approximately 1,000 acres, a population of about 500,000 had to sustain itself, thirteen persons to a room, and many thousands without a roof over their heads. Nearly 60% of the population was left without a means of making a living.

In Warsaw, as in other occupied towns, the Germans designated a *Judenrat* (Jewish council) as the body responsible – with their own lives – for the enforcement of orders in the Jewish community. After the establishment of the ghettos, the *Judenrat* was given control of the police, economic management, and all matters of food supply, housing, and education. Although this seemed to be giving Jews a great deal of managerial autonomy, in reality the Germans created the *Judenrat* solely for their own convenience. *Judenrat* members had no option whatsoever but to respond to every command or caprice of their masters. They were often charged with collecting punitive contributions, one method of reducing the Jewish population to penury. As might be expected – and this indeed was part of the German plan – the *Judenrat* often attracted the fierce hostility and hatred of the Jewish population, deflecting these emotions from the real executioners. The role of the *Judenrat* remains a subject of controversy in the study of the behaviour of Jews under German occupation.

The Germans appointed Adam Czerniakow as head of the Warsaw *Judenrat* – it mattered little to them who would act as their puppet. Czerniakow kept a diary in which he noted his daily dealings with various German officials – a diary that remains a most important source of knowledge of that period. It shows Czerniakow, much maligned by his contemporaries, as an almost heroic figure, pleading and arguing with his implacable masters with great courage and dignity, wringing from them small concessions here and there, trying to persuade himself and those around him, in the face of mounting evidence to the contrary, that the worst would not happen. When it became clear, even to him, that 'resettlement' was a euphemism for murder, he refused to put his signature to a directive ordering the deportation of children, and took his own life. He was condemned by many as a coward, and his contemporaries comment bitterly in their diaries: he should have warned the ghetto, he should have issued a call for resistance. Later judgements are kinder to him. This points to the agonizing moral dilemmas that often faced people in those apocalyptic times, dilemmas to which there was and is no answer.

The Warsaw Ghetto was a vast concentration camp with a simple ultimate purpose – to exterminate the Jews through hunger, through cold, through disease. As time went on, it became common to see corpses on the street. Bands of children roamed the alleyways searching for food scraps. Even though the gates were guarded and the penalty for leaving the ghetto without permission was death, the residents tried to survive by smuggling food from the outside. Risking their lives, children proved the most effective smugglers and supporters of their families.

The German governor, Hans Frank, stated in a report, 'It is not necessary to dwell on the fact that we are sentencing the Jews to death. If the Jews do not die of starvation, it will be necessary to step up anti-Jewish measures, and let us hope that, too, will come to pass.' Frank's vision soon materialized in the fulfilment of the Wannsee

Conference decision on the 'Final Solution'. In July 1942, under the pretext of 'resettlement', a mass deportation to the death camps began and continued, with short pauses, until mid-September. During those seven weeks some 265,000 Jews were transported to Treblinka and murdered in the gas chambers. Some of the victims, lured by the promise of food, presented themselves voluntarily at the Umschlagplatz – the railway siding from which the human cargo was packed into cattle trucks and dispatched to the death camps. The deportation drastically reduced the ghetto population; 35,000 inhabitants were permitted to stay – mainly workers employed in German workshops and their families. In addition, some 25,000 Jews were hiding in the ghetto illegally.

Under such conditions, as a defiant gesture and in a quixotic attempt 'to die as human beings', Jews organized resistance. A few hundred desperate people, gathered from the whole spectrum of Jewish society, formed battle units, arming themselves with a few pistols, submachine guns, and Molotov cocktails. In all, their defense amounted to very little. On 19 April 1943, when German troops entered the ghetto finally to liquidate the last remnants of the population, they met with armed resistance. To their surprise and shock, the Jewish fighters inflicted losses on them and forced them to retreat. The outcome of the battle was, of course, never in doubt for a moment. General Juergen Stroop crushed the uprising with tanks, heavy artillery, and flame-throwers. Avoiding open street combat, he systematically burned the houses, block by block. German bombs and hand grenades killed the fighters huddled in bunkers and canals. In spite of that, the battle continued sporadically until 8 May 1943. As a final, triumphant act in the war against the Jews, General Stroop blew up the Great Synagogue in Warsaw and wrote in his report: 'The Jewish residential district is no more.'

The Warsaw Ghetto uprising had an enormous effect on the morale of the Jews and non-Jews around the world. The longest battle against the Germans in occupied Europe before April 1943, the uprising story has become a legend.

We owe a great deal of our knowledge of that period to the effort and initiative of one man, Emanuel Ringelblum (1900–1944). A teacher, historian, and social worker, he is one of the unsung heroes of our time. From the initial outbreak of war, he became one of the chief organizers of Warsaw self-help and mutual assistance committees. He kept a chronicle of events and, at his inspiration, in the autumn of

1940, a group with the cryptonym 'Oneg Shabbat' (The Joy of the Sabbath) started writing bulletins describing and documenting the situation. Under his guidance, Oneg Shabbat developed a network of reporters all over the country who collected information in response to a prepared questionnaire. They thought, rightly, that every scrap of paper relating to Jewish life would be of inestimable historical value. Thus they collected official posters, public announcements, diaries, letters, advertisements, packaging, copies of the monitored foreign radio broadcasts and, above all, newspapers and news sheets of the many underground groupings. They commissioned special reports on various aspects of life and fed news items to the Polish underground press.

The Germans took little interest at first in what the Jews were doing among themselves. Jews could write, talk, curse, and gossip almost openly. They could discuss in the streets and cafes the illegal news sheets that circulated freely in the ghetto. Semi-official and clandestine committees sustained the fabric of communal life on all levels, alleviating hunger, providing education, organizing cultural events, setting up projects for medical research, generally keeping up the spirits and the morale of the population. Behind the facades of the tenement houses, around the large, typical Warsaw courtyards, cultural and religious life took on new forms adapted to the unprecedented, immediate needs.

The network of Oneg Shabbat was the first to obtain eyewitness reports of the mass murders by gas in Chełmno, the first to raise the alarm in the Polish underground press and, finally, abroad. On 26 June 1942, the BBC broadcast news of the extermination of Polish Jews, based on reports sent by Ringelblum. He noted: 'By alerting the world to our fate we fulfilled a great, historic mission. Maybe this will save some hundreds of thousands of Polish Jews. The near future will show. I don't know which one of our group will remain alive, whom fate will choose to make use of our archives, but of one thing we are certain – that our sacrifices, the risks taken, the tension of constant danger, our toil and suffering, have not been in vain.'

As the noose tightened, the danger of losing the archives caused serious concern. A few months before the liquidation of the ghetto, all materials were assembled, packed into sealed milk churns and metal containers and buried in a cellar deep under the ghetto buildings. After the war, in 1946 and 1950, two parts of the treasure were found under the mountain of rubble which was all that remained of the ghetto. The third part must be considered beyond retrieval, and the sense of its loss is haunting.

The recovered collection consists of some forty thousand pages, mostly still awaiting analysis and publication. The largest and the most important archive of the era, it remains a priceless source of what we currently know and may yet know about the life and death of the Warsaw Ghetto and the destruction of Polish Jews.

Ringelblum gave of himself unstintingly to the last. In March 1943 he was persuaded to leave the ghetto and find shelter on the 'Aryan side'. On April 18, the day before the last deportation and the eve of the ghetto uprising, he re-entered the ghetto, wishing to spend Passover with the last survivors. He was caught in a roundup and sent to a concentration camp near Lublin. When his location became known, a team smuggled him out of the camp and brought him back to his Warsaw hiding place, reuniting him with his wife and son. He continued writing; amazingly, without access to books and sources, he wrote one of his key studies, *The Relations Between Poles and Jews in the Second World War.*

In March 1944 the Gestapo discovered Ringelblum's hiding place which reputedly housed 60 people. All of the Jews and the Polish family who sheltered them were taken to the Pawiak prison and shot – within a stone's throw of the ghetto.

In one respect, at least, the Germans were unlucky in their choice of victims. The Jewish people were determined to leave a trace of their fate, at whatever cost. Feeling abandoned by God and man, they were haunted by the thought that the world would not know how they lived and died. Writing made dying easier. The last entry in Chaim Kaplan's diary before his deportation to Treblinka was his anguished cry: 'If I die – what will happen to my diary?'

Primo Levi, in *The Drowned and the Saved,* imagines members of the SS taunting their victims: 'However this war may end, we have won the war against you, none of you will be left to bear witness, and even if someone were to survive, the world would not believe him. There will perhaps be suspicions, discussions, research by historians, but there will be no certainties, because we will destroy the evidence together with you. And even if some proof should remain and some of you survive, people will say that the events you describe are too monstrous to be believed; they will say that they are exaggerations of Allied propaganda and will believe us, who will deny everything, and not you.'

Warsaw Ghetto

Because of these writers and scribblers, the truth has been recorded, has become known to the world, and no one but a maniac or pervert will deny it. These testimonies give us a picture of consummately hideous times. They show us the depth to which humans can descend, and they document how hatred can bring hell on this earth.

The photographs were handed to me by Willy Georg, a former soldier in the German army, to whose doorstep I was led by friends who knew of my consuming interest in this field. Willy Georg is now over eighty years old – of a generation of Germans with whom I am not at ease without further probing. I am satisfied that he is not suspect: a man of good education and a fairly prosperous background, a professional photographer; at the age of thirty, when these photographs were taken, he still held the humble rank of *Funke* – a radio operator. This does not point to someone who was favoured by or benefited from membership in the Nazi party.

How did these photographs come to be taken? Willy Georg has a clear recollection. He was stationed with his unit in Warsaw (in a district called Mokotów, he thinks). Known to his colleagues and superiors as a professional photographer, he was earning extra money to send home by taking snapshots of his fellow soldiers. One day, in summer of 1941, his officer called him and said, lightheartedly: 'There are some curious goings-on behind that wall. I am issuing you with a pass to enter the enclosed area through one of the gates. Take your Leica, and food for the day, and bring back some photos of what you find.'

He did as he was told. He entered the ghetto, walked around, snapped what he saw on four rolls of film, loaded the fifth. Toward evening a German police detachment entered the ghetto, spotted him, and told him to hand over the camera. They opened the back and removed the film; Georg said nothing about the four rolls in his pocket. His credentials verified, he was led outside the gates. He developed the film himself in a photo laboratory in Warsaw. He is proud of his professionalism: after half a century, the film looks as crisp as new. He sent the film home, to his wife in Munster. He gave it little thought in the intervening years, until lately, when he felt the time was approaching to make his final dispositions.

He felt shocked to the core, he says, when he saw these photos anew and recalled those times. It would have been tempting to ask him how he felt then, fifty years ago, when he came, unprepared, upon that horrific scene, unlike anything he could have encountered before. But there would have been no point in this: all he would have said is what he thinks of it now, or, rather, what he thinks would be appropriate to say to me now. He remembers how polite these people were to him. Although he might not have known it, they had to be polite: a Jew encountering a German was obliged by order to doff his cap and step off the pavement.

This photographic record is not unprecedented. Other photographs still exist that were taken in the ghetto by the Germans around that time and later. (The most famous image – of a small boy in a peaked cap, with his hands raised – stems from one such source.) A team from the German Propaganda Ministry assembled a collection that is now in the official German archives in Koblenz. These photographs were made with the explicit purpose of showing the degradation of that subhuman race, of their indifference to the suffering of their brethren (look how they pass the corpses lying on the street without batting an eyelid!), of people allegedly enjoying themselves playing cards in coffee-houses. These photographers and their masters were clearly unaware of the reverse effect of their work – ultimately, the images degrade not the victims but those who created them.

Willy Georg's snapshots, on the other hand, were totally spontaneous; they simply record the passing scene. The people caught in these photographs – busy, feverish, emaciated, oppressed, but still living a life of sorts – are unaware of the unthinkably cruel end that awaits them shortly. Virtually none will escape a horrible death. One's instinct is to shout a word of warning – run! hide! – but it is too late. At that stage nothing, but nothing, they could have done or left undone would have had the slightest effect on their fate.

To many of us who grew up within or next to that human landscape and who remember it lovingly, these people – shameful to confess – did not at that time look attractive. These misty eyes, beards, sidelocks, crooked noses – one looked away, embarrassed by what a non-Jewish onlooker might feel or say. It now seems clear that these faces, etched with worry and wisdom, lit with inner light, otherwordly, Rembrandtesque, were inexpressibly beautiful. Set against that rogue's gallery, the flower of the 'master race' – Goebbels, Goering, Streicher, Frank, and Hitler himself – little more need be said.

These photographs give a last glimpse of a people about to be murdered, leaving the world forever and irreparably the poorer for it.

Warsaw Ghetto

The lessons of their lives become more valuable as the time approaches when there will be no living witnesses, and future generations might find such things beyond belief.

Introduction to the album of photographs
In the Warsaw Ghetto – Summer 1941, Aperture, New York 1993

13 • *Witnesses*

THE extermination of the Jews by the Germans during the Second World War has given rise to an explosion of writing in all branches of literature.

There is a categorical imperative to continue to record, to relive, to analyse, to understand, to transmit. Every book, every journal, memoir or poem, every case history, every document, every scrap of testimony is a gift to the future – and it is all that will remain after us. The direct testimony of eyewitnesses is self-evidently of supreme importance. The time is approaching when there will be none of them left to speak to us. This book is one of the last of its kind.

On 6 September 1939 the German Army entered Kraków and, for the 60,000 Jews who lived there, some with roots extending over many generations, the world which they knew collapsed, overnight, never to recover. Even though their ultimate and not far distant fate was not yet apprehended, the pattern of persecution leading inexorably to their physical destruction emerged from the start. *Bekanntmachungen*, edicts of increasing severity, pasted on the walls, marked the stages.

First, the separation from the rest of the population – all Jews had to wear armbands with the Star of David. Then, the destruction of the economy. Shops had to be clearly marked – an invitation, smartly taken up, to robbery and looting. Money, except for a pittance, had to be surrendered; anything of value was confiscated and not to be destitute became illegal. Personal freedom was restricted – every Jew had to register, was forbidden to change his address, was not allowed to use the railways.

These edicts were brutally enforced and were accompanied by continuous harassment, raids, man-hunts, searches, beatings. Jews found themselves outside the law, a free prey to brutes and scoundrels – of whom there was no shortage.

The next stage came when the Jewish population was locked in ghettos, where the conditions were very harsh and degrading. Escape from the ghetto was punishable by death. Slave labour detachments taken from the ghetto and put to work beyond human strength led to a rapidly rising death rate. Special work camps, like the one on the periphery of Kraków, in Płaszów, were only thinly veiled instruments of slow destruction.

The pace quickened when the way led through a KZ, a concentration camp proper, where calculated cruelty was the norm and where the inmates were often reduced to walking corpses. And so to the final stage, the extermination camp pure and simple, death factories which had no other purpose than to gas and burn human cargoes as quickly and efficiently as the state of the art – Zyklon B and the crematoria – permitted.

It calls for a painful mental effort to envisage this apocalyptic world, for which there is no analogy in history. There have been wars, foreign occupation, oppression, persecution and murder on a massive scale; such horrors continue to abound, but it is totally without precedent that a whole people, without exception, should be separated from its surroundings and condemned to death, and that this verdict should be carried out with the utmost efficiency, overriding war-aims and – in view of the magnitude of the task – involving tens of thousands of Germans operating the various stages of the gruesome mechanism of extermination. This is the background against which the story of our authors unfolds. Historical events take on flesh and become more real when seen through the prism of individual lives of people who we think are like us.

Miriam was born and brought up on her Father's smallholding, not far from Kraków, from which the family eked out a modest livelihood. Lack of means prevented her from continuing her studies at Kraków University, but she kept her links with the socialist youth organisations and at the outbreak of war this gave her entry to the underground resistance movement and contacts which she was able to put to good use. As contemporary photographs testify, she was a woman of arresting presence – a dubious asset in the circumstances, but, providentially, she was totally free of Jewish features and thereby hangs the whole tale.

Mordecai, born in Tarnow, an auto-didact, a man of great sensitivity and intelligence, clear-headed and self-assured, had no hesitation in deciding what he must do when darkness fell.

These two, separately and at first unknown to each other, but clearly of similar cast of mind, which made them later into ideal partners, assumed roles which, as will transpire, were nothing short of heroic. They themselves remained unaware of this dimension: ordinary people, you might say, who had greatness thrust upon them and took it in their stride, not fearlessly, but by overcoming fear and in full knowledge of the consequences – with the comforting feel of the phial of cyanide in their pocket, since no one knows the limits of endurance under torture. It would have been easy for them to slide into relative safety and merge with the surroundings – with their 'good looks' and impeccable speech, their chances of survival were reasonable.

Instead, whilst being vulnerable in the extreme, particularly the man, they courted constant danger. They plied their errands of mercy in places the prudent would shun like the plague: in railway stations, assisting people on their journeys; in crowded shops which were used to deposit and pick up printed matter for distribution and where they could be recognised by former acquaintances or friends (even those with the best intentions could, unwittingly, be dangerous); in offices, seeking rubber-stamping of fake documents.

Having secured for their wards 'good papers' – an identity card, a birth certificate, a confirmation of employment in the right firm – there was always the problem of finding a hiding place: for some it was a cellar, a loft, a dark room at the end of the corridor; for others a place in a convent or orphanage. There followed frequent visits – to pay 'rent', or to deliver the money allowance or a message from the family. Few of these hiding places remained permanent – a careless word, a suspicious noise, a disturbance in the neighbourhood made it imperative to move, and quickly. All this took place under the prying eyes of a suspicious and jumpy population, the Gestapo, the police and hordes of informers and blackmailers. Even reading about it, 50 years on, one's heart misses many a beat and one is challenged to think whether in similar circumstances one would have found the inner resources to act as they did.

In the eyes of the ghetto-dwellers the world outside the wall, on the 'Aryan' side, was normal. Although it was far from that in any accepted sense of the word, its dangers were of a different order, and it offered a possibility of survival at least to those few who had the necessary equipment, that is the looks, the language and the physical and mental stamina to withstand the terrible stress of the situation, of pretending to be someone else, of never lowering one's guard, of living every minute of day and night in mortal dread of discovery.

One could have the appearance of an angel, yet the tell-tale details which could give one away were legion; the eyes could be cornflower-blue but their uncontrollable sadness was hard to disguise

– dark glasses in themselves were highly suspect. Men, of course, carried their death sentence with them, ready for inspection.

As important as the physical mimicry was the mastery of characteristic Polish forms of speech and behaviour, particularly in religious settings – how were Jews or Jewesses to know when to cross themselves, when to kneel down or get up during Mass – a moment's hesitation could mean that the game was up. The learning of prayers and the minutiae of ritual was imperative.

The masking of one's feeling in public was a further ordeal, testing endurance to breaking point, particularly after the details of the death camps became known. How to hold back the 'tears by which a Jew is known', how to react when the topic of the murder of the Jews was raised in conversation with the Poles, as happened all too often – to feign indifference, to condemn? Miriam speaks at one point of how, risking all, she simply could not hold her tongue. Mordecai mentions how hard it was to keep up the pretence when a Jew whom he was helping and whom he tried to console, would burst out, bitterly, 'It is easy for you to talk ...'

In many cases the strain proved too much. Having taken the enormous risk and trouble of getting themselves established on the 'Aryan side', some of these wretches returned voluntarily to the ghetto to live and die with their own people. And how can one come to terms with the situation where a mother and her child, having been given shelter and hospitality by Polish friends, cannot endure the thought that her presence so greatly endangers her hosts that, one day, she simply leaves, never to be heard of again? What were the feelings of these people then?

In their understandable resentment of the misfortunes that engulfed them Jews were often not sufficiently sensitive to the Polish situation and the agonising choices facing their neighbours. Only by comparison with the terminal tragedy of the Jews does the fate of the Polish people appear tolerable. By any other standards their sacrifices, their suffering and their losses during the war mark them out as the great victims of their history – and geography.

The extent and nature of the support given by Poles to Jews in their pathetic efforts to survive outside the ghetto walls has been and remains the prickliest issue in the post-mortem analysis of Polish–Jewish relations. It is the Jewish perception that, on the whole, the Poles have not emerged from the infernal trial with credit. They are accused, at best, of indifference and, at worst, of abetting the

Poland, what have I to do with Thee ...

Germans in their murderous design – the notable exceptions being those few thousand celebrated in Jerusalem as 'The Just Among The Nations' and, surely, the many, unrecorded, who did not live to tell the tale. It is revealing, in view of the indictment, that the indifference and hostility came as no surprise; it was what the Jews had been led to expect through the many years of uneasy cohabitation – the sowing of hatred would not yield a harvest of compassion.

The Poles counter, with justice, that effective aid on a massive scale was simply not possible, in view of the power and the utter ruthlessness of the Nazi forces, to whom the extermination of the Jews became an overriding war-aim. Giving aid in individual cases was perilous in the extreme and called for readiness to risk one's life and that of one's family – the Decree of 10 December 1942 issued by the Governor General set the death penalty not only for the Jews caught outside the ghetto but also for all who gave them shelter or aid of any kind. This was no mere threat and many paid the ultimate penalty.

Despite that, in 1942, an organisation was set up by the Polish underground in Warsaw and Kraków, under the name 'Żegota', with a network thinly spreading over the whole of the 'General Government', for the specific purpose of helping the Jews on the 'Aryan side'. The aid took the form of finding accommodation, supplying false documents, distributing money, protecting them against blackmail, reclaiming them by bribes or cunning from the hands of the police or the Gestapo. The activity of Miriam and Mordecai Peleg was carried out under the aegis and within the framework of 'Żegota', and as we know from the evidence available to us, many people owed their lives to this organisation.

In the controversy which bedevils Polish–Jewish relations to the present day, objective evidence is hard to come by. Here the testimony of Miriam and Mordecai is of singular value. Their integrity and trustworthiness are beyond question. Their daily engagement with both Poles and Jews gives them a unique viewpoint from which as true a picture can be drawn as is humanly possible. No study of that period and problem can disregard this case-history.

The purpose of *Witnesses*, as Miriam Peleg-Marianska sees it, is to try 'to express in human language things which are not human.' One cannot know how this will strike the reader, remote from that time and those events. Sensitivity differs and man has shown a great capacity to endure the suffering of others. But one thing will surely come through: it is people like Miriam and Mordecai, living in those

Witnesses

consummately hideous times, who allow us to hold on to the belief that goodness has a chance in the eternal contest with evil.

Introduction to *Witnesses – Life in Occupied Kraków*
by Miriam Peleg-Marianska and Mordecai Peleg, Routledge, London and New York 1991

14 • *Saints or madmen?*
A meditation on Ephraim Oshry's *Responsa from the Holocaust*

THIS IS one of the most extraordinary documents of our time, of any time. A large claim this – let us consider the evidence.

Ephraim Oshry was a young rabbi in Slobodka, a suburb of Kovno in Lithuania, at the time when the German armies occupied that territory in the last war. That part of the world was famed for its Yeshivas, founded early in the nineteenth century – Slobodka, Mir, Volozhin, Ponieviezh – presided over by great sages and scholars, attracting students from all over the world. For those who believed that the study of the Torah was the highest of human pursuits, that territory was hallowed ground, 'the second Eretz Yisroel', and Vilna was named 'the Jerusalem of Lithuania'.

Rabbi Oshry was an eyewitness of the entry of the German army into Kovno on 25 June 1941, a date which marked the beginning of the end of Lithuanian Jewry. The Lithuanian 'fifth column', the Fascist grouping which comprised a substantial portion of the population, went instantly on a murderous rampage against their Jewish neighbours. Armed with guns and axes they broke into house after house, killing whole families. Rav Zalman Ossovsky, the Rabbi of Slobodka, was bent over a folio of the Talmud when the mob forced the door, he was tied to his chair and decapitated. The head was put into the window for passers-by to see. That day many hundreds were put to death, among them a large number of Yeshiva students.

With varying degrees of intensity the murder and plunder continued for two months. However, that proved merely to have been a prologue; a pogrom following historic precedents; an idyll, by comparison with what was in store – the systematic programme of total extermination. As elsewhere, the process began by forcible transfer of the Jewish population into the confines of the work camps and ghettoes, in the course of which thousands were left homeless and died of exhaustion. It was an intermediary stage prior to despatch to the sites of mass execution and death camps.

In the crowded ghetto behind the barbed wire, with just about enough space to turn around, life, of sorts, went on. The physical hardship and psychological oppression created conditions in which human beings tend to lose their humanity – which was the additional purpose of the enterprise. The space was constantly shrinking, as the population became decimated by disease, hunger, daily murder and finally 'resettlement'.

In this purgatory the young Rabbi Oshry carried on his ministry. He proved himself to be a man of great authority, courage and faith, a veritable tower of strength. He was brought face to face with human and theological problems of agonizing complexity. People came to him with questions because – he says – 'they were not always sure what the Torah required of them'. He noted the questions and wrote down his brief rulings on paper torn from cement sacks. For some time he had access to the sources which he had to consult: there was in the ghetto a large store of sacred books – the Germans collected them in order to exhibit them later as 'artefacts of an extinct race' – and Oshry, providentially, was put in charge of those stores. Oshry packed the notes he made into cans and buried them in the ground. He vowed that if he survived he would expand his notes into full-length 'responsa'. Happily, he did survive and on the day of the liberation of the ghetto he recovered his notes.

Rabbi Ephraim Oshry lived for some years after the war in Rome where he founded the Yeshiva 'Me'or Hagola' for survivors. He now lives in New York where he occupies the pulpit of 'Beth Hamedrash Hagadol' and is the president of an organization of rabbis who survived the camps. As promised, he elaborated and expanded his original 'responsa' and published them under the title *Sheilos Utshuvos Mima'amakim* in five volumes. The book under review is a short selection, containing 112 'responsa', translated into English (published by Judaica Press, New York). On the face of it, it is a traditional item of rabbinical literature in the customary form but, because of the time and place when it was started and the nature of the problems it tackled, it is unlike anything else ever written. The background and context of the questions that are raised – quite apart from the answers – provide a record, detailed, authentic and immediate, of life in circumstances which numb the imagination. Everybody's daily existence hangs on a thread, depending on the whim of the commander, the guard, the distant masters in Berlin; on an additional piece of bread or a spoonful of soup; life around is brutish and dangerous in the extreme; there is a systematic and seemingly irreversible destruction of all one holds dear; parents look on helplessly at the suffering of their children. And people come to the rabbi to ask what to do.

The scene is the classroom where Oshry teaches his students Talmud. A woman bursts in, screaming that the Germans have just shot dead her husband and three children. Her father-in-law, Reb Zalman Sher, dies of a heart-attack on hearing the news. The question put to the Rabbi is: since it is impossible to know if the Germans will allow them to make arrangements for the funeral, is it permissible to make the *tahara* – the preparation of a corpse for burial – *in advance* rather than *as close* to the funeral as possible? (Oshry permitted immediate *tahara*.)

On 4 Elul 5701 – 27 August 1941 – the Germans captured stray dogs and cats and brought them into a house of study in the ghetto in Slobodka where they shot them. They then forced a number of those present to rip apart a Torah scroll and use the sheets of parchment to cover the carcasses of the shot animals. The participants and the witnesses of this desecration later asked the Rabbi to prescribe a programme of penitence. Oshry ruled that all those who saw the scroll being torn were to rend their garments. Those who were forced to tear the Torah scroll with their own hands were obliged to fast; if they could not fast because of debility they were excused. Those who were not present but only heard of it from others were to make a contribution to charity.

In September 1941 the Kovno ghetto contained some 30,000 souls, among them 10,000 labourers. The Germans ordered the *Judenrat* to distribute among them 5,000 permits (the so-called *Jordan Schein* from the name of the German commander) which would entitle them to stay in the ghetto with their families; the implication for the rest was clear. The labourers besieged the office of the *Judenrat* and fearful scuffles began, with many trying to grab the permits by force. The question was put to Oshry; was the *Judenrat* permitted to obey Jordan's order and distribute such permits? On what basis could they determine whose life was more significant than another person's? A further question was asked: is it permissible for anyone to grab a permit to save his life? For by grabbing a *Jordan Schein* for oneself, one was condemning another man and his family to death.

A similar event took place several months later in Kovno (and countless other places). The Kovno Rabbi, Rav Avrohom Dov Ber Kahana-Shapira, in a responsum to the *Judenrat* whether to obey the German order to gather the whole of the ghetto population without exception in the central square (to cooperate in the process of extermination), rules: 'If a decree is issued that a Jewish community be destroyed and a possibility exists to save some part of the community, the leaders of the community must gird themselves to take every possible measure to save *as many as can be saved.*' Oshry's responsum was similarly phrased. As to the second question of grabbing a permit by force, he says that, initially, no Jew is ever allowed to do anything that places another Jew's life in danger. Nevertheless, according to the principle that one must save whoever can be saved, it seemed that each labourer was entitled to do whatever he could to save his life and that of his family.

On 6 Cheshvan 5702 – 27 October 1941 – 48 hours before the Black Day of the Kovno ghetto, when some 10,000 men, women and children were taken away to slaughter and the German purpose of total extermination was made apparent to everybody inside, one member of the community came to Rabbi Oshry with the following problem. Since it is known from former practice that women and children are shot in front of the men, the petitioner cannot endure the thought that he will witness such a scene. He asks, therefore, whether he is permitted to take his own life. This would have the additional advantage that he would be buried in the Jewish cemetery in the ghetto. Responding, Oshry denies him the permission to commit suicide. It would mean surrendering to the enemy, who welcomed such confusion and despondency among the Jewish captives. It also showed a lack of trust in God's ability to save the Jews from the hands of their oppressors. Oshry notes with pride that he knows of only three instances of suicide in the Kovno ghetto.

Standing in the central square in Kovno (*Demokratiaplatz* no less) with the whole of the ghetto population, some 30,000 souls, awaiting the final 'selection'. Oshry is approached by a man with the following query: what is the precise formula of the blessing which a martyred Jew should utter as he dies to fulfil his very last *mitzvah*? He wished to tell this to as many people as possible so that when their turn came they should use the right words. Oshry offers him the formula which he, Oshry, himself intended to utter: *asher kideshonu bemitzvosov vetzivonu lekadeish shemo berabim.*

In the winter of 1942, several months before Passover, many Jews in the ghetto began to think about how to secure some matzah. Most basic foods were not available, let alone white flour from which matzah is baked. Moshe Goldkorn who worked in an outside brigade

Poland, what have I to do with Thee ...

came into contact with Lithuanians who were ready to barter goods for flour. In the course of time he managed to smuggle into the ghetto, bit by bit, each crossing of the gate fraught with danger, enough flour to bake matzah for nearly 100 Jews, each of whom would receive one olive-sized piece, enough to fulfil the commandment on Passover Eve. After preparing the oven according to the *Halacha* the matzah was baked in one of the bakery workshops.

Two days before Passover, Goldkorn was stopped at the gate and searched – a small bag of flour was found on him. He was beaten black and blue and had all his teeth knocked out. He came to Oshry with the following problem: 'With my knocked out teeth how can I fulfil the commandment of eating an olive-sized piece of matzah? I come from a Hassidic family whose custom is never to eat matzah that is 'soaked' on Pesach. I cannot break that custom and yet I cannot bite anything which is not softened.' Oshry ruled that he be allowed to soak the matzah in water even though he is descended from Hassidim whose custom is not to do so, in order that he may fulfil the *mitzvah* for which he had risked his life. However, he must obtain from a *beit-din* an annulment of the implicit vow of the tradition of his forebears not to eat soaked matzah on Pesach.

There was an absolute prohibition by the Germans on bringing food into the ghetto from the outside – the meagre ration of those working outside had to be consumed so that it was not shared with one's children and family. Oshry notes a case of a man who saved a piece of bread and hid it between his thighs, hoping to sneak it past the guard. He was caught, beaten and kicked, so that his testicles were crushed. He came to Oshry with the following: 'I am prohibited from living with my wife (Deuteronomy 23:2) and I can have no children. Since I am a *kohein* I have always been 'called up' to read the portion of the Torah as the 'first reader'. Now I am blemished and therefore forbidden to read as the 'first reader'. Is there any way I can still be treated as a reader and a *kohein*?' Oshry is unable to rule against Deuteronomy 23:2 which forbids a man who has had his testicles crushed to live with his wife. But as for his status as a *kohein* Oshry is ready to interpret the Law entirely in his favour.

On 20 Iyar 5703 – 7 May 1942 – the Germans decreed that any woman found pregnant would be killed. Oshry was asked whether, in the circumstances, contraception is permitted. The answer was – yes. He also ruled that in view of the threat to the woman's life abortion was permitted.

Saints or madmen?

A question was put whether a person could be permitted to buy a baptismal certificate which, if he could subsequently escape to the forest, would enable him to join the partisans. Oshry opines that there is no way that this may be permitted, even if one expected to owe one's life to such a transaction.

These are some cases chosen at random, out of hundreds, thousands. Each one a glimpse of hell, reflecting dilemmas which no man should be asked to face, showing sentient beings at the extreme of the human condition. Each one a text for meditation.

There is another series of cases put to Oshry after the liberation but arising from circumstances of the war. For instance: is a Jew allowed to enter church premises to search for Jewish children hidden and protected there by the priests in order to get them returned to the fold? (Yes, he is.) The children saved by the Gentiles now had to be 'saved' from the Gentiles. Oshry was himself involved, often at risk to his life, in the searches and 'recovery' – and this is a story apart. The process took time and some of the boys found were six or seven years old. The question arose: Is anaesthetic permitted in circumcision? One boy refused to be circumcised unless he was promised that he would suffer no pain. Oshry permits the use of an anaesthetic (even though to feel the same pain as our forefather Abraham felt is a merit) on the grounds that, since that particular boy had already lived among Gentiles, if we caused him pain he might rebel against other commandments of the Torah and leave the fold. Immediately after the liberation there was a severe shortage of *tefillin*. Many sets were found in Gentile homes. Was it permissible to use such a set immediately without waiting for an inspection to check whether they were kosher or not? Oshry records that when he ruled in favour of immediate use people cried for joy.

There was a case of the *mamzer* rabbi, born in a union which, in retrospect, was deemed unlawful. The story goes back to October 1941 when a rumour spread in the ghetto that all husbandless women would be put to death. By that time, as experience taught, nothing was past belief, and the rumour caused panic among single women who scurried round for husbands at all costs. One woman, whose husband had been taken away by the Germans and disappeared without trace, assumed that he was dead. She found herself a new partner and married him. The couple escaped from the ghetto, survived and, after the war, moved to another country. Here they had a son who, in the fullness of time, studied in a Yeshiva and became the

Poland, what have I to do with Thee ...

rabbi of a community. One day, out of the blue, a man turned up declaring, and proving, that he was the first husband of the rabbi's mother, wrongly presumed dead. It had taken him a long time to come upon the trace of his wife but when he discovered that she had married another and had borne him a son, he felt outraged by his wife's 'betrayal'. He was determined to track her down, force her to divorce her second husband and publicly reveal her shame. However, by that time the woman was no longer alive and his wrath turned upon her son, the product of that bigamous marriage; the man would spare no efforts to have the rabbi cast out from the Jewish community.

Rabbi Oshry tried to persuade the vengeful man to remain silent – publicizing such an issue constitutes in itself *chilul Hashem*, a desecration of God. The young rabbi's life was in ruins anyway. Oshry ruled that he should resign his office for although, according to the Law, a *mamzer* is not disqualified from being a rabbi, 'people will not listen to him'. He also made the necessary arrangements for him to divorce his wife for it is forbidden for a *mamzer* to be married to a Jewish-born woman unless she herself was similarly begotten.

What is one to make of these people?

In the context of the Holocaust, where other people despaired and lost direction, they maintained their unshakeable faith – despite daily evidence to the contrary – in God's ultimate loving purpose. Where other people felt helpless and rudderless, they searched for answers and knew where to look for them. Risking torture and death for defying the German order forbidding communal prayers and teaching, they studied the Torah and observed the *mitzvot*, convinced that 'Jewishness' had to be preserved and only thus could it be preserved. They refused to be dehumanized and maintained a feeling of infinite superiority over their oppressors. This was spiritual resistance of a high order. It was undoubtedly a source of enormous inner strength in the fight for survival. On the other hand, at a time when every flicker of energy had to be summoned to want to live another day, it was an awesome hindrance if one insisted on fasting on Yom Kippur, strove to observe *kashrut* and had to ask the rabbi whether it was permissible, if there was no other way of getting a meal, to cook on Sabbath and – a further question – whether it was permitted to eat what another Jew thus cooked. And if a piece of paper like a certificate of baptism, which could prove to be a life-saver, had to be refused.

What is this phenomenon? Is it human, perchance superhuman?

Saints or madmen?

Where is its place in the sum of things? To the lay, secular, rational mind the questions and the responsa might appear absurd, grotesque, eerie, not to say insane. But one would have to be quite devoid of feeling not to perceive that we witness here a dimension of spirituality which is transcendental. One may not be able to comprehend it or even remotely empathize with it but it is impossible to shrug it off. Whether one is inclined to shake one's head in disbelief or weep with compassion, one cannot but stand in awe in the face of this degree of devotion and trust in God.

Must we not try to form a balanced view of the mental landscape of these, our brethren, even though, to them, our own is meaningless and unworthy and we ourselves are apostates and scoffers who will burn in hell? In fact, if hell, by the best definition, is separation from God, for all we know we are there already.

The Jewish Quarterly, No. 128, 1987

15 • *All our yesterdays ...*
On the album by Roman Vishniac

ROMAN Vishniac's album of photographs[1] taken between 1934 and 1939 in Poland, Czechoslovakia, Rumania, Carpathian-Ruthenia, Hungary and Lithuania, entitled *A Vanished World* is a work of genius. It is a document of enduring value: potent, evocative and inexpressibly sad. Those who remember and those who want to imagine what these people and these places were like, having seen these photographs, will be thinking in his images.

In all weathers, sunshine or dusk, in the street or in basement hovels, with an unerring eye for subject and composition and artistry which conceals art, time and again Vishniac captures these astonishing images which bring to mind the great Dutch Masters. A passing moment is caught in a blinding flash of insight and now fixed for as long as books are printed.

We have known of Vishniac from former exhibitions and publications (*Polish Jews*, Schocken Books, New York 1947, *Life of the Six Million*, 1969) and the appearance of some of his photographs in other albums (*Image Before My Eyes*, Schocken Books and YIVO, New York 1977, Franz Hubmann's *The Jewish Family Album*, Routledge and Kegan Paul, London 1975), but this album is the long awaited selection – 200 of the best.

Roman Vishniac, now 86 and living in New York, where he has just been made an honorary citizen, is a truly remarkable man and the story of how these photographs were taken could be the subject of a picaresque novel.

Vishniac was born in Russia and studied medicine and zoology at Moscow University. After the Revolution he moved to Berlin where he became an eminent specialist in microphotography.

After the access of Hitler to power he was possessed by a sombre premonition that the threats uttered in *Mein Kampf* would be fulfilled. As if guided by an inner voice he embarked on this improbable venture: armed with a Rolleiflex and a Leica camera he made his way through Eastern Europe, through town and village, casting a compassionate eye upon the Jewish scene. He operated without flashlight and, mostly, with a camera hidden from view. This he thought advisable because orthodox Jews often refuse to be photographed, but also a stranger wandering through the countryside with a camera in that part of Europe in those days (as now) was courting trouble. In fact, Vishniac was taking grave risks; repeatedly he was manhandled and pushed over frontiers – only to re-enter at another point. He was arrested 11 times, spent time in various prisons, his negatives were often confiscated. He covered enormous distances and took over 16,000 photographs – of which he managed to smuggle out 2,000 negatives which were hidden throughout the war by his father in Vichy France. He himself landed in a concentration camp in Clichy from which he escaped early in 1941, across Spain and Portugal to America. It did not take him long to re-establish himself as an outstanding scientific photographer in New York. All in all, one might think, a good Jewish life.

Turning the pages of the album ... that dreamy, downy-cheeked boy with eyes like saucers pulls at the heartstrings; like those other boys in the 'cheder', so innocent and yet knowing, one wants to embrace them; like that other boy in the oversize peaked cap and arms raised, in that famous photograph from the Warsaw ghetto (taken by a Nazi for a souvenir), which has become a Jewish icon.

Those three 'Hassidim' in full regalia, kaftan, tallit, shtreimel – caught in a graceful movement like a ballet-group, leaving the synagogue after morning service, still in full flight of argument, a telling point made with a characteristic gesture.

A bleak, snow-swept street corner, the nameplate reads 'Street of Isaac', in the heart of Kazimierz in Jewish Kraków – where else would streets be named after Patriarchs? – an old wall bruised and bespattered, ghostly figures in emptiness, strangely moving ...

By way of contrast – a bustling courtyard in Nalewki on a warm day, every one of the hundred windows in the tenement open to air the tiny rooms which also serve as offices, shops, workshops; a motley crowd streaming in all directions; signs offering ribbons, corsets, underwear, sewing-thread, aprons, trunks, umbrellas. A little segment of what, multiplied a thousandfold, formed the greatest concentration of Jewish life on earth ...

One is startled by the singular beauty of these people. If one could, for 1/100th of a second, forget what happened to them a few years or months after the Vishniac snapshot, one could simply be enchanted. But one knows the imminence of massacre, one knows that the whole

Poland, What have I to do with Thee ...

scene is an ante-room to hell – one smothers the impulse to shout a warning. This is still not graspable: that within four years this thousand-year-old civilisation had vanished without trace, smashed, stamped out, annulled, burnt ... Nothing of it remains – only by some miracle would a single soul captured in these pages have remained alive. How is one to adjust to this eternal absence?

Vishniac has earned our admiration and gratitude. His work will not be supplanted or amplified (other than by himself from hitherto unpublished stock) – it will become, in fact already is, a classic of its kind. It is therefore important not to let pass the inaccuracies and the bias which permeate the notes and captions. The notes which precede the photographs and can be read virtually as a continuous narrative are often ill-informed and misleading. They were written by Vishniac recently, in old age, many decades after the events. With all due respect, memory plays him false or his emotions get the better of him, which is understandable – but the notes distort the perspective and blemish the book as a source of information. The Polish Government and population, to take the example of that country alone, have enough to answer for without being accused of things they did not do and could not help.

For example: on p.20, an orthodox Jew in his 'bekeshe' (kaftan) and round peaked cap is said to have been dismissed, under pressure of the boycott committee, after twenty years' service – it is fanciful to imagine that a man like him would have worked for a non-Jewish Polish firm or institution in the first place.

Note to pp.27–28 says: 'After the boycott transporting freight by handcraft or on their back was the only occupation permitted to Jews of Warsaw' – the assertion is quite absurd and should not have got past the editors. A note to p.65 speaks of rules of employment for Jewish office girls as opposed to their non-Jewish counterparts – there were no such discriminatory rules as those described. Note to p.66 says about a 'bagel seller': 'On Jewish streets nobody had money to buy anything but ordinary bread'– no, no; some had little, some had more, some had plenty; 'bagels' were within the means of most. Note and caption to photo No. 178 – a face of a Jew through a small window in an iron gate – allegedly the 'Endeks', the *pogromschschiki* are coming to beat him up. Would they but try! They knew better than to trespass on this territory at risk to life and limb.

Vishniac repeatedly refers to the boycott – as if this was the main reason for Jewish poverty. This was not so. Poverty preceded the boycott and had deeper causes. The boycott was villainous but its effects were probably marginal; it made some Jewish traders a bit poorer and no Polish trader any richer. A great many Jewish shopkeepers and artisans never saw a non-Jewish customer anyway. It was possible, in the larger towns, for a Jew to live totally within his milieu, only in very marginal contact with the surrounding local population. The shopkeepers who served Gentile customers were proverbially cheaper than the less experienced and less industrious competitor. The buyers would mutter under their breath but would not be ready to pay more elsewhere; and big business, as is its nature, did what it found profitable, regardless.

Vishniac focuses on Jewish poverty – the ragged shopkeepers with their bare shelves, the beggars, the pedlars, the artisans in their sunless hovels, which were also their kitchens and bedrooms, often with one bed for the whole family. Indeed poverty was dire and widespread. But it was not a specifically Jewish poverty which contrasted with non-Jewish wellbeing. On the contrary, urban squalor knew no boundaries and the Gentile unemployed workman suffered the same, if not worse, hardship and degradation. The countryside could be harsher still: the smallholder or landless peasant led, in a bad year, a pitiful existence. Vishniac concentrates almost entirely on the poor and the orthodox – as a photographer he found them the more picturesque and as a man he felt the greater affinity with them – it is his prerogative. But the result is a very partial and one-sided view.

The idea that Jewish existence in Poland was always one of unredeemed gloom and oppression is ill-founded. There were lights as well as shadows, the manifold fabric of Jewish life was woven of many strands and some of its brightest and most life-enhancing manifestations have taken place on Polish soil.

World War I brought Poland political independence, after nearly 150 years of being partitioned between Russia, Prussia and Austria. The socio-economic problems of unifying the country, its respective parts differing in structure, law and traditions were formidable. The minorities – Byelorussian, Ukrainian, German and Lithuanian with their separatist tendencies and conflicting demands – also the perennial Russian threat under a new guise, made for conditions which were a breeding ground of injustice. Rising Polish nationalism, the chronic economic depression and unemployment led to predictable effects. The Jews represented a 10% minority, predominantly urban, distinguishable and competitive. Between the age-old Russian antisemitism and the lethal influences from Germany, the Poles would have to have been saints for their own brand of antisemitism, religious, political and economical, not to have come to the fore – and saints, decidedly, they were not.

In the middle 1930s anti-Jewish discrimination, as it had always been the core of 'Endecja' and other right-wing parties, gained government support, and whilst the Constitution continued to guarantee equal rights, discriminatory measures were enforced. The then prime minister, General Slawoj-Skladkowski, uttered his infamous 'Owszem' ('why yes, by all means') in support of an economic boycott of Jewish enterprises. (Ironically, the said general lived in Palestine during the war and died in Israel in 1952.) Riots at the universities and picketing of Jewish shops were defined as 'natural instincts of cultural self-defence and the tendency for self-sufficiency.' But against this background of menace and uncertainty Jewish life was throbbing – tumultuous and irrepressible. A degree of oppression was accepted as natural, this was after all the Diaspora-Galuth, another chapter of an old story, what else would you expect?

It is important to remember that there existed a considerable area where the division between the Polish and the Jewish world was blurred and the long cohabitation had resulted in mutual acceptance, tolerance and harmony. This had produced a cross-fertilisation with an untold enrichment of both cultures. As in that nursery rhyme about the girl with the curl in the middle of her forehead – a Pole, when he is good, he is very, very good ... There is a native specimen marked by noble spirit, romantic dash, contempt for danger, idealism, which any society would be proud of.

Antoni Slonimski, one of the finest Polish poets and the grandson of Hayyim Selig Slonimski, the founder and editor of the Hebrew newspaper *Hazefira*, has a poem about 'the two unhappiest nations on earth'. Their paths have parted for ever.

When the Polish Jews perished, a part of Poland perished with them. But the Poles have hardly shed a tear over this loss. There was a momentary unease – and a pretence that, somehow, the Jews had never been. There was a widespread relief that the intractable 'Jewish problem' in Poland had been solved in a way for which the Poles could not be blamed. What would have happened if at the end of the war millions of Jews had surfaced to claim their position and property does not bear thinking about. Indeed, the welcome accorded to the pitiful remnant which emerged from their hideouts, from the camps,

All our yesterdays ...

the bunkers, the forests, gives an inkling of the nightmare that would have followed.

When the Jews and their children were murdered and their environment annihilated, 'one of the roots from which history grows'– as George Steiner puts it – was torn up, the genetic pool from which this specific tradition arose has been blotted out. 'The absence from our present needs, our evolutionary hopes' – to use his own words – 'of the strains of moral, psychological, cerebral quality extinguished at Belsen and Treblinka constitutes... the slow, sad vengeance of the unremembered dead.'

The Jewish Quarterly, No. 113, 1983/84

NOTE

1. *A Vanishing World* by Roman Vishniac, Allen Lane, 1983.

16 • Reflections on the unspeakable

IT IS well-nigh impossible to sustain a rational discourse about Auschwitz. The very word lacerates a raw nerve. It means many things. It is not only a physical place in Poland, where there is a museum, visited, through the years, by millions of people of all nationalities, religions and ages, wanting, for their own diverse reasons, to see the site where, not long ago, was enacted one of the most horrific events in human history. It is also an abstract notion which fills us with awe and profound unease. It is a symbol – holding different meaning to different people.

To Jews, Auschwitz is the symbol of the Holocaust. They are surprised and outraged at any attempt to invest it with a different meaning. But, for Poles, Auschwitz is not, primarily, a 'Jewish' camp, but a symbol of the German rape of their country and the persecution of their nation – and they have their very good reasons for perceiving it thus.

It is salutary to bear certain data in mind, for sometimes we talk and act as if we did not want to be confused by the facts. (Auschwitz, by the way, is the name the Germans imposed on the very ordinary Oswiecim and one should really try to revert to the original name. But like the word 'holocaust' – which is wrong, misleading, inappropriate, an alien import – it has gained such a firm grip in all languages that the battle against it must be considered lost.)

Auschwitz was opened in June 1940 as a concentration camp for Polish political prisoners. The Hitler–Stalin 'Boundary and Friendship Treaty' contained secret provisions for the 'elimination' of the potential opponents of both regimes. In April and May of 1940 the Soviets murdered about 15,000 Polish POWs, 45% of the pre-war Polish officer corps, in the Katyn Forest and other locations. At the same time, the Germans, honourably keeping their side of the bargain, sent 20,000 Poles to concentration camps. It was the beginning of their grand design to destroy the spiritual and political elite of the nation.

Auschwitz was situated in the territory incorporated into the Reich from which most Poles were removed to create a no-man's land. On

Reflections on the unspeakable

14 June 1940, the first transport of Polish prisoners arrived in Auschwitz and for the next 21 months the Poles were the only inmates of that camp. (The first Jewish prisoners, women from Slovakia, arrived in Auschwitz towards the end of March 1942.) Referred to as the *Stammlager*, the main base camp, Auschwitz I, where Poles always formed the majority, was a slave-labour camp, the hub of over 40 sub-camps in the vicinity. Many thousands of inmates perished there from hunger, overwork, disease, sporadic executions. But there were also many survivors.

In October 1941 the Germans started building a sub-camp, Brzezinka (Birkenau), about two miles away from the base. This became known as Auschwitz II: the gas chambers and the crematoria were sited there.

From May 1942 the majority of the Jews arriving in Auschwitz-Birkenau were sent straight from the railway-ramp to the gas chambers. The precise figure cannot be established but most recent research sets the number of Jews gassed and burnt there at one-and-a-half million.

Of the six death camps – Belzec, Chelmno, Sobibor, Majdanek, Treblinka and Auschwitz – this last is the only one where most of the physical fabric has survived – the Germans, having dynamited the installations in an attempt to cover up the traces of their crime, left the camp in haste, escaping from the Russian advance.

The former administration buildings, the barracks, the watch-towers, the pylons with the barbed wire, the ruins of the gas chambers and crematoria and the fields themselves form the structure of the 'Museum' which the Polish Government established shortly after the end of the war. The purpose of the Museum was to show Polish martyrdom and the danger of Fascism. In accordance with the official historiography, the victims were 'people' distinguished by their nationalities, 28 of them, listed in alphabetical order: Jews, with letter J, between Italians and Letts. There was no mention that virtually all of them, of whatever nationality, were Jews, murdered there for no other reason. To the Communist 'historian' this was an irrelevance. Various nationalities were given their own section in which to tell their own story – the Bulgarian, for instance, illustrated the glorious achievements of their Communist Party. But a Jewish exhibition section was only opened in 1978 and to this day, despite some improvements introduced since, is totally inadequate in form and substance.

Poland, what have I to do with Thee ...

With the sweeping changes in Poland and elsewhere, there is a call for correcting the falsification of history, and not only in this respect. The Polish authorities responsible for the Museum show an open-minded and far-reaching willingness to listen to and, if possible, implement the advice of the 'Jewish side'. There is, of course, no single, authoritative Jewish voice in this matter and no agreed view on what to tell and how to tell it. (Some years ago, at a World Conference of Polish Jews in Jerusalem, I heard Prime Minister Shamir addressing the audience with the following words: 'If Jews in Europe had followed Jabotinsky's warnings and come to Palestine in their masses, there would have been no Shoah'. Recently, I heard General Barak, the head of the Israeli Army, deliver a moving speech to a group of soldiers and school children from Israel in front of the 'Jewish barrack' in Auschwitz. 'We came here fifty years too late ... Only a strong Jewish state and a strong Jewish army are a guarantee that this will not happen to Jews again.')

An International Auschwitz Council, with a strong Jewish representation, was recently called into being by the Polish authorities. The Organisation of Camp Survivors with their headquarters in Belgium, guards, understandably, their claim to have their voice heard. The Yad Vashem has undoubtedly the greatest expertise and moral authority to offer guidance. Various American institutions bring their influence (and money) to bear in these matters. An independent group of writers and scholars from nine countries came together at Yarnton Manor in England in May 1990, under the aegis of the Oxford Centre for Hebrew Studies and in the presence of specially appointed representatives of the Polish Government. They formulated a set of recommendations and desiderata concerning the policy and the practical arrangements on the camp site of Auschwitz. A similar group was reconvened recently in Kraków and Auschwitz to monitor progress since the 'Yarnton Declaration' and to reinforce and update a further set of proposals. Since it is solely the Polish authority which has power – and by the same token the duty – to preserve and present Auschwitz, it is imperative that the guidance offered be practical, well thought out, based on exact knowledge of local conditions and directed, with due delicacy, through channels which are sympathetic and effective. In this respect the 'Yarnton-Kraków' group has good credentials and a significant role to play.

The questions which arise are many and complex. Leaving aside the philosophical issues, which are in a category of their own, and touching only on practical problems: which 'history' is the Museum to show and through which texts, images, captions, exhibits, artefacts? Having acknowledged and shown the predominantly Jewish victims of Auschwitz, how should due weight be given to the very large numbers of non-Jewish victims? How is the dignity and the integrity of the site to be preserved in view of the nature of mass tourism? How is the vulgarisation of the place to be prevented, with thousands of people of all cultures and ages milling around, in need of occasional relief and refreshment, looking for 'souvenirs' to take away? How is orderly and thoughtful behaviour to be ensured? How are people to be prevented – the terrain is vast and cannot be strictly supervised – from placing in various spots, no doubt with the purest intention, their own signs, plaques or symbols? This is an enormously sensitive issue. As I have said elsewhere, to Christians, the cross is a sign of love and hope: how are they to be made to understand that to most Jews it symbolises oppression, persecution, the Church's triumphalism, the intention to convert 'the stray brothers'? Can they see that the cross, in what is perceived as a Jewish cemetery, offends the deepest Jewish sensibilities? How are the guides, who every day of their working life have to relate the gruesome story in accurate detail, to be educated? How are they to retain their freshness and sincerity, and not get numb or even blasé? Standing on the site of the gas chamber one must, to preserve one's sanity, use all one's strength to repel the imagery which assaults the senses. How and where is the viewer, the pilgrim, given an overview of Jewish society and culture – what these millions of murdered people believed in and created and stood for and what was lost to the world with them?

Now consider the problems of the physical preservation and restoration of the site and its contents. Through the ravages of time and weather the fabric of the camp is threatened; it disintegrates, rots and crumbles. How is one to deal with it? The watch towers round the camp, for instance, the most well-known feature of that bleakest of landscapes, have been completely rebuilt, with new materials – thus losing their 'authenticity'. Was this wrong? They would have otherwise disappeared ... Is this a precedent to be followed or avoided? The barbed wire around the perimeter of the camp has rusted and soon there will be no trace of it: replace it with new? preserve it at all costs? let it go? What about the most telling and poignant exhibits in their showcases: the human hair, the mound of shoes, the suitcases with their names: they change colour, mould, rot.

Poland, what have I to do with Thee ...

What is to be done?

What is to be done with the piles of bricks which are the ruins of the gas chambers and crematoria, dynamited by the Germans? Rebuild them in their original shape? Conserve them as they are at the moment? Let nature take its course? Half of the original wooden barrack at Birkenau has been removed and taken to the National Holocaust Museum in Washington. It would have disintegrated if left on site – so the argument runs – and the Holocaust Museum needs genuine relics; they have a better home now. Is this an act of piety or cultural vandalism? Battered and confused by all these perplexing dilemmas, one may well ask: DOES ALL THIS MATTER?

The 'Yarnton-Kraków' group came up with many constructive suggestions. To implement them, even some of them, will cost money, a lot of it. The Polish Government will give some but, for reasons all too obvious, not much can be expected from that source. It has been suggested that funds should be sought from UNESCO; Auschwitz-Birkenau is listed as part of World Heritage, but it is only one of many competing causes. However, millions of dollars are spent on the Holocaust museums in the United States, new ones are planned all the time. Would not a moment's rational thought make clear where such funds should go in the first place?

The Jewish Quarterly, No. 146, Summer Issue 1992

17 • A peculiar people

CONTEMPLATING the massive contribution to contemporary European culture which is, by some reckoning, attributable to Jews or people of Jewish origin, one would want to know what were the sources of such creativity, what kind of people were those who gave rise to it, what was the soil and the climate in which this phenomenon grew?

To try to convey this in a few pages is like an attempt to pour the ocean into a hole in the ground, but at least a little of the story can be told, and let it begin thus:

Once upon a time, in the basins of the Rivers Oder, Vistula, Niemen, Dniepr and Dniester there lived a people like no other, the Jews. They arrived in that part of the world gradually, over centuries, by diverse routes – some from Spain and Portugal, some from the West, some from Asia and Africa. They spread over a vast territory and their characteristics differed. But they had important things in common. They were all exiles, their ancestors were driven away from their erstwhile homeland, the Holy Land, and they were destined to live dispersed among other peoples who claimed a better title to the land and who, most of the time, treated them as unwelcome intruders.

Other groups in history, exposed to similar conditions, have long disappeared, intermingling with other races and nations – the Jews, mysteriously, survived. Some want to see in this very fact proof of the existence of God, but in terms of rational discourse, other reasons will have to be found. One of them was that Jews shared a singular religion which kept them apart, a faith in One God, based on a Book, which they called the Torah, the Bible, which is not only the greatest work of literature ever written, but also prescribes, in minute detail, the way they should live and worship. The Book assures them that they are God's Chosen People – and if that means being chosen to suffer, then so be it. The Book also contains a promise of redemption, at the end of days, when Messiah comes. The Book told them also 'to be fruitful and multiply' and this they did, prodigiously.

They cared little for man-made borders; whether the destination was named Bukovina or Bessarabia, Volhynia or Podolia, Galicia or

Poland, what have I to do with Thee ...

Lithuania – when oppression increased they moved to join their brethren in another place where life was, for the time, more bearable. They often gained an autonomy of sorts, developed their own institutions, judiciary, tax collections, schools. They established famous 'Yeshivot' – *sui generis* academies of Talmudic learning, wherein they maintained the age-old tradition of intensive, day and night study to which they attracted students from far and wide, even from the Western Hemisphere.

There was a cult of learning, although for most of them study was confined to the Bible, the legal codes and commentaries and the rabbinical writings. Illiteracy was unknown, all children were taught to read on their father's knee. The social standing of a man was tied to his learning, following the saying that 'the learned man takes precedence over the High Priest'. This developed the sharpness of intellect which proved so effective when it had a chance to spill over to other spheres – in philosophy, in science, literature, art or business.

A predominant and distinguishing feature of the internal landscape of those people was a high degree of spirituality – a conviction that 'not by bread alone', that no matter how humble or oppressed, man must aspire to some higher ideal, however defined. There was an underlying belief in the ultimate rightness and justice of the world. One might think that this belief would have been extinguished by the all-too-tangible evidence to the contrary.

If spirituality was one hallmark, internal dissent was another. Throughout history (and to the present day) Jews have not been at peace with each other. Communities were often shaken to their foundations by fratricidal strife due to depth of conviction (some call it fanaticism) and lack of tolerance which tends to afflict people who claim to hear voices from on high. Sadducees against Pharisees, Hassidim against the so-called 'Mitnagdim', Zionists against Bundists, Orthodox against Reform, Lubavitch against Satmar, Traditionalists against Assimilationists, 'Peaceniks' against 'Settlers'. Jews have been turbulent people, people 'who do not sleep themselves and keep others awake'.

One of their most important cultural achievements is the development of their own language, Yiddish, which formed a strong bond, across borders, between the diverse offshoots of the people. It was estimated that on the eve of World War II there were 11 million speakers of that language worldwide, from Ukraine to Holland and in America.

A peculiar people

Yiddish is a curious mixture of German, Hebrew, Polish and a small component derived from the language spoken by the surrounding population. To the unaccustomed ear it sounds unattractive, and many considered it to be a jargon, not worthy to be called 'language'. It was lively, adaptable, colourful, witty. Its grammar was flexible to the point where it was hardly possible to commit a grammatical error (would that other languages had this gift!). It flourished not only as a means of oral communication but also as a medium of literary expression. There were thousands of newspapers, magazines and pamphlets printed and published in Yiddish – printing was one of the crafts, like shoemaking, tailoring and watch-repairing, which became a Jewish speciality.

YIVO, the institute of Jewish Research, founded in 1925, with headquarters then in Wilno, and now in New York, has in its archives hundreds of thousands of books, manuscripts, theatrical collections, letters, photographs and sundry items recovered from the Nazis after the war.

Yiddish literature was an influential and inseparable feature of Jewish life. Jewish theatre gave scope to playwrights like Goldfaden and Anski, whose play *Dybbuk* achieved widespread fame. Actors like Abraham Morewski, the Turkow brothers, and Esther Rachel Kaminska performed the classic repertoire in their own theatres or on tour and had a wide following. Great writers arose, of whom the literature of any nation would have been proud – J. I. Perec, Shalom Aleichem, Mendele, the Singer brothers, of whom the younger, Isaac Bashevis, won the Nobel Prize and brought prestige to the language in which he wrote. During the war Itzhak Katzenelson wrote in Yiddish, in the Warsaw ghetto, an elegy on the destruction of the Jews, which is amongst the most moving documents of our time.

The Founding Fathers of Zionism, with the exception of Theodor Herzl – Weizman, Sokolov, Jabotinsky, Borochov, Ben Gurion, Achad-Ha'am – all coming from the same East European background and undoubtedly Yiddish speakers and orators themselves, perceived that the future Jewish nation for the creation of which they strove should have a language not associated with the miseries of the Diaspora, but one going back to their source in Palestine. It was a near-impossible task to raise Hebrew from the dead and set it, as a matter of principle, against Yiddish, which was very much alive and kicking. The fact that in that battle, Hebrew, 'the holy tongue', prevailed over Yiddish, 'the mother's tongue' (*Mame-loshen*), and is now a sign of Israeli identity, the natural language of people born there, the 'Sabras', used for all daily needs, for scientific pursuits, as well as for worship, as of old, is one of the miracles associated with the rebirth of the Jewish nation in its old land.

The fences which separated the Jewish communities from their neighbours were strong and tall, for they were erected and kept in good repair by both sides. The indigenous population was, on the whole, quite ignorant of what the Jew was really like. They held on to a stereotyped image of something dark and sinister. The Jewish communities were inward looking, sufficient unto themselves, other than on the margin where the need to earn a living made them enter the outside world. They felt, and for good reasons, threatened and at the not so tender mercies of the native population. The contempt shown to them they reciprocated, they had an idea of their own value ('When the natives were still in the trees – Jews already had diabetes!') and the humblest of them would not want to swap places with the princes of that hostile world.

In the second half of the eighteenth century, in the aftermath of the Chmielnicki massacres and the upheavals brought about by the false messianic and kabbalistic movements of Sabbatai Zevi and Jacob Frank, there arose in the South East of the Polish-Lithuanian Commonwealth a new religious movement, Hassidism. Jews are good conductors of ideas and Hassidism swept over the Eastern part of Europe like bush fire. It was meant to revitalise Judaism by leading people back to the traditional tenets of Judaism in a spirit of love and joy. By 1900 there were more that a million Hassidim in the world, including almost one third of pre-war Polish Jewry. In the course of 200 years Hassidism has produced some 1,500 teacher-leaders, outstanding practitioners of the movement, attracting devoted followers to this or that 'Tsaddik' and his Court.

At the time when Jews in that part of the world had little to rejoice about, Hassidism preached joy in simply being a Jew and in the performance of everyday drudgery. Against the traditional view that learning was supreme, Hassidism accorded every Jew, however humble and unlearned, equal rank in communion with God, in a mystic bond and ecstatic prayer, induced by violent body motions, shouting and singing.

The founder of this revolutionary movement, the 'Baal-Shem-Tov', preached that the essence of religion is in feeling, not reason; ceremonial details are unimportant; it is necessary to live and serve

A peculiar people

God in a cheerful and happy mood. The life of the Russo-Polish Jew became thus brighter at heart but darker in intellect. The telling of stories of the great, miraculous deeds of the Tsaddiks was a continuous, life-enhancing activity, stimulating the imagination, a sort of worship in itself. Martin Buber, an inspiring writer, thinker and spiritual leader, collected and wrote down the Hassidic stories, a literary genre *sui generis*. Hassidism – although nothing was further from what Hassidism thought – created a climate which was favourable to the development of art.

By a curious linguistical coincidence, in the Jewish encyclopedias the word 'Hassidism' is preceded by 'Haskala' (which means, roughly, enlightenment). This is most appropriate not only in linguistic but also in historical terms. Towards the end of the eighteenth century a new movement, under that name, sprang up and spread among the Jews of Eastern Europe. To start with, it meant to substitute the study of the Talmud with modern subjects, stressing the poetical and critical works of Hebrew literature. It meant, further, to fight obscurantism, superstition and Hassidism, to encourage Jews to adopt agriculture and handicrafts, abandon their exclusiveness and acquire the knowledge, manners and aspirations of the nations among whom they dwelt. Moses Mendelsohn, the German philosopher and man of letters who was 'the Father of the Haskala' directed Jews towards 'the broad highway of human culture'.

The Vilna Gaon, one of the greatest spiritual leaders of his day and the fiercest opponent of Hassidism, was also an opponent of the 'Haskala'. He foresaw, correctly, that the first step on the path of so-called progress would set many Jews on the slippery slope of assimilation and, perish the thought, conversion (a suspicion which Mendelsohn shared).

Jews were ready to welcome and take advantage of the Enlightenment and the Emancipation which dawned in Europe. With the new spirit spreading and with Jews, at least formally, obtaining equal rights of citizenship in most countries, they began to spill out from their ghettoes onto the world scene. That process of contradictory pulls, challenges and conflicts often tore the guts out of Jewish communities, but the release of talents impacted on every walk of life, for all the world to see. If some latter-day Goebbels arose and wanted to separate the 'Jewish' contribution to culture from the rest, he would have little joy. Modern culture is unthinkable without that particular input; without the eternal rebel, the outsider, the dissident, the Jew.

Poland, what have I to do with Thee ...

One could preen oneself and bask in the reflected glory of the great many artists and men of letters who have immeasurably enriched the human heritage – from Antokolski to Zadkine and from Babel to Zamenhof – all of them had their roots in or around Odessa and Czernowitz and Vitesbsk and Warsaw.

Chaim Nachman Bialik, the greatest of modern Hebrew poets (born in Zhitomir, died in Tel Aviv) is known to have bemoaned the fact that so much Jewish talent goes to the 'goyim's' credit. He need not have worried, should not have begrudged it, there is enough to go round. Such is the blessed chemistry of art – nobody gets poorer, all get richer.

It is worth mentioning that among the consumers of Art, among those who create interest and demand, without which the supply would wither, among those who buy, spread and propagate Art, who read books, go to theatres and concerts, there has always been an inordinately high proportion of Jews. That also is no mean contribution.

* * *

... And then there arose in the West a mighty leader, Hitler, who became the head of the German nation. He preached a gospel of hate against the Jews and vowed to destroy them. His armies overran and conquered the lands where most of them lived and Jews were murdered by the million. In the course of a few years the world of European Jewry, a thousand-year-old civilisation, was destroyed and is no more. One utters these words but their full meaning cannot be grasped.

We who are in a state of perpetual mourning for that vanished world seek solace in dwelling on the matchless heritage left to us, and to humanity, for all times.

Published in *Europa-Europa – catalogue of an exhibition*
'Das Jahrhundert des Avantgarde in Mittel- und Osteuropa', Bonn, May 1994 (in German)

18 • A Beloved Teacher

YITZHAK Katzenelson, the author of the elegy in Yiddish, 'The Song of the Murdered Jewish People' – which was written in the Warsaw Ghetto and is probably the most moving document of that time, has written the following in a tribute to his father:

'When did he learn the Bible by heart?
The Commentaries of Onkelos and Martin Luther?
The Talmud, the Codes, the Midrash, Shakespeare and Heine?
When did he read Gogol, Thucydides and Plutarch?
When did he study the Holy Zohar?
When did he sleep?'

The immeasurable and ungraspable loss lies in that the human type which Katzenelson described here, has perished and will not recur. Those who constituted the civilization of the Jews of Eastern Europe and who were the main victims of the Shoah, are no longer a part of the human landscape.

The *shtetl* was full of them: amateur scholars, perhaps not as well versed in secular literature as Katzenelson's father, but totally at home in Jewish religious writings, masters of vast and complex texts. And yet for most of them – excepting the rabbi in office and the son-in-law of some magnate – studying could have been only a partial pursuit, a hobby, as it were, for their waking hours were mainly consumed in laboriously earning a living. Providing for the family was seen as the overriding duty of the father.

A Polish poet, Antoni Slonimski (the grandson, incidentally, of Selig Slonimski, the founder and editor of the first Hebrew journal in Poland, *Hatsefira*), describes the *shtetl* in one of his poems as 'a place where the cobbler was a poet, the watchmaker a philosopher and the barber a troubadour'.

I knew many such souls, but one particularly remains in my memory. Benzion Rappaport – a simple teacher, my teacher in the Hebrew school in Kraków, where Hebrew subjects – the Bible, Jewish history and literature were taught concurrently with the Polish curriculum. Benzion Rappaport was one of a number of Hebrew teachers in that school.

Poland, what have I to do with Thee ...

Biblical studies were his speciality and it was commonly known, although he himself never made much of it, that he was immensely learned not only in this, but in a variety of secular subjects. His position was not easy – to deviate from the traditional, orthodox teaching, would endanger his job, and yet he wanted at all costs to implant in us the spirit of free, far-ranging, open-minded enquiry. More important than the formal lessons during which he usually had his nose stuck in a book – almost literally, for he was very shortsighted – whilst we were left to our own, noisy devices – were the discussions we had with him after the bell had rung for the break. Then he felt freer to speak his mind and we soon learned to take advantage of it. 'You do not have to believe, literally, in every word of the Scriptures to remain a good and observant Jew' – he used to say (when have we heard that, in different places, since?).

I remember one occasion, before Pesach, we were re-reading the Haggadah, and he explained the miracle of 'the parting of the Seas' – *Yam suf*, what we call the Red Sea, he told us, is clearly a 'sea of reeds' the waters thickly overgrown with bulrushes, papyrus. Jews could cross it, light of foot, even though laden with the riches they carried. The Egyptians in pursuit, in heavy chariots, sank.

One of us, innocently, must have repeated this at home.

An irate parent came to complain that Rappaport was teaching us to disbelieve in miracles. He had to defend himself:

'Is the Exodus less of a miracle because of that explanation? Is Moses less of a prophet and leader because he did not, literally, split the Sea but knew the best way to go?'

In one of those discussions with him, I remember pronouncing with the self-assurance of a teenage know-all:

'There is nothing easier than the facile acceptance of faith, as a package, just like that, on somebody's say-so.'

He shook his head indulgently.

'There is one thing easier still – a facile rejection. You can be an unbeliever, an iconoclast, an agnostic if you wish. But, please, not a shallow one. In both cases, it is the shallowness which is unworthy.'

On another occasion I remember asking him the following:

'To accord a learned man high praise, they say sometimes: 'he knows Shas', the whole of the six books of Mishnah, by heart – in my own family they say this about my grandfather. Surely this is hyperbole and cannot be taken literally? No human brain could retain millions of words and recall them at will, and they are not like an orderly sequence of an actor's part, but often quite random. Surely, this is not possible?'

Rappaport took a deep breath:

'I understand your scepticism but I want to assure you that it is possible. It requires, of course, not only a talent and love for the matter, but above all constant application *yomam v'layla*, day and night study, poring over the texts in the conviction that they interpret the word of God. There are people who have done it and' – here he smiled shyly – 'I have very nearly done it myself.'

I was overcome by admiration and embraced him and he uttered a blessing.

Rappaport was the one who was preparing me for my *bar-mitzvah*. I used to go to his home – a room and a kitchen, full of books stacked on the floor – to be taught how to put on the *tefilin*, how to read the portion of the Torah, what prayers to say in the morning. He also wrote the *drasha* for me, the address which I learned by heart and delivered to the congregation. It was composed in beautiful Hebrew. (I remember it to this day, and it is my 'party piece' during our school reunions in Israel.)

Next morning after the ceremony in the synagogue, before going to school, I applied myself to *shacharit*, the full, adult morning prayers. These, as we know, are quite long and take time. I took the *tefilin* from the embroidered bag, put them on as he had taught me, opened the prayer book and set out to read the text, under my breath; verse after verse, page after page. For the first time in my life I came to school late. And so the next day and the day after that – as my mother watched with increasing impatience and anxiety. She certainly did not want to be the one who stopped me from praying. But, on the other hand, to make me get up earlier, she feared, would also not do me any good and probably arouse my resentment against the whole procedure. What should she do? She went to consult Rappaport.

He took me aside and what he told me I have never forgotten.

'Dear boy' – he said – 'remember that going to school, learning, is also a form of worship, equally – or, perhaps, even more pleasing to God than prayer, and coming late to school is an affront to Him. I know that *shacharit*, the morning prayer, is long – maybe too long for youngsters like you, who knows? We have to shorten it to enable you to get to school on time. We have to extract from it the essence, what is most important in it. The most important thing is the question man has to put to himself when he raises his eyes to heaven: *Ma chovato b'olamo* – 'what is my duty in this world?' Every morning, before you begin your day, ask yourself this question – but seriously, not just casually. Every day afresh – and think about it a minute. Do not try to answer it – there is no short answer to it, it will not come to you quickly, maybe it will never come to you – it matters not. The thing is to realise that the question is important, that you have a duty to perform and have to search for it. Give it a thought – that's all. Then go to school – on time.'

It is true that since that day I have never put on *tefilin* again and in that sense, one could argue that Rappaport had led me astray. But I like to think that, on the contrary, he gave me a complete lesson in morality. And if sometimes, often, I do not live up to it, at least I feel that I know it and am conscious of my failing.

There is another reason why I shall never forget Rappaport. It was June 1945. The war had just ended and its conclusion found me in the British Army, in Norway. I was a sergeant in the Intelligence Corps, charged with the task of interrogating members of the German Army of occupation and weeding out the criminal elements among them before their repatriation to the Fatherland. News reached me, via London, that my mother was alive, having miraculously survived the war. Almost instantly I was on a plane to Germany, to the Headquarters of the British Army on the Rhine, where I picked up a staff-car and a driver (this took some doing, but there was no stopping me) and started on my journey to Kraków, via Warsaw. We drove through the Ruhr in Germany and, I confess, my heart leapt for joy when I saw the destruction wrought on that territory by the Allied Air Force. But coming to Warsaw – or rather to what was supposed to have been Warsaw on the map – a pile of rubble stretching for miles, a landscape riven with moonlike craters, I realised that the bombing of the Ruhr had been a picnic by comparison.

One of the few buildings in the centre of Warsaw still standing with its roof was the 'Hotel Polonia' where the British Embassy was located and I pulled up in front of that building to report my presence (and draw coupons for petrol for my further journey).

In the hotel lobby a crowd of people were milling around, hustling and shoving, transacting business. In that crowd – a heartstopping moment this – I spot a familiar face, a former school-mate of mine! We shake hands, embrace, it appears that he has just arrived from Palestine, in search of survivors.

As we talk, feverishly, exchanging information about mutual

friends, a Polish peasant who, I notice, has been observing us for a while, comes up to us. 'You are Jews?' he asks. 'Indeed we are', we reply.

He takes out from his breast-pocket a bundle of papers, pages from an exercise book, covered in Hebrew hand writing, in fading ink. With it a scrap of paper, scrawled in Polish. 'Pious soul,' the message reads, 'this is a man's life work. Give it into good hands.'

We look at the Hebrew manuscript, we can hardly believe our eyes. It appears that this is the writing of Benzion Rappaport, which he threw out of the window of the train taking him to the death camp in Belzec, on to an open Polish field. A man, the one who now stands in front of us, finds it, deciphers the Polish message, safeguards the manuscript. When the war ends, he travels to Warsaw to look for Jews to hand it over to. They are hard to find, but in the crowded lobby of the 'Hotel Polonia' he spots two Jews – two former pupils of Benzion Rappaport.

We saw to it, of course, that the manuscript was published in Israel. The book carries the title *Teva v'ruach*, 'Nature and Spirit'. It is a collection of essays on the glories of German philosophy, on Hegel, Kant, Schopenhauer, and Rappaport's own thoughts on religion, on ethics, on the method of scientific enquiry.

The pity, the horror and the irony of it all ...

Judaism Today, No. 1, Spring 1995

19 • Booksearch! From Przemysl to the British Library

MY FATHER'S family hails from Oswiecim, Oshpitzin in Yiddish, a *shtetl* which the Germans renamed Auschwitz and gave cause for it to be one of the most sinister sounds in any language. My Father was one of fifteen children, so it will be clear that there were at one time hundreds of Scharfs in Oswiecim, from the patriarch Elias to the four-year-old Chanele.

There were many rabbis among them, which added lustre to the family name, and also, as was natural, some 'no-goodniks' which detracted from it. But the figure of whom one spoke with awe and pride belonged to a previous generation – Rabbi Moshe Yaacov Jekel Scharf, born in 1784, died in 1869, the 'official' Rabbi of Oswiecim for 50 years. To be one of his descendants, in direct line, was a *yichus*, a distinction one had to try to live up to, as my father never tired of telling me.

Rabbis were often known not by their family name but by the title of the book which they had written, like *Megale Amukot* or *Chofetz Chaim*.

The books of Moshe Yaacov stood, of course, on the bookshelves in our drawing-room, among the other *seforim* – the large volumes of religious books, bound in their characteristic, mottled, yellow-brown covers. I remember in particular one slim volume, with a red flash and gold embossing – my father would look at it lovingly and occasionally stroke its spine in passing. Not that he would have understood a great deal of the text, that was not the point. He knew that the book, those books, belonged to another realm and formed a spiritual resource which made life meaningful.

And so I always remembered where the book stood, the spine and the binding, but – I confess – I had forgotten the title and therefore could not, on those occasions which called for it, bask in his glory. This caused me some distress through the years – since my memory is, on the whole, reasonable and I have a total recall of a myriad trivial details of that time. Yet I had forgotten the title of my great-grandfather's book – shame on me.

There was, of course, a way of finding out, but I was too ignorant to think of it. Bernard Friedberg (1876–1961), a fellow Cracovian (yes, you find them everywhere), among other important works on Hebrew printing, published a bibliographical lexicon *Beit Eked Sefarim* in four volumes, which is the standard, indispensable work and – as I now know – Moshe Yaacov Scharf's books (note the plural) feature in it.

However, the spirit moves in mysterious ways, and the other day a little book fell into my hands, entitled: 'From Oswiecim to Auschwitz – Poland Revisited' by Rabbi Moshe Weiss (Mosaic Press P. O. Box 1032, Oakville, Ontario, Canada). Rabbi Weiss, who now lives in Canada, but was born in Oswiecim, travels to Poland at frequent intervals, visiting various places in search of traces of Jewish life and the remaining Jews, to whom he brings aid and comfort. Describing his recent visit to Oswiecim, he mentions that Moshe Yaacov Scharf, a disciple of the Sanzer Tzaddik, was a Rabbi there for 50 years and, bless him, he mentions the title of the book: *DARKEI YOSHER*!

To see it suddenly, in black and white, was for me like a shaft of light across a darkened sky. *DARKEI YOSHER*, of course! How could I have forgotten? *DARKEI YOSHER* – 'The Ways of the Just'.

Since this happened on a Monday, the day on which I attend Rabbi Louis Jacobs' Talmud lesson, I told him of my great joy at this rediscovery. Next morning he phoned me to say that the book, indeed, appears in Friedberg's Bibliography, that it contains 192 pages and had been printed in Przemysl, near Kraków, in the year 1872. He thought that a copy might be found in the British Library.

I confess I had thought this highly improbable: a little Hebrew book, published more than 120 years ago, in Przemysl, in an edition of – what would it have been? – 200, 300 copies, how could it be expected to have found its way to the shelves of the British Library?

To go there, I dug up my old Reader's Ticket to the Reading Room in the British Museum – and thereby hangs another tale.

I came to London from Kraków shortly before the outbreak of war, and I have this vivid recollection how, the very day after arrival, I stood on the steps of the British Museum and pinched myself to prove that I was not dreaming, that I was in England, in London, at the gateway to this glorious temple.

I went to the office and applied, there and then, for a Reader's Ticket, to which I proved my title: I was a working journalist, a foreign correspondent for my paper in Kraków and had been admitted as a postgraduate student at the London School of Economics, intent on completing my thesis begun at the Jagellonian University in Kraków. I entered the Reading Room – I thought I was in Paradise. I thought I should happily spend the rest of my life there.

World events intervened, there was little time for such cosy dreams, life took a different course, years went by in other pursuits. But 30 and some years later, at 'retirement', I felt this nostalgic tug at the heart as I stood, once again, in the office of the Museum, filling in an application form for a Reader's Ticket. The last item on the application form read:

'Have you had a ticket before?'

'Yes,' I said jokingly to the man behind the counter, 'I have had a ticket before, before the war' – and I waved in front of him the old, faded card, which I had retained as a souvenir.

'You don't require a new ticket, you want a renewal', said the man, apparently in all seriousness.

'It was a long time ago', I stuttered.

'Not long for a Museum', he said, took the ticket from my hand, and in the space provided, after former renewals which read '10 July 1940', '31 January 1941', he put a stamp '14 December 1972'.

I keep this as a rare document, a museum specimen of sorts. I find this, somehow, enormously endearing and reassuring. 30 years on, 30 miles of bookshelves later, with World War II in between, empires risen and fallen and the world changed beyond recognition, the man said: 'It is not long for a Museum.'

And so, armed with that renewed ticket, I went on to the British Library – the Hebrew books are no longer housed in Bloomsbury, but in Orbit House near Blackfriars Bridge. I presented my request to the Librarian, Ms Ilana Tahan. A few buttons pressed on the computer – a breathtaking moment this – yes, the book is catalogued and available. In a few moments it appears in front of me on my desk.

I handled the book tenderly, overcome by a strange feeling. There it was, as if flown from my old home, a fragment of life that is no more. Bookshelves of *seforim*, religious books, stood in thousands of Jewish homes – not only the orthodox where they sometimes occupied half the living space, but in many ordinary homes, where no member of the household would open them any more, a sort of natural backdrop, without which the room felt cold and empty. If you add to this the books in the synagogues and yeshivot and *shtiblech*, through the land, one is clearly talking about vast numbers, millions of books. It is a measure of the destruction, of the uprooting of a civilisation, that one does not find any religious Hebrew books in Poland, other than by accident, some tattered copies among the bric-a-brac in a flea market.

After all this excitement, you may well be curious about the content of the book. All I am able to say, for the moment, is that the text is extremely difficult to follow, even for somebody not entirely ignorant in these matters.

The front page says that this book is a collection of 'innovations and wonderful explications of most of the chapters of the Mishna, both in the casuistic (*pilpul*) and in the straightforward manner'; brought to the printing house by Rabbi David Scharf, the son of Moshe Yaacov; printed by Zupnik and Partners, in Przemysl, in 1872.

The inside page carries the 'imprimatur' and fulsome commendation of the great Rabbis, Chaim Halbersztam of Sanz and Josef Natanson of Lwow and Galicia. It is printed, as was customary for works of that kind, in the 'square' Rashi alphabet, without vowels, of course, or punctuation. And if that was not enough of a trial, virtually every line of text contains one or more of the *rashe tevot*, the shorthand, where single letters stand for words or phrases. (When I see the *lamed-kof*, denoting that the question under discussion is easy to answer – *lo kashe*, I am inclined to cry out for mercy – it is difficult! Very difficult!)

When one tries to follow the argument and breaks through the many qualifying clauses, one finds innumerable references to other passages in the Scriptures and the Talmud – in fact the whole strength of the argument seems to be derived from these scattered quotations.

How these passages were recalled by the authors and marshalled at will, without the aid of lexicons or concordances or a card index, boggles the mind (and how infinitely easier is the work of modern scholars, when a 'search' button will instantly bring to the screen every mention of a word in the whole text).

To ask why the Rabbis with such prodigious minds and creative talents, which makes one's own endowment look so puny, devoted their entire lives to the study of problems which, for thousands of years, had absolutely no relevance to any contemporary issue, would show a misunderstanding of what such writing is. For the Rabbis and their disciples and followers, the preoccupation with these problems and the treatment of them was simply (well, perhaps not so simply) a form of worship, a labour of love of God. How could one think that this was not enough, that there was something better, more practical to do?

Poland, what have I to do with Thee ...

Finally, can one guess or explain how such a book found its way from Przemysl to the British Library? One must know whom to ask, and in this case it was obvious to me that the person who knows everything there is to be known in these matters is Professor Chimen Abramsky, not only a leading scholar on Jewish subjects but, in one of his previous careers, a bookseller of Jewish books. Indeed, as it transpires, he knows of Zupnik, the nineteenth-century printer in Przemysl in Galicia, at that time in the Austro-Hungarian Empire. Zupnik, like other printers, and there were many of them, circulated their 'catalogues' or loose sheets of books they printed, to the Jewish booksellers, wherever they found them. One such, the best known in England, was Yaacov Lifschitz, who – according to Abramsky – supplied the Museum, in the course of years, with many hundreds of Jewish books. It is almost certain that it was he who spotted *Darkei Yosher* on Zupnik's list, thought it worthy of purchase and persuaded the Librarian to acquire it for the collection – wouldn't Moshe Yaacov be surprised.

End of story – but not quite. The computer tells me that the book was reprinted in Baltimore in 1969, by Y. Sh. Gotteher – and I confess that I find the whole thing utterly amazing.

Judaism Today, No. 2, Autumn 1995